The Politics of Everyday Life

The Politics of Everyday Life

Making Choices, Changing Lives

PAUL GINSBORG

Yale University Press
New Haven and London

Copyright © 2005 by Paul Ginsborg

For information about this and other Yale University Press
publications, please contact:
U.S. Office: sales.press@yale.edu   yalebooks.com
Europe Office: sales@yaleup.co.uk   www.yalebooks.co.uk

Set in Minion by MATS, Southend-on-Sea, Essex
Printed in Great Britain by St Edmundsbury Press Ltd, Bury St Edmunds

ISBN 0 300 10748 X

Library of Congress Control Number: 2005925106

A catalogue record for this book is available from the British Library.

10 9 8 7 6 5 4 3 2 1

For permission to reprint lines from 'Fall 1961' by Robert Lowell and
'Essential beauty' by Philip Larkin, grateful acknowledgement is made to
Faber and Faber Ltd.

For Ayşe, con tenerezza

Contents

Acknowledgements

I would like to thank two people who have helped me a great deal in the preparation of this book: Christian De Vito, who was an excellent research assistant in its earlier phases; and my librarian friend, Silvia Alessandri, for her constancy, intelligence and quickness of wit, without which this work could not have taken on its present form. The staff of the Biblioteca Nazionale in Florence and of the British Library in London have always been helpful and efficient. I am very grateful to Andrew Gamble and Stephen Morris for reading the manuscript, and for their constructive criticisms. The responsibility for errors that remain in the text is entirely mine.

Introduction

This is a book which has its origins in the experience of civic action at a local level. The city in which I live and work, Florence, is known throughout the world for the beauty of its artistic monuments and for the greatness of its medieval and Renaissance past. In many ways the city lives on and in that past. In 1877 Henry James wrote: 'She sat in the sunshine beside her yellow river like the little treasure-city that she has always seemed, without commerce, without other industry than the manufacture of mosaic paper-weights and alabaster Cupids, without actuality, or energy, or earnestness, or any of those rugged virtues which in most cases are deemed indispensable for civic robustness.'[1] Such a portrait is no longer a faithful one. Modern Florence boasts an unusually active civil society, made up of a network of voluntary associations, a flourishing trade union movement which derives its strength from a densely industrialised hinterland, a university with some 60,000 students, and a tradition of radical, socially oriented Catholicism. Contemporary Florence, which has some 370,000 inhabitants, is one of the cities of Europe with the highest number of bookshops per head of population.

In January 2002 a small group of Florentine university professors decided to organise a protest against the government of Silvio Berlusconi, who had come to power in Italy in June of the previous year. It seemed to us that his government represented a dangerous model for the rest of the democratic world. Here was one of the richest men in Europe taking hold of the Italian republic; a media magnate who owned most of Italy's commercial television and its largest publishing house, a man who at the time of his election was on trial on a number of charges, which varied from bribery of tax inspectors to corruption of magistrates. Once in office, he added to the control of his own

---

1. Henry James, 'Italy revisited', in James, *Portraits of Places* (London: Macmillan, 1883), p. 57.

television channels that of public radio and television, notoriously the vehicle of Italy's ruling political elites.

The new government also moved swiftly towards curbing the power of what has probably been in recent decades the most independent judiciary in Europe. When the judicial year of 2002 began, many judges and magistrates protested by deserting the traditional opening ceremonies in their cities, leaving their black gowns draped over the empty seats. To us in Florence it appeared essential not to leave them to fight a lonely defensive battle. We were alarmed by the threat which Berlusconi posed to democracy, if not to its formal procedures then certainly to its substance. But we were also dismayed by the lack-lustre quality of the centre-left opposition, which seemed unable to grasp the historical significance of the moment, and insisted instead on the need for dialogue and to avoid excessive alarmism.

The group of university teachers, students and trade unionists which gathered in my house in Florence decided to organise a symbolic march of protest – from the offices of the rector of the university, in Piazza San Marco, to the steps of the eighteenth-century Courts of Justice in Piazza San Firenze, which is situated just behind the Palazzo Vecchio, the historic seat of Florentine government. On the banner that opened our march was a paraphrase of one of the final considerations of Alexis de Tocqueville's *Democracy in America*: when the autonomy of the judiciary and the freedom of information are under attack, then democracy is in danger. We expected a few hundred people to join us. On the day of the march, 24 January 2002, the skies opened and rain poured down incessantly, decisive proof of what Silvio Berlusconi had often maintained – that God was on his side.

Instead, defying the weather, some 12,000 people marched behind the university teachers that afternoon through the central streets of Florence. They were a mixture of the city's middle classes – those who worked at various levels in the professions and public services, teachers and students, as well as delegations of workers from some of Florence's factories. A substantial contingent came too from Florence's Social Forum – the city's 'new globals', who were to organise the extraordinarily successful European Social Forum in Florence later in the same year. When the march arrived at the Courts of Justice, many magistrates under their black umbrellas were waiting for us in silence on its steps. I made a brief and faltering speech from the microphone of the loudspeaker van lent to us by the city's trade union federation, the Camera del Lavoro, after which we sought refuge, soaked but happy, in the nearest pizzeria.

In the following months, the tide of protest in Florence flowed into a much vaster, nationwide movement against the Berlusconi government, a movement which culminated in the enormous demonstration of 23 March 2002, organised by the CGIL, Italy's largest trade union. On that day between two and three million people, coming from all parts of the peninsula, gathered in and outside the Circo Massimo in Rome. This was the largest single voluntary demonstration in the history of the modern Italian state. Mussolini had organised parades of similar size, but they had been regimented affairs. In September of the same year, another massive demonstration gathered in Rome, to protest against Berlusconi's tampering with the legal system. This time it was organised spontaneously by the network of civil society organisations which had come into being to defend Italian democracy from the government's marauding instincts. Some 800,000 people gathered in Piazza San Giovanni and the adjacent streets.

In Florence, the committee which had organised the march of 24 January decided to transform itself into a Laboratory for Democracy. At its first meeting, in the Casa del Popolo of S. Bartolo in Cintoia on the periphery of Florence, some 800 people turned up. We wanted, if at all possible, to avoid being a fly-by-night social movement, here one day and gone the next. Instead we tried to organise for the medium term, privileging various lines of action. One was obviously the need to continue to mobilise against the Berlusconi government. Only if protest was continuous and widespread would the government be checked in its attempts to realise the most controversial parts of its plans, such as the limitations of workers' rights and the undermining of state education through insufficient funding. But we also wanted, given our intellectual training and vocation, to open up our city to wider debates: on immigration and security, education and welfare, gender, control of the mass media, consumption patterns. Was it possible to invent new ways of connecting these themes to our daily lives and to the government of our city?

We were also troubled because the municipal government, for some years in the hands of a centre-left coalition, was seemingly unable to come to grips with the city's principal problems. Among them were very severe air pollution from heavy traffic, the social and economic differences separating centre and periphery, the absence of cheap housing for young people and of autonomously organised meeting places, and the way in which the city's streets were being transformed by mass tourism, as ordinary shops closed and leather and fashion shops overran the city centre. Our city was in the hands of major commercial interests who appeared to be uncontrollable, while at the same time determining the quality of life of each of us.

Behind these problems lay more profound ones concerning the nature of local democracy. Our representatives, who conducted their meetings in the Palazzo Vecchio, often in the splendid rooms adorned by Vasari and his school, seemed unable to turn their gaze outwards to the city. Like their counterparts in most of the regions of Italy and indeed of Europe, they were for the most part self-referential in their attitudes, content to manage an existing state of affairs, and to enjoy the power that it conferred. We asked ourselves if local democracy had necessarily to assume so mundane an aspect. Or was it possible to invent new forms of democracy, in which people could take an active part, and through their participation foster a culture of citizenship? These were not new themes in the history of democracy, nor ones that had ever received a satisfactory answer, at least in the modern world, but they were ones which had an obstinate habit of not going away.

The Florentine Laboratory for Democracy asked more questions than it could possibly answer, and set in train more work groups than it could possibly sustain. The normal demands on our time – those of our families and of our work in the first place – made it difficult indeed to sustain the energies and rhythms that the Laboratory imposed. But however much our time flew away just when we wanted it to settle slowly around us, and however limited our achievements, we wanted to contribute to two processes: that of defending democracy and at the same time that of renewing it. In order to underscore these ambitions, in the summer of 2004 we ran our own candidate for mayor of the city, a university professor of English literature called Ornella De Zordo. With few resources and no previous experience, she gained 12.3 per cent of the vote.

I wrote at the outset that this book draws its inspiration from an experience of local civic action, one that I have briefly described above. However, it also takes its impetus from the global situation in which we all find ourselves in the wake of the rapid transformations of the last three decades. As is immediately apparent, these two instances, the local and the global, are intimately linked. Very many of the questions raised by our Laboratory for Democracy can only find meaning and answers from an analysis that goes far beyond the city of Florence. The same is true of the national political situation which Italians are now experiencing. Silvio Berlusconi is only one, albeit a highly significant example, of the ambitions and almost unlimited power of present-day media magnates. They are the product of, and in turn shape, a global culture of conspicuous consumption, and their television channels communicate a particular view of the normal and the possible. Dissatisfaction with democracy, too, is not peculiar to the city of Florence. In every country where democracy has triumphed (and we shall see in chapter 5 how it has extended ever further around the globe), disaffection with its workings, though perhaps not with its essence, has grown.

Time and again, those who wish to make their own street, or neighbourhood, or city a better place to live in are pushed almost immediately into making connections between their own lives and the larger and more distant forces that shape them. Waging war on traffic pollution in the historic centre of Florence, for instance, means coming face to face with a global model of individual mobility, with a particular Italian model of overfilling a small peninsula with an excessive number of cars, and with a specifically Florentine preference, even passion, for fast-moving, noisy and polluting scooters and motor-bikes.

These concentric rings of connection, between the material culture of everyday life, larger communities, and worldwide patterns of consumption and production, have very extended histories. They are the result of long-standing relations between the 'North' of the world – its rich and developed regions – and the 'South' – its poor and developing areas. The chains of connection that have been drawn across the world fundamentally benefit only one restricted part of it. They do not derive from impulses of equity and solidarity, or from a sense of mutual responsibility. Rather their driving force has been primarily, though not exclusively, economic profit and national power. In chapter 1 of this book I shall analyse the principal dichotomies which have emerged as a consequence of these relations. Suffice it to say here that the forces driving forward the globalisation process of the last thirty years have taken as their raw material already existing disparities, as well as the whole history of colonialism and imperialism, and have built upon them in an uneven and unpredictable way.

The distinction by compass point, between a partially invented 'North' and 'South', is hardly satisfactory. There are parts of the South of the world, like Australia, that belong substantially to the 'North', and much of the 'South', like India, Bangladesh, China, Indonesia and Vietnam, that is clearly of the East. On the other hand, to distinguish numerically rather than geographically, in terms of First, Second and Third worlds, is even more unsatisfactory. From 1989 onwards, with the demise of Soviet Communism, the greater part of the Second World ceased to exist as such; to continue to talk of a 'Third' World without a 'Second' is only confusing. Even the distinction between 'developed' and 'developing' regions of the world begs many a question. How do we wish to define development? And to what degree is it desirable that other countries and regions of the world follow the same development trajectory as ourselves? In the era of globalisation, we lack the most basic vocabulary to describe global relations. Along with a majority of commentators and researchers, I shall continue to use North and South in the absence of anything better.

The destruction of the Twin Towers and the subsequent invasions of Afghanistan and Iraq have brought the relations of North and South, between rich and poor, between the powerful and the powerless, into the sharpest of focuses. Not because Bin Laden comes from a poor family (quite the opposite), nor because al-Qaida represents in some perverse way the whole of the South (which it certainly does not), nor even that the Twin Towers symbolised the whole of the North (though this last affirmation has more of a ring of truth about it). No. September 11, 2001 conveyed with terrible clarity a relatively simple and novel message: that certain global hatreds, which are not the mechanical products of the injustices of globalisation, but which certainly draw their sustenance from them, have been translated into a willingness for self-sacrifice on the part of small groups of individuals who aim, by immolating themselves, to inflict unlimited violence upon an indiscriminate number of unknown others.

Nor is this all. The events of the last three years have injected again into vast sectors of public opinion in the developed world (and not only there) an emotion that had been largely absent for some forty years: fear for our own survival, for the survival of those closest to us, and for the survival of the human species in general.

Georges Lefebvre, the distinguished French historian, once wrote a book entitled *La Grande Peur*, which analysed the way in which many peasants were gripped by fear of marauders setting out from Paris in the wake of the revolution of 1789.[2] The psychosis of fear in that case concerned mainly the requisitioning of grain, the killing of chickens, and the plundering of farms. From September 2001 onwards, the 'great fear' has been far more cosmic: of a 'dirty' nuclear bomb left in a suitcase in Central Park or Hyde Park, of kamikaze killers unleashing widespread destruction in American or European cities, of uncontainable bacteriological warfare. A growing number of newspaper articles inform us in a chilling, matter-of-fact way of the capacity of very small numbers of people to kill very large numbers of us, perhaps all of us.

Such global awareness of danger is not new. In the 1950s and 1960s, at the height of the Cold War, the fear of annihilation by atomic warfare was

---

2. Georges Lefebvre, *La Grande Peur de 1789* (Paris: Armand Colin, 1932); Eng. trans. *The Great Fear of 1789* (London: New Left Books, 1973).

widespread. In the cinema Stanley Kubrick made us laugh at our fears, though he did little to allay them, with his extraordinary black comedy, *Dr Strangelove* (1964). But new elements are present in the preoccupations of today. Our world is menaced not just by nuclear destruction, but also by our constant misuse of it, and by our capacity to modify it beyond recognition or recall. These are all themes to which I shall return in chapter 1.

These cumulative menaces to human existence have introduced a new relationship between fear and time. Much more so than forty years ago, there is a feeling that time is running out. To the absence of time in our own lives is added the anguish of the possible absence of global time.

The net result of these gathering concerns is the fostering in very many people of an uneasy combination of two sensations: those of urgency and powerlessness. We feel that something must be done before it is too late, but we have little idea of what we as individuals, or as families, or as groups of friends or as workmates can possibly do to stem the tide. We would like to connect our everyday lives and our individual actions to making the world a better place to live in – even a possible place to live in – but we do not know how.

This book tries to answer such a dilemma. It argues for the need to 'reappro-priate', to take back under our own control, the sorts of lives we live and the contexts in which we live them. It offers a strong critique of the prevailing model of modernity in developed countries, a model which is being exported and imposed on the rest of the world. While respecting the opinion of those who argue that the market and liberal democracy in their present forms offer the best possibilities for human emancipation, this book begs to disagree with them. Francis Fukuyama wrote after 11 September 2001 that 'modernity is a very powerful goods train which will not be derailed by recent events, however painful and unprecedented they are'.[3] I believe, on the contrary, that the model of modernity he has in mind is an unsustainable one. The goods train must be filled with other goods, and the lines on which it travels must radically change their direction.

In order to achieve, or even to approach such a transformation, we need to start with ourselves; not in a puritanical or fanatical or guilt-laden manner, but in a realistic one, with what each of us feels capable of. We have to rethink the choices we make on a day-to-day basis, the ways we use our time, the family lives we live, the sorts of things we consume, the quality of democracy we are

---

3. F. Fukuyama, 'La fine della storia dopo l'11 settembre', *la Repubblica*, 19 Oct. 2001.

able to exercise. We have to question, to use Vernon Lee's resonant expression, 'the vital lies that are essential to our existence'.[4] The task may appear gargantuan, but the accumulation of alternative practices at an individual and familial and civic level produces a notable cumulative effect. The individual, the local and the global are inextricably intertwined, in positive as in negative ways. Passivity and indifference at the first two levels, the individual and the local, contribute greatly to collective dismay at the third.

Naturally, a small text of this sort does not pretend to have all the answers. It is not a work of economics, though political economy is present, but instead one of politics of a rather peculiar sort. It suggests some 'ways out' – some responses to the growing collective awareness that we simply cannot go on like this. It does so primarily with reference to the themes of self-government, autonomy and control from below which have long been debated in the European working-class movement. But it tries to do so in a novel way – by discussing choice with reference to consumption patterns, time, television, family life, all themes scarcely present in the previous political debate.

Often here I have used a collective 'we', and the reader has the right to know from the outset which 'we' it is that I have in mind. As must be obvious from the examples I have chosen and the Florentine Laboratory for Democracy of which I am part, the 'we' in the first instance is a Western democratic one, the urban educated population of the North of the world. Given its central role in consumption, its experience of democracy, and its privileged economic position, this part of the global population, though derisory in numerical terms, is highly influential in economic and political ones. Potentially it has a very powerful role to play. At the moment it is the willing subject of what appears to be a consumerist paradise, but it may not stay that way. Different forces, I believe – fear, necessity, dissatisfaction with lives dominated by lack of time and the endless cycle of work and spend, even what Immanuel Kant called

4. Vernon Lee was an English woman writer resident in Florence at the beginning of the twentieth century. Commenting on the recent publication of the novel *Una donna*, written by the Italian feminist Sibilla Aleramo, Lee wrote in 1907 that Aleramo's book 'should make us reflect whether the institutions which have appeared tolerable or propitious to us, the fortunate, are for that reason innocent or sacrosanct; it should make us ask whether we render ourselves complices of evil by denying its presence, refusing to think, to shake our prejudices, to look the truth in the face, even if that truth deprives us of those beliefs that are dearest to us, the vital lies [. . .] that are essential to our existence'; Vernon Lee (Violet Paget), 'Commenti e frammenti. A proposito del romanzo "Una donna" di Sibilla Aleramo', *Il Marzocco*, 27 Jan. 1907, quoted in C. Gori, *Crisalidi. Emancipazioniste liberali in età giolittiana* (Milan: Franco Angeli, 2003), p. 70.

'a feeling which dwells in every human heart and which is more than mere pity and helpfulness [. . .] a feeling for the Beauty and Dignity of human nature'[5] – will push it towards reconsideration. This book intends to help it on its way.

However, I do not intend the 'we' of this book to be limited to the educated classes of western Europe and northern America. Many of its themes, both in the positive and the negative – from the growth of civil society to the pervasive cultures of clientelism and corruption, from gender battles to deliberative democracy – have as much relevance for India and Brazil, the Russian Federation and South Korea as they do for Italy, Britain or the United States. The most interesting medium-term experiment in participative democracy at a local level comes from the Brazilian region of Rio Grande do Sul, and in particular from its capital, Porto Alegre, which has a population of some 1,300,000 persons. It does not come, unfortunately, from a city like London, or Florence, and even less from New York, which has recently elected its own Berlusconi-like figure, Michael Bloomberg, as mayor, after an electoral contest characterised by the massive use of private wealth and media influence. To this theme, too, I intend to return.

I am aware that to use the word 'reappropriation', to take back control of one's own destiny, makes little sense for vast sections of the world, because their inhabitants have never been able to exercise such control in the first place, even on a very limited scale. Very many have still to attain a minimally satisfactory standard of nutrition and living, a basic education, fundamental civil and political rights. They are still prevented from exercising as individuals what Martha Nussbaum has called, in her fine book *Women and Human Development*, the central human functional capabilities.[6] The poor women of India, who are the subjects of Nussbaum's book, are impeded by male violence, by the dowry system, by family structures and culture, by lack of education and by the lack of property rights from realising their own capabilities. They are unable to enjoy decent health, to live a full span of life, to move freely from place to place, to have their own bodily boundaries treated as sovereign, to be free from overwhelming fear and anxiety, to participate effectively in political choices that govern their lives.[7]

5. I. Kant, *Beobachtungen über das Gefühl des Schönen und Erhabenen* (1764), ch. 2, p. 4, quoted by Pepita Haezraki, 'The concept of man as end-in-himself', in R. P. Wolff (ed.), *Kant: A Collection of Critical Essays* (London: Macmillan, 1968), p. 295.
6. 'The basic intuition from which the capability approach begins, in the political arena, is that certain human abilities exert a moral claim that they should be developed [. . .] This must be understood as a *freestanding moral idea*, not one that relies on a particular metaphysical or teleological view'; M. Nussbaum, *Women and Human Development, the Capabilities Approach* (Cambridge: Cambridge University Press, 2000), p. 83.
7. For the full list of the central human functional capabilities, see below, pp. 18–19, n 12.

They inhabit, therefore, a very different world from that of Florence. Our world seems cosy and complacent by comparison, and their needs would seem to dwarf ours into insignificance. Yet it is all too easy to draw the wrong conclusions from such a reflection. I once heard one such, 'the count yourself lucky approach', from a conservative Anglo-Indian lady living in Cambridge: 'Why are you making such a fuss about workers' conditions in the West', she asked me, 'when there are so many much poorer people in the rest of the world?' Another approach is not material but cultural relativism: 'You must understand that other people in other parts of the world have different values and traditions. You should not just impose your values, even decent ones, on them. Such "universalism" is tantamount to cultural colonialism.' A third is a self-sacrificing and often self-denigratory 'Third Worldism', very popular in Europe in the 1970s but still with its following today. Its exponents stress that the real battles for human emancipation are only to be fought in far-flung and extremely poor places. The populations of the First World, by contrast, are irretrievably corrupted by the capitalist system.

All of these points of view have something to be said for them (especially the second). However, it is not by separating our worlds, as these approaches suggest, but by connecting them that the compelling imperatives of the South are best served. One version of that connection is globalisation in its present form. The realisation of human functional capabilities does not appear to come very high on its list of priorities. In its place we can try and suggest a whole number of mutually profitable modes of connection, which take as their point of departure the redefinition of our own needs. I shall try and examine this central proposition throughout the course of the book.

Furthermore, although it may not at first be apparent, many of the needs of North and South are similar if not identical. Uneducated Indian women have no more need of corrupt officials who draw regular salaries and then provide no schooling than do Italians of corrupt politicians and administrators who demand illicit cash compensations for the 'public' services they offer. Patronage and clientelism are always demeaning, whatever their context, though often there is little else available. Arbitrary male power, both inside and outside the family, displays many of the same characteristics the world over. When Bangladeshi or Zambian women try to build the associations of a nascent civil society, they encounter many of the inherent difficulties of organisation, of continuity and of lack of support from local government that their counterparts experience in materially far richer countries. All over the world people have the same interests in trying to exercise some form of democratic control over their own lives. They are subject to the same television transmissions and advertisements, which have become the most powerful cultural instruments of our time. Finally, while it is true that people everywhere would like to live in peace, they all too often, for one reason or another, find themselves accepting or even supporting the horrors of war. With globalisation, the world has become a much smaller place, more dangerous than ever, but it also has the potential for the creation of an unprecedented commonality of interests.

1   We can't go on like this

In the modern world a series of binary categories dominates economics and politics. The most important of them are riches and poverty; power and powerlessness; male and female; profits and ethics; legality and illegality; human reproduction and environmental conservation; war and peace. Not all these separations and contrasts, as will be immediately obvious, are equally sharp, or of the same quality; but all are overlapping.

Each of them has a very long, contentious and far from linear history. Each has been rendered more impelling by the developments of the last thirty years, by the rapid development of what Martin Shaw has called 'a common consciousness of human society on a world scale'. With the increase in intensity of global relations, writes Shaw, 'the understanding of human relations in a common, worldwide frame comes to predominate over other, more partial understandings.'[1]

The radical economic transformations of the last three decades have done much to foster this common frame. Many national economies have become integrated, albeit with differing degrees of intensity, into supranational economic organisations, such as the World Trade Organization, the European Union and NAFTA, the North American Free Trade Agreement. Meetings between the leaders of the world's principal economies have proliferated, as have the publicity and security which surround them. The major trans-national companies, which once bore the name of 'multinationals', have organised their production, promotion and retailing on a world scale, and have correspondingly increased their influence, as well as their geographical and organisational flexibility. Company fusions and takeovers have increased

1. M. Shaw, *Theory of the Global State: Globality as Unfinished Revolution* (Cambridge: Cambridge University Press, 2000), p. 11.

in rhythm and size. Financial markets have been revolutionised by information technology and deregulation, and have assumed an unprecedented importance in the capitalist world system as a whole. The only seeming alternative to such a system, that of the state socialism of the 'Second World' countries, has collapsed ignominiously. Global capitalism has become one.

Riches and poverty

There are many aspects to poverty, and the economic one is only the most obvious. Let me concentrate on it as a start. At the beginning of the new millennium the richest 5 per cent of the world population enjoyed an income 114 times larger than the poorest 5 per cent. The income of the richest 25 million Americans was the equivalent of that of almost 2 billion of the world's poor. By itself the Walton family, owners of the Wal-Mart chain, enjoy an estimated wealth equal to the GDP of the whole of Egypt.[2]

These gross inequalities are not stable. China and India, two of the most populous nations in the world, accounting for some two-fifths of the world's inhabitants, have seen their GDP per capita grow very significantly in recent decades. In East Asia as a whole (accounting for some 31 per cent of global population), GDP per head rose by a remarkable 5.9 per cent per year between 1975 and 2001; in South Asia (accounting for another 22 per cent of world population) at 2.4 per cent per year. As Martin Wolf, a fervent supporter of globalisation, has written, 'Never before have so many people – or so large a proportion of the world's population – enjoyed such large rises in their standards of living.'[3]

However, this is far from the whole of the story. In spite of Asia's rapid growth, absolute and proportional gaps in living standards between the world's richest and poorest countries have, as Wolf himself admits, continued to grow. Furthermore, comparing national or international per capita income is only *one* way of measuring inequality, and a controversial one at that.[4] It masks the divisions of wealth *within* countries, the presence of severely

2. United Nations Development Programme (UNDP), *Human Development Report No.14* (Oxford: Oxford University Press, 2003), p. 59; *Atlante di le Monde diplomatique* (Italian edn, Paris and Rome: Le Monde diplomatique, 2004), p. 103.
3. M. Wolf, *Why Globalization Works* (New Haven and London: Yale University Press, 2004), p. 141, with accompanying statistics.
4. F. Bourguignon and C. Morrison, for the World Bank, have attempted to chart the progress of world income inequality from 1820 to 1992 in their article 'Inequality among world citizens', *American Economic Review*, 92, 4 (2002): 727–44. Their

underprivileged sectors of the population in the global North and privileged elites in the South. According to the United Nations Development Programme, between 7 and 17 per cent of the populations of industrialised countries remain in a state of relative poverty.[5] These disparities have increased over the past thirty years. Nor is the wealth of each of these countries a good guideline to its capacity to restrict or eliminate poverty. The United States, certainly the richest of the developed nations, has the highest percentage of its population living in relative poverty (some 17 per cent). As for the elites of the South of the world, by and large they have earned an unenviable reputation for corruption and for feathering their own nests. To them we shall return.

In economic terms, Asia has made great strides forwards, with China now the most dynamic nation of all, but entire other regions of the world have entered into states of comparative or absolute decline. The tragedy of sub-Saharan Africa has many facets; one of them is that its share of world per capita GNP has diminished drastically in the period 1975–2000. The same is true for Latin America, though its crisis has been less severe.[6]

To explain these differences of trajectory, it is essential to understand that the relationship between poor and rich countries is not a casual, but a structural one. It depends on their respective positions in the world division of labour. During the transformations of the last thirty years, it has been the developed countries of the North, and the United States in particular, that have dictated their own terms, both at a macroeconomic and at a local level.

In particular, policy towards developing countries has changed, with the triumph of what John Toye called the 'counter-revolution' in development theory. Both the International Monetary Fund (IMF) and the World Bank, fundamentally dependent on the US, abandoned the development-friendly

conclusion is that global inequality among individuals rose steadily from 1820 to 1980, but then fell. On the other hand, R. P. Korzeniewicz and T. P. Moran, in their detailed article 'World-economic trends in the distribution of income, 1965–92', *American Journal of Sociology*, 102, 4 (1997): 1000–39, argue on the contrary that the world became a less, not more equal place between 1965 and 1992, with inequality accelerating sharply during the 1980s.

5. UNDP, *Human Development Report No. 9* (Oxford: Oxford University Press, 1998), p. 28. table 1.8. The international standard-of-poverty line is drawn at the point where a family of two persons has an income inferior or at most equal to that of the average per capita income of the nation in question.

6. For an exemplary comparison, Giovanni Arrighi, 'The African crisis', *New Left Review*, NS, 15 (2002): 5–38.

policies of the preceding thirty years. The global South was invited to open up its economies to world market competition, to encourage the free flow of capital, and to reduce state sectors, which were often corrupt and inefficient. Markets were to reign supreme. The increased use of 'conditional aid', conditional that is on toeing the neoliberal line, was to be the instrument for forcing change upon recalcitrant elites.[7]

Both Latin America and sub-Saharan Africa have suffered severely from this shift, as they have from the general macroeconomic policies of the United States. Their plight, therefore, is not merely an endogenous affair, the result of natural disasters like the great Sahelian drought and famine of 1983–5, or the incompetence of local elites, as in Argentina. It is, to a considerable degree, the product of significant choices in political economy taken by analysts and politicians at the core of the world economy. Their choices have contributed to a dramatic bifurcation in the fortunes of developing countries, with East Asian countries in particular moving rapidly forward, but others, in other continents, being left far behind. The effects of such key policy decisions taken in New York or Washington constitute an object lesson in the need to understand human relations in a common, worldwide frame, in a 'global' fashion; and to realise how crucial, potentially, is the pressure of informed public opinion in the industrialised democratic countries

It may be objected that decisions such as those described above, heavy in consequences for whole regions of the world, seem far beyond the reach, if not of our comprehension, then certainly of our influence. This is not necessarily the case. Two examples are worth citing immediately to demonstrate in their different ways the possibilities of politics, even in the realm of macro-economics. One is characterised by the actions of elite analysts working from above to influence the direction and content of North–South relations. The other is the experience of a mass international campaign from below which aimed, and partially succeeded, in changing the governmental policy of the industrialised nations.

On 14 July 2001, two months before the catastrophic events in New York, the Harvard economist Jeffrey Sachs wrote in *The Economist* arguing for a massive increase in foreign aid from the richest countries, especially the US, to the poorer ones. In 1999 the US spent just 0.1 per cent of its GDP on foreign

---

7. John Toye, *Dilemmas of Development* (Oxford: Oxford University Press, 1993). For a more recent and essential critique, see Joseph E. Stiglitz, *Globalisation and its Discontents* (New York: Norton, 2002).

aid, a figure which had declined from nearly 0.8 per cent in the early 1960s. Italy was the next lowest spender in Sachs's graph, followed by Great Britain. At the top came Denmark (1 per cent of GDP), Norway and the Netherlands.

'Much of the poorer world', wrote Sachs, 'is in turmoil, caught in a vicious circle of disease, poverty and political instability':

> Through all of it, the US barely lifts a finger. It somehow thinks that sending the impoverished and unstable governments down Pennsylvania Avenue to get loans from the IMF and the World Bank will do the job, but even some staff of those organisations now publicly acknowledge that they have failed: making loans when grants are needed, imposing excessive austerity by collecting rather than cancelling debts, and failing to find partner-institutions with the scientific expertise to tackle underlying problems of disease, low food production, climatic stress and environmental degradation.[8]

Sachs couched his appeal to the United States and its allies as much in terms of self-interest as anything else: 'Large-scale financial and scientific help from the rich nations is an investment worth making not only for humanitarian reasons, but also because even remote countries in turmoil become outposts of disorder for the rest of the world.' Many doubts can be raised about the efficacy of aid strategies, and the way in which money has been squandered in the past. None the less, Sachs's campaign represents one important way of trying to reverse the immense damage done in the last thirty years. When Silvio Berlusconi, a man not known for a particular sensibility to the African tragedy, begins to argue on one of his television channels for the need to increase Italy's foreign aid to 0.33 per cent of GDP by 2006, then it is clear that the parameters of global discussion on these issues have been effectively shifted.

A second example concerns the massive debts incurred by some of the poorest countries in the world. The campaign of Jubilee 2000 was launched from London in 1996 with the aim of forcing the cancellation of unpayable debts by the year 2000. Countries like Uganda, Mozambique and Niger were crippled by the debts deriving from intergovernmental or IFI (international financial institutions) lending to them in the late 1980s and early 1990s. The original sum had grown rapidly into a much larger amount because many of

8. Jeffrey Sachs, 'What's good for the poor is good for America', *The Economist*, 14 July 2001.

the debtor countries, afflicted by war or civil war and by the collapse of primary commodity prices, had been unable to service their borrowing.

The campaign grew rapidly out of its London base. In 1998 a British opinion poll revealed that 69 per cent of public opinion wanted the British government to celebrate the millennium by cancelling Third World debt rather than building the Millennium Dome. (The Dome was a useless and costly construction enthusiastically backed by Tony Blair and some of his colleagues to celebrate 'Britishness', but which proved a cultural and economic disaster.) At its height the campaign of Jubilee 2000 involved groups of varying strength and character in sixty-eight countries, from Angola to Japan, from Sweden to Togo.

Not all that the organisers wanted was achieved. By the end of 2000 the debt had been partially cancelled, and only promises had been made about the rest. Ethiopia, with almost half of its population living in extreme poverty, is still spending $100 million on debt servicing, more than it spends on health.[9] However, the campaign had been exemplary in many respects. It had forced the question of poor nations' debt high up the international political agenda. It had communicated to ordinary people all over the world the idea that they could contribute, in a minimal but functional way, to altering the overwhelming imbalance in global riches and poverty. It had given courage to the representatives of the poor debtor nations. As Ann Pettifor, the former director of Jubilee 2000 UK, has written, 'The growth of a social movement in the North that supported their human rights and called for international financial justice encouraged developing country representatives to strengthen their negotiating stances and to appeal over the heads of bureaucracies like the IMF to the electorates in Western countries.'[10]

Both these initiatives, on the level of foreign aid and on debt cancellation, touch only marginally the structural economic relations between North and South as they have developed historically. Yet they are immensely valuable. They give the idea of targets to which governments can aspire, and by which they will be judged. In addition, a campaign like that on Thirld World debt can set in motion a process best described as subversive in a positive sense. It encourages people to question accepted truths and expert opinion, to inform themselves, to

9. Kevin Watkins, 'Africa's burden of debt is still far too heavy', *Financial Times,* 22 Sept. 2004.
10. Ann Pettifor, 'Why Jubilee 2000 made an impact', in Helmut Anheier, Marlies Glasius and Mary Kaldor (eds), *Global Civil Society 2001* (Oxford: Oxford University Press, 2001), pp. 62–3; see also Meghnad Desai and Yahia Said, 'The new anti-capitalist movement: money and global civil society', in ibid., pp. 60–4, box 3.4.

try and reach an understanding of human relations in a common, worldwide frame, to contribute with varying degrees of intensity to a collective movement.

Power and powerlessness

In 1999 a team of researchers working for the World Bank carried out interviews with over 20,000 poor people in twenty-three different countries in Africa and the Middle East, Eastern Europe and Central Asia, Latin America and the Caribbean, South and East Asia. The interviews revealed, time and again, that poverty and powerlessness were very closely connected and that the latter, in the words of the research's coordinator, Deepa Narayan, was 'at the core of the bad life'. Powerlessness was generally described as the inability to control what happens, the inability to plan for the future, and the imperative of focusing on the present. In Zawyet Sultan, Egypt, the condition known as *el-ghalban* and *ma' doom el hal*, words used to indicate the poorest, signify helplessness and having no control over sources of one's living, and therefore no control over one's destiny.[11]

The powerlessness that derives from poverty, but is not identical with it, blights most of the central human functional capabilities listed by Martha Nussbaum: it prevents adequate care of the body, leaves the living places of the poor isolated, unserviced and stigmatised, and allows little possibility of education. It is the antithesis of political participation.[12] There are many ways of illustrating it, but perhaps none more evocative than that of powerlessness in the hospital. Always allowing, and it is a big allowance in many of the rural

11. Deepa Narayan et al., *Voices of the Poor: Crying Out for Change* (Oxford: Oxford University Press (for the World Bank), 2000), p. 36. See also the companion volumes, *Voices of the Poor: Can Anyone Hear Us?* (Oxford: Oxford University Press, 2000), and *From Many Lands* (Oxford: Oxford University Press, 2002). The World Bank's definition of 'participation' which underlies these volumes has been the subject of much criticism, but the testimonies collected are of undoubted value.
12. Nussbaum, *Women and Human Development*, pp. 78–80. Given the importance of Nussbaum's approach for the arguments sustained in this book, it is worth listing here, even in abbreviated form, what she calls the 'central human functional capabilities': 1. *Life.* Being able to live to the end of a human life of normal length. 2. *Bodily health.* Being able to have good health including reproductive health. 3. *Bodily integrity.* Being able to move freely from place to place; having one's bodily boundaries treated as sovereign. 4. *Senses, imagination and thought.* Being able to use the senses, to imagine, think and reason – and to do these things in a 'truly human' way, a way informed and cultivated by an adequate education. 5. *Emotions.* Being able to have attachments to things and people outside ourselves. 6. *Practical reason.* Being able to form a

areas of the world, that the poor are able to reach medical services of one sort or another, there is no guarantee that once there they will be treated properly. Quite the opposite is very often the case. As a fisherwoman from Konada in India noted bitterly, 'If you don't know anyone, you will be thrown to the corner of a hospital!' In Padre Jordano, Brazil, a participant in a discussion group recounted that 'when we go to hospitals we know we will have to wait beyond the expected time [. . .] There comes somebody who is "higher" than us and jumps the queue.' A woman's group at Madaripur, Bangladesh, reported that the duty doctor in the hospital regularly ignored them and gave preference instead to patients wearing good clothes. Make poor and sick people wait: that is one of the many ways of marking them out. Their time is not precious, and they have no resources for, or possibility of, recourse.

The examples quoted above are revealing of another fundamental aspect of global power relations – those that exist between patrons and clients. This unequal dyadic relationship, with one person dependent and behoven to another, is one of the most diffuse in the modern world, as it was in the ancient world. It is fundamentally a societal relationship, but it is also found in many forms of government, in the real operations of states, even democratic ones. Sometimes it takes the name of patronage, a denomination which accentuates the role of the patron's munificence and influence; sometimes that of clientelism, in recognition of the service performed and the subordination established.

For the very poor, to gain access to the lowest rung of a clientelist ladder, that is to find a patron, may be the only way, certainly the most usual, to break out of a condition of total powerlessness. Patron–client relations, which obviously take different and complex forms, are of predominant importance in many parts of the world: in the Middle East and the Mediterranean, in Latin America and South-East Asia, in Japan and India, in eastern Europe, and in some parts of black Africa. They are far from absent, if less prominent, in the English-speaking and in the other European democracies.[13]

conception of the good and to engage in critical reflection about the planning of one's life. 7. *Affiliation.* a) Being able to live with and toward others. b) Having the social bases of self-respect and non-humiliation. 8. *Other species.* Being able to live with concern for and in relation to animals, plants, and the world of nature. 9. *Play.* Being able to laugh, to play, to enjoy recreational activities. 10. *Control over one's environment.* a) *Political.* Being able to participate effectively in political choices that govern one's life. b) *Material.* Being able to hold property (both land and movable goods), not just formally but in terms of real opportunity.

13. S. N. Eisenstadt and L. Roniger, *Patrons, Clients and Friends* (Cambridge: Cambridge University Press, 1984).

In ancient Rome clientelism was a formal pact established between patron and client, in which the client swore loyalty to his master, but received in return a series of legal guarantees as to the conduct of the patron on his behalf.[14] In most modern forms, by contrast, the client rarely has rights or powers; agreements are most often personal and informal, often covert and without legal binding. Powerful patrons are mostly middle-aged or elderly men, to whom other men and women are often locked in hopeless dependency. Patron–client relations, as Leopoldo Franchetti wrote long ago in his classic study of late nineteenth-century Sicilian society, may inspire a devotion 'which knows neither limits, nor scruples nor remorse'.[15] They are not, though, the stuff of which citizenship is made. The dominant social values they foster are those of submissiveness and gratitude, not of equality and mutual respect.[16]

Not all power is explicit, or easily legible. In the advanced democracies, but not only there, our capacity to interiorise power relations, to delimit by ourselves the realm of the possible, is extensive. We imbibe behavioural codes that are not unilateral or totalitarian or especially disciplinarian, and which furthermore appear to offer great freedom of choice, but which none the less convey us effortlessly into a life of normalcy and convention. The process is one of the great magics of modernity. In a famous passage Michel Foucault described this transformation, with prison architecture as his example and conveying metaphor:

The heaviness of the old 'houses of security', with their fortress-like architecture, could be replaced by the single, economic geometry of a 'house of certainty'. The efficiency of power, its constraining force, have, in a sense, passed over to the other side – to the side of its surface of application. He who is subjected to a field of visibility, and who knows it, assumes responsibility for the constraints of power; he makes them play spontaneously upon himself; he inscribes in himself the power relation in which he simultaneously plays both roles; he becomes the principle of his own subjection.[17]

14. See, for example, E. Deniaux, *Clientèles et pouvoir à l'époque de Cicéron* (Rome: École Française de Rome, 1993). For an interesting comparison between modern clientelism and that of ancient Rome, see L. Roniger, 'Modern patron–client relations and historical clientelism: some clues from ancient republican Rome', *Archives Européennes de Sociologie*, 24, 1 (1983): 63–95.

15. Leopoldo Franchetti, *Condizioni politiche e amministrative della Sicilia* (1876; Rome: Donzelli, 1993), p. 40.

16. See also below, ch. 4, pp. 153–6.

17. Michel Foucault, *Discipline and Punish* (Harmondsworth: Penguin, 1979), pp. 202–3.

Such interiorisation is endemic in modern societies but it should not be considered absolute. Power is never concentrated in a single source or a single historical actor, however powerful these may appear. Rather it is diffuse, more scattered in its specific instances than general, and capable of being created. 'Power over', the dominant expression of power even in democracies, often finds itself checked and contested by the 'power to'.[18]

Many of those individual figures who are most powerful in the modern world feel themselves strangely constrained. Such is the case of the chief executives of the great transnational companies, some of whom were recently interviewed by Noreena Hertz.[19] Fifty-one of the hundred biggest economies in the world are now corporations, while only forty-nine are national states, and the hundred largest corporations now control about 20 per cent of global foreign assets. Yet the group of men in charge of them appears highly vulnerable. 'What we fear most', said one of them, 'is consumer revolt.' Another admitted, paradoxically, to a feeling of powerlessness: 'If people think corporations are powerful, they haven't been in a corporation. We are by no means powerful – we are confined and restricted in what we do. Consumer choice doesn't allow us to have unfettered power.'[20] And to the vulnerabilities identified by Hertz we can add those engendered by the remorseless need to satisfy shareholders' hunger for dividends. The command posts in the corporations are thus notoriously insecure and falls from grace are frequent and dramatic, though always accompanied by extraordinary and unjustifiable economic compensation.

To build power from below is certainly a much more arduous, less remunerative, and less possible occupation than exercising it from above. Yet even in the most unpropitious circumstances the human capacity for solidarity, resistance and organisation finds spaces in which to flourish. The workers' movement in Italy gathered its first strength in the late nineteenth century, in the little towns of the eastern Po plain, when the habitués of the cafés and those of the taverns came together: artisans, doctors, students on the one hand, landless labourers in the direst poverty on the other.[21] In the rural areas of contemporary Bangladesh we can find something similar. Martha Chen has recounted the activity of the Bangladesh Rural Advancement

18. Angus Stewart, *Theories of Power and Domination* (London: Sage, 2001).
19. Noreena Hertz, *The Silent Takeover: Global Capitalism and the Death of Democracy* (London: Heinemann, 2001).
20. Ibid., p. 163.
21. Tiziano Merlin, 'L'osteria, gli anarchici e la "boje!" nel basso Veneto', *Annali dell'Istituto Alcide Cervi*, 6 (1984): 171–201.

Committee (BRAC), an indigenous private development agency which has helped very poor women, often heads of households, to enter the labour market at 'food for work' sites, and to create elements of power through collective action:

> In 1977, Saleha Begum's group, the Pachbarol Working Women's Group, collectively husked paddy for sale and cultivated potatoes and sugar cane on leased land [...] The women in Saleha's village took advantage of all that BRAC had to offer: they attended non-formal education classes; they negotiated loans; they received training in poultry rearing, fish culture, silkworm rearing, and agriculture; and they selected women from their group to be trained as paramedics, paraveterinarians, and paralegals.[22]

The interaction of the powerless members of a society with a democratic and enabling group, such as BRAC, is of crucial importance. It can initiate a cycle which runs counter to the processes which always put the poor and the powerless in last place, which make them wait, which pay no attention to them in hospitals. It can set in motion a realisation of individual capabilities inconceivable in a condition of individual isolation. It can oppose the subservience characteristic of patron–client relations and of many familial ones. None of these 'ways out' are guaranteed total success, but they put into play different dynamics from those habitually linked with the exercise of power.

Male and female

In historical terms, power has been predominantly male. In the Hellenic world the polarity between male and female was linked with others, all of which stressed the inferior qualities of the feminine. Aristotle's medico-philosophical reflections stressed that man was warm, dry, animated; woman cold,

22. Martha Chen, 'A matter of survival: women's right to employment in India and Bangladesh', in Martha C. Nussbaum and Jane Glover (eds), *Women, Culture and Development: A Study of Human Capabilities* (Oxford: Clarendon Press, 1995), pp. 43–4. See also Martha Chen, *A Quiet Revolution: Women in Transition in Rural Bangladesh* (Cambridge, Mass.: Schenkman, 1983), and the official website of the organisation, www.brac.net. Starting from a very modest base, BRAC today has more than 26,000 regular staff and 34,000 part-time teachers, active in more than 60,000 villages and all 64 districts of Bangladesh.

humid, inert. Woman's menstruation was an imperfect version of man's production of sperm, which was rarified blood obtained by an intense process of 'cooking'. The better the cooking of the sperm, the more chance of a male child. Such distinctions were not limited to the Western world. In Taoist philosophy *yin* is feminine – the earth, cold, shade, the north, rain, inferiority; *yang* is masculine – the sky, warmth, sunlight, the south, impetuosity, superiority.

In every part of the world the social and cultural representations of difference, and of male dominance within that difference, have been translated over the centuries into a terrifying catalogue of arbitrary powers. In the public sphere men have excluded women; in the private they have secluded them, as well as exercising a habitual violence on their bodies. Research carried out in the early 1990s in Chile, Mexico, Papua New Guinea and South Korea established that two-thirds of married women continued to be subject to domestic male violence.[23] In the northern Indian and Bangladeshi villages studied by Martha Chen, men have historically confined their women to limited spaces, above all to the household. Markets, roads and towns are forbidden to them. Nor can high caste women in northern India look for work, even if they and their families face destitution and famine. Still today, global poverty wears a female face: of 1.3 billion poor people, 70 per cent are women.[24] One informed comparison of the female/male ratio in the global North and South found more than 100 million women to be 'missing' in the South. This constructed figure reveals a hidden and tragic process, of which the selection of male newborns and malnutrition of girl children are the main elements.[25]

Male dominion takes many forms and patriarchy has expressed itself in any number of variations and guises. Often male power is exercised with the consent and support of females, some of whom, usually matrons of a certain age, exercise their own power within a patriarchal system. This was the case with the mother of the Turkish pasha, or of his first wife within the harem.[26]

23. UNDP, *Human Development Report No. 6* (Oxford: Oxford University Press, 1995), pp. 44–5.

24. Ibid., p. 36.

25. Amartya Sen, 'More than a 100 million women are missing', *New York Review of Books*, 20 Dec. 1990, p. 61, quoted in H. J. Steiner and P. Alston (eds), *International Human Rights in Context: Law, Politics, Morals* (Oxford: Oxford University Press, 2000), pp. 165–8. For the dramatic situation in India, see David Gardner, 'Where have all the girls gone?', *Financial Times*, 8–9 Feb. 2003.

26. Ayşe Saraçgil, *Il maschio camaleonte. Strutture patriarchali nell'Impero ottomano e nella Turchia moderna* (Milan: Bruno Mondadori, 2001), p. 38.

However great the variations between systems, certain male codes of conduct, the prioritising of specific values, can be recognised again and again: virility, heroism, honour, aggression, discipline and control. No group of men better expressed these values than those who built the European world empires on the basis of the segregated occupations of soldiering and sea trading: 'It was on those towers that the Portuguese captains had stood, scanning the sea for the ship from Lisbon that brought them blessed news of home [. . .] those gallant, swarthy men, in breastplate and hauberk, who carried their adventurous lives in their hands.'27

In the second half of the twentieth century, in many though not all parts of the world, the iron grip of male dominion loosened. Faced with the mobilisation of the feminist movement, the spread of women's education, and the changing conditions of the international labour market, men have retreated. Their legal powers have become more limited. They have moved, so one distinguished history of the European family has suggested, from patriarchy to partnership.28

There is clearly some truth in this, but none of us should be fooled or fool ourselves. Male chameleons are all around. Male power takes on different colours, more accommodating and more egalitarian, but much of its essence remains. As Françoise Héritier has written in this regard, 'Everything can be adjusted and perhaps inequalities are thinning out, but asymptotic regression does not mean disappearance.'29 Nowhere is this clearer than in the field of sexuality. In the vast, closeted empire of pornographic films – a semiotic cavern mainly of American manufacture – the sexual narrative is almost always the same: a woman exists in such films to worship the phallus, and to be taken, preferably simultaneously, both in the vagina and in the anus; her own orgasm is quite irrelevant, and the climax of the film comes with her oral consummation of the man's or men's 'hot' sperm. The long-term effects of such repetitive narratives on male ideas of their own sexuality can hardly be underestimated. In another and connected twilight world, that of prostitution, it is no exaggeration to say that female slavery has been reintroduced into some parts of southern Europe at the end of the twentieth century. Nigerian, Albanian, eastern European women in general, ensnared by male criminal

27. W. Somerset Maugham, *The Narrow Corner* (1932; London: Penguin, 1967), p. 102.
28. M. Mitterauer and R. Sieder, *Vom Patriarchat zur Partnerschaft. Zum Strukturwandel der Familie* (Munich: Beck, 1984).
29. Françoise Héritier, *Masculin/féminin. La pensée de la différence* (Paris: Odile Jacob, 1996), p. 13.

groups who promised them regular jobs in western Europe, are forced nightly to sell themselves many times over to members of the wealthy indigenous male population. Refusal or attempted flight usually means death at the hands of their 'protectors'.

In global terms, the fight for female emancipation has taken various significant steps in the last thirty years. In the fields of health and education especially, the condition of women in poor and developing countries has changed for the better. The significant decline in global birth rates between 1970 and 1990, from 4.7 live births per woman in 1970 to 3.0 in 1990, has meant that women have become progressively liberated from the burdens and dangers of excessive procreation. Fatalities at birth have decreased by more than half. In the same years, the fight to realise women's human capabilities through education has taken great strides. Women's illiteracy decreased between 1970 and 1990 by 50 per cent in the Arab states, by 26 per cent in South-East Asia, by 13 per cent in Latin America. In the field of tertiary education there has been a vertical rise in the enrolment of women in Latin American and Caribbean universities, while in most countries in the Organisation for Economic Co-operation and Development (OECD), though not Switzerland, not only are there more women than men at university, but their academic performance is superior.[30]

Signs of progress are much more muted in other fields. Women are systematically penalised in labour markets all over the world, and their wages and salaries are nowhere equal to those of men for the same work performed. Female representation in the public institutions of a country remains woefully sparse, even though women often obtained the suffrage more than fifty years ago. In many democratic countries there occurs a dispiriting if fascinating process of dilution by which women's votes are not translated into women's presence in politics, and women's professional capabilities do not succeed in penetrating the higher ranks of public administration. In a recent study of 502 senior civil servants in Japan, just three were women.[31] In Italy a woefully low number of women have become members of parliament, presidents of regions, senior civil servants and so on. As is well known, the four Scandinavian countries, Sweden, Finland, Norway and Denmark, have the best record in this respect and consistently head the gender parity tables of the

30. UNDP, *Human Development Report No. 6* (1995), pp. 29–30.
31. Paul S. Kim, *Japan's Civil Service System: Its Structure, Personnel and Politics* (New York: Greenwood, 1988), p. 40.

United Nations Development Programme.[32] However, even in the cold and civilised North the number of women MPs and cabinet ministers only reaches one-third of the total, while the OECD average is under one-sixth.[33]

Nor is it at all safe to claim that it is the Western democracies that are most attentive to the question of gender parity in the political sphere. It was India, not Britain or the United States, that in 1993 took the dramatically necessary but much contested step of legislating for an obligatory minimum of 33 per cent of women as councillors in local governments (*panchayats*), thus revolutionising representation at a local level.[34] Those democracies that boast most about their long-standing democratic values are often in reality staid and tired.

In a renowned article on the development of citizenship in the modern Western world, T. H. Marshall identified three areas of rights which were gradually acquired as democracy developed, and which constitute the basis of citizenship: civil rights, such as equality before the law, the right to own property and freedom of worship, which he identified principally with the eighteenth century; political rights, whose acquisition was to be located primarily in the nineteenth century; and social rights, such as those concerning health and education, which were the terrain of struggle and achievement in the twentieth century.[35]

Marshall's typology was precious and innovative at the time of its construction (1950), but it has been justly criticised on gender grounds. Feminist critics have pointed out that his scheme took no account of women or of the very uncertain trajectory of their achievement of rights.[36] Often

32. UNDP's *Human Development Report No. 6* (1995) suggests two ways of measuring gender disparity. The first, the index of human development co-related to gender (GDI), examines the amount earned by women as a percentage of a country's total income, women's life expectancy, literacy rates and levels of education. The second, the gender empowerment index (GEM), takes into consideration the number of women members of parliament, and the percentage of women administrators, managers and professional and technical workers in any given country, as well as women's overall income. While the first index aims to measure the development of women's capacities, the second shows to what extent women are able to put those capacities to use; see pp. 72–98, esp. tables 3.1 and 3.5 on pp. 76–7, 84–5.
33. Ibid., p. 52, table 2.8.
34. UNDP, *Human Development Report No. 13* (Oxford: Oxford University Press, 2002), p. 70.
35. T. H. Marshall, *Citizenship and Social Class* (Cambridge: Cambridge University Press, 1950). For a revisitation, Tom Bottomore, 'Citizenship and social class, forty years on', in T. H. Marshall and Tom Bottomore, *Citizenship and Social Class* (London: Pluto Press, 1991), pp. 55–93.
36. See S. Walby, 'Is citizenship gendered?', in Walby, *Gender Transformations* (London: Routledge, 1997), pp. 166–79.

women, especially in developing countries, receive political rights while still being denied fundamental civil rights. In Bangladesh women are now political subjects, but as we have seen they are still far from having control over their own bodies, full property rights, or the right to engage in all forms of employment. In the industrialised democracies, too, women's civil rights have often lagged behind their political ones. In France, women could vote from 1946 onwards, but they remained legal subordinates within the family until 1976.[37] As for social rights, such as pensions and social benefits, they are still overwhelmingly determined by the pattern of male work and male headship of families.

However, even these criticisms do not get to the heart of the matter. It is worth returning to the nature of difference in order to invert its habitual ordering. Millicent Fawcett noted at the beginning of the twentieth century that women could be adequately represented by men so long as the two sexes resembled each other completely, but, seeing as they did not, women's difference found no adequate expression in the present system.[38] A century later, her point is still largely unmet. The adequate expression of difference in the public sphere is not just ensured by the numerical presence of women. It is, rather, a question of culture, of a different way of setting agendas, choosing priorities and conducting business; a question of institutions and administrations, through being gendered in a different way, behaving in a different way.

A number of assumptions lie behind such bold affirmations. One is that it is possible to identify, if only in broad terms, specifically male and female values and behaviour, and that the time-honoured dominion of one (male) set of values has been not only to the detriment of women, but to all of us. Another, closely related, is that the ancients were right in perceiving gender difference, but wrong in the hierarchies they deduced from their observations and reflections.

To pretend the exact inversion of those ancient lists would be foolish indeed. So too would be the claim that women's behaviour incarnates every virtue and natural superiority. Everywhere there are women who have fully espoused, whatever the cost to themselves, typically male values of aggression, control, and unbridled individual ambition. In the Mediterranean countries,

---

37. This was the date of the new French family code, whose Article 215 states that 'spouses are mutually bound to a community of life'. None the less the husband remained the manager of the couple's communal property until 1985; Mary Ann Glendon, *The Transformation of Family Law* (Chicago: University of Chicago Press, 1989), pp. 90f.

38. Quoted in Héritier, *Masculin/féminin*, p. 292.

and not only there, such women are admiringly said to have male attributes. Sexual identities are more confused, overlapping and interchangeable than ever before.

None the less, it is still crucial to argue that female difference and specificity emerges constantly in a distinctive and recommendable form and content: both with regard to certain moral *virtues* such as caring, peacefulness, patience, and attention to intimate and everyday relations and needs; and with regard to certain moral *abilities*, such as that of perceiving intuitively the needs of others and being able to respond resourcefully to those needs.[39] The conscious transposition of such values to the public sphere would be a marvellous thing. And if care became the ethical basis of citizenship? Our parliaments, guided by such ideas, would be very different places.

Profits and ethics

Ethics and economics are not usually linked in the modern world. 'Business is business' has been a common refrain since the eighteenth century, and it is almost a matter of common sense, at least in the North of the world, that this should be so. As *The Economist* declared recently with disarming frankness: 'Businesses are ultimately interested in one thing: profits [. . .] If businesses think that treating their customers and staff well, or adopting a policy of "corporate social responsibility", or using ecologically friendly stationery will add to their profits, they will do it. Otherwise they will not.'[40] To question such a hierarchy of values is generally considered to be woolly minded, or out of touch with reality. Or even feminine, we might add.

It was not always so. For a long time the academic discipline of economics was considered to be a branch of ethics. Adam Smith was Professor of Moral Philosophy at the University of Glasgow, and one of his principal works, little used by those neoliberals who bowdlerise his thought, was *The Theory of Moral Sentimentes* (1790). The need to revive the links between economics and morals appears to be of prime importance at the present time. Otherwise we risk being governed by interests and processes that are unlikely to withstand a measure of ethical scrutiny.[41]

Those who believe most fervently in global capitalism would argue that it is

39. Nussbaum, *Women and Human Development*, p. 242.
40. See the survey 'Globalisation and its critics', *The Economist*, 29 Sept. 2001, p. 4.
41. For a renowned treatment of this theme see Armatya Sen, *On Ethics and Economics* (Oxford: Blackwell, 1987), esp. pp. 22–8.

indeed able to withstand such scrutiny. In other words, both the profit motive and the market economy (often wrongly considered to be indissolubly linked) enjoy a moral standing of their own. The argument in their favour is based on a number of planks. One is consequentialist. The 'invisible hand', as Adam Smith famously called the workings of market forces, brings unintended but unavoidably beneficial consequences *for all*. Men acting in their own self-interest in conditions of market freedom produce the best guarantees for the general enrichment of society. Not all men will profit equally, but all will profit. In recent times this has been referred to, in rather miserly terms, as the 'trickle down effect'; or else, more generously, as 'the rising tide that lifts all boats'.

A second argument has to do with rights. The rights to operate in the market and to buy, sell and own (unlimited) amounts of property are inalienable. They constitute one of the pillars of modern freedom and cannot be interfered with, at the cost of limiting freedom itself. The market offers to all who form part of it different paths to a single good: protection from coercion, which constitutes the essence of Isaiah Berlin's 'negative' freedom and, so some would argue, the essence of freedom itself.[42]

A third is essentially historical. For all its cyclical fluctuations and manifest inequalities, no better economic system than capitalism has yet been invented. Capitalism has led to the creation of extraordinary amounts of wealth for significant parts of the world, and the promise of its further extension. To call it seriously into question would be to kill the goose that laid the golden egg. Furthermore, convincing alternatives are not in abundant supply, either at a theoretical or empirical level. Marx may have been unrivalled as an analyst and critic of nineteenth-century capitalism, but the Marxist planned economies of the twentieth century in practice killed liberty, as well as entrepreneurship, without being able to achieve economic superiority. Thus their demise.

Such arguments must be tempered by a number of considerations. As we have seen briefly above, the rising tide of global economics, dominated above all by American needs and desires, has not lifted all boats, only some, and has cast down others in the most dire of fashions, as in contemporary Africa. Some

---

42. 'The consumer is protected from coercion by the seller because of the presence of other sellers with whom he can deal. The seller is protected from coercion by the consumer because of other consumers to whom he can sell. The employee is protected from coercion by the employer because of other employers for whom he can work, and so on. And the market does this impersonally and without centralised authority'; M. Friedman, *Capitalism and Freedom* (Chicago: University of Chicago Press, 1982), p. 15.

people and corporations, working in the 'casino capitalism'[43] of present-day financial institutions, have made the most extraordinary profits. Others, equally hard-working and talented, often in socially responsible jobs, have had no such opportunities. Others still, in the South of the world, have been briefly picked up and then thrown down by the fluctuating needs of the 'invisible hand'. Capitalism in its present form is too unpredictable, too unequal in its effects, too globally divisive to appear ethically convincing.

The same sort of argument can be made with regard to rights. Property rights and market freedoms, however important, cannot be considered inalienable, but must rather be measured in terms of their consequences. As Amartya Sen has argued with reference to major human disasters such as famines, the contingency of ownership, transfers and terms of trade can easily lead a particular occupational group or section of a population into destitution and even decimation, without anything illegitimate or perverse having happened from a rights' perspective. But, so he continues, it is not easy to understand why such rights should have an absolute priority over the life and death of millions of people.[44]

Even in less extreme circumstances, bold and blind is the apologist of the capitalist system who fails to notice that in it the freedoms of some are necessarily accompanied by the unfreedoms of others. Some (the minority in both the North and the South of the world) command, control, are enriched and consume conspicuously. They own and bequeath extensive property. Others, especially in the global North, have some say but less control. They too consume, but at most will leave a house and a car. Others still, especially in the global South, have no say and no control. They consume minimally and leave nothing to speak of. Under global capitalism, the position of these social groups is necessarily interdependent, as is the degree of their respective freedoms.

The third argument, the cautionary historical one which stresses the need not to abandon an economic system which has brought unprecedented if unevenly distributed wealth, is certainly the strongest. It is made stronger still by the absence of alternatives. Faced with it, many commentators have concentrated on the different roles of economic and political agents – of firms and governments. Precisely because markets and firms are driven by competition and profits, there are many things they cannot do, and many others that they do but should not do.

---

43. Susan Strange, *Casino Capitalism* (Oxford: Blackwell, 1986).
44. Amartya Sen, 'The moral standing of the market', in E. F. Paul et al. (eds), *Ethics and Economics* (Oxford: Blackwell, 1985), p. 6.

By contrast, so the argument runs, it is the task of governments, both national and supranational, to safeguard public and general interests. If they are democratically elected, governments have a legitimacy which no economic agent, however large, enjoys. Theirs is the task, therefore, to make the distinction between public ethics and business practice; theirs the responsibility for regulating conflicts regarding 'positional' goods, the ones that are in limited supply and the object of fierce competition; theirs the obligation to limit the inherently rapacious nature of economic actors under capitalism, to impose rules where the market is incapable of doing so. All this while leaving intact the functions which the market performs best – to provide incentives, guarantee the circulation of ideas and information, and to stimulate competition and innovation.

Such stuff is the mainstream discourse of present-day liberal and social-democratic reformism. As a programme of political action it is more often announced than practised, and more than once the hopes of a serious political alternative have evaporated in the face of the substantial subordination of 'left' or 'centre-left' governments to neoliberal ideas. But even if such governments were to do what they say they intend to, I wonder whether that would be enough.

Montesquieu, hardly the most economically radical of political thinkers, wrote in *Mes Pensées*: 'Riches are a wrong that have to be righted, and one could say: "Excuse me if I am so rich!"'[45] Behind this eighteenth-century statement, startling to twenty-first century ears, lies the perception of riches being a relational problem. To be rich, especially to be *too* rich, is to express oneself in relation to others in less than ethical terms. And one does not need to have a particularly Marxian sensibility to hear that same unease echoing across the centuries.

In the era of globalisation concerns such as these are of great relevance. While the daily incomes of those who work in the financial markets or at the summit of the great corporations seem absurdly and immorally inflated, a worker in Starbucks told Naomi Klein, '"You can buy two grande mocha cappuccinos with my hourly salary."' And Klein comments: 'All the brand-name retail workers I spoke with expressed their frustration at helping their stores rake in, to them, unimaginable profits, and then having to watch that profit get funneled into compulsive expansion.'[46]

---

45. C. L. de Montesquieu, *Mes Pensées*, part 6, 'Cupidité et libéralité', no. 1130, in Montesquieu, *Oeuvres complètes*, ed. R. Caillois, vol. 1 (Paris: Gallimard, 1949), p. 1290.
46. Naomi Klein, *No Logo* (London: Flamingo 2000), p. 264.

Are there any glimmers of a more ethically convincing, more democratic economic system? In the face of the relational problem of riches, some authors have suggested a rule of limitation. The distance between the average income of the richest fifth of a nation and its poorest fifth should not exceed the ratio of five to one. This is a project for 'equitable inequality'.[47] Others have talked of the slow introduction of 'market socialism', based on local producer and consumer cooperatives which should never exceed a certain size.[48] Such suggestions have much to recommend them in ethical terms; they leave open a window for individual economic incentive, and they would make society less polarised. However, they are as yet untried, and there must be doubts about their practicability and enforceability.

There seem to be no easy answers. The nineteenth-century dream of the cathartic and liberating moment of socialist revolution, which would create the conditions for a more humane, post-capitalist world, appears to have been consigned by the history of the twentieth century to the rubbish heap. What might be suggested instead is a critical traversing of the sheer faces of the capitalist system, with the intent of introducing counterdynamics to those now operating. Successful experiments with economic alternatives could become global reference points, and in this way accumulate momentum. A journey of this sort could only be successful, we should insist, if ethics and economics are very firmly roped together.

Legality and illegality

The last thirty years of world history do not comfort us very much in this task. If we contemplate the framework of regulations and norms within which capitalism operates, not only has deregulation been the order of the day, but explicitly illegal economic practices have greatly extended their influence. Legal and illegal economies now increasingly intertwine. They both use the same financial and communication networks, the same forms of transport, sometimes the same lawyers. In many countries administrators and politicians, in return for bribes or votes, or both, turn a blind eye to the activities of the illegal sector, often while simultaneously insisting on the need for law and order. Technological transformations, too, have come to abet lack of

47. See the discussion in Giorgio Ruffolo, *La qualità sociale* (Rome: Laterza, 1985), pp. 224ff.
48. David Schechter, *Radical Theories: Paths beyond Marxism and Social Democracy* (Manchester: Manchester University Press, 1994), pp. 124–49. D. Schweikart et al., *Market Socialism. The Debate among Socialists* (London: Routledge, 1988).

detection. 'Dirty' money is laundered more easily than ever before. The container revolution in maritime transport has provided excellent cover for shipments of cocaine and other drugs.[49]

The transnational illegal economy has become a world unto itself.[50] According to the geographer Teresa Isenburg, its landscape is defined both by the flows that animate it, and by its ethico-structural profile.[51] It has no fixed confines but rather contaminates continuously the larger world with which it is in constant contact. Its driving forces are those of rapid accumulation, clan loyalty, male virility and violence. Its culture is that of superstitious religiosity, opulent and ostentatious consumption, blackmail and betrayal: the world of Tarantino's films. Its consequences are vertiginous social mobility or early death – sometimes both in the course of abbreviated and violent lives.

'Traffic' is the word most often used to describe the illegal economy's principal activities: traffic in illegal immigrants, offering them no guarantee of surviving the journey for which they have paid considerable sums of money; in drugs and toxic substances; in prostitutes, who are often reduced, as we have said, to slavery; in human organs; in protected animal species; in arms and in materials needed to construct nuclear weapons. Vast flows of money accompany all these tradings. The IMF estimated in 1996 that every year 500 billion dollars deriving from illegal trafficking is 'cleaned' and recycled by the international financial system, with its highly convenient offshore havens.

The illegal world is not just one of traffic, but one which inhabits entire geographical spaces. In recent times the central part of the valley of the Magdalena river in Colombia has been reduced to a Hobbesian 'state of nature'. Its natural resources have rendered the valley a site of considerable foreign investment: by Texas Oil for petrol, by the United Fruit Company for

49. It has been estimated that in US ports the thorough inspection of one previously sealed container takes five customs officers some three hours. Under the 'streamlined' US Customs inspection procedures only 3 per cent of the nearly 9 million containers that enter the country every year are now subject to inspection; P. B. Stares, *Global Habit: The Drug Habit in a Borderless World* (Washington DC: Brookings, 1996), p. 69.

50. André Bossard, former general secretary of Interpol, has noted that transnational crime is distinguished by two key characteristics. First, a border must be crossed, either by the perpetrators, their victims, the goods and services being transacted, or the orders directing such transactions. Second, the activity must be recognised as a criminal offence by at least two states, either by treaty, convention, or similar national laws; as quoted in H. R. Friman and P. Andreas (eds), *Illicit Global Economy and State Power* (Lanham, Md.: Rowan & Littlefield, 1999), p. 5.

51. Teresa Isenburg, *Legale/illegale, una geografia* (Milan: Edizioni Punto Rosso, 2000), p. 25.

bananas, by more than one economic agent for the mining of emeralds. Here there was once a tradition of trade union organisation and even of agrarian reform (the law 200 of 1936). But the trade unionists were killed off by paramilitary groups and the valley 'reorganised' at the behest of mine and ranch owners, of banana exporters, of segments of the army and the traditional political parties. Terror has become the order of the day. The peasants have been forced off their land by some 6,000 paramilitaries, organised in 140 different groups.[52]

The central Magdalena valley in Colombia is an extreme example of occupied space, lost to any semblance of legality. There are others like it and they are terrible places. However, they constitute only a fraction, at least up until the present time, of the inhabited territory of the globe. In many other parts of the world, the tension betwen legality and illegality takes other forms, less dramatic but equally insidious. Official codes of behaviour and the rule of law exist, but they are undermined from within by clientelism and nepotism, by bribery and corruption.

These semi-legal and illegal practices can be viewed as being situated along a single continuum, or else, in an image beloved of Antonio Gramsci, as interconnected carriages of a train. Patron–client relations lie at one end, wholesale cooperation with illegal armed organisations at the other. There is no necessary and inevitable passage from one end to the other, and any individual can stay in the carriage of his or her choosing, or even get off the train. However, if a given collective, be it a corporation or nation-state, does not take its distance in a determined fashion from all such practices, and fails to establish its own sense of limits to certain behaviour and its own culture of public ethics, then it will soon be infested by the daily practice of illegality.[53]

The entire history of Latin America can, to varying degrees, be read in these terms. As the historian Anthony McFarlane has written about the development of independent South American states:

In political cultures where freedom was traditionally seen in essentially negative terms, as freedom from the state rather than freedom within it, and where escape from the impositions of the state by evasion or bribery

52. Ibid., pp. 87ff.
53. J. Scott, *Comparative Political Corruption* (Englewood Cliffs, N.J.: Prentice Hall, 1972), pp. 79–80, on the need for states to create a sense of limit and of propriety among its citizens. For a recent and useful discussion of these themes, L. M. Macedo Pinto De Sousa, 'Corruption: assessing ethical standards in political life through control policies', Ph.D. thesis, European University Institute, San Domenico di Fiesole, 2002.

was commonplace, the construction of integrated national states built on basic liberal principles was to prove highly problematic. Although the Spanish crown had been swept away, corruption remained as an important device for distributing power and resources in societies where family and personal ties continued to overshadow the formal obligations which bind state and citizen in a modern polity.[54]

There exists, of course, the danger of treating the problem of legality and illegality in oversimplistic or Manichean terms. Illegality is not a single corpus. Circumstances, it can be argued, dictate the creation of grey areas and fine lines of distinction. In post-Communist Russia, with the helter-skelter commercialisation of society and the lack of clear legal sanctions, not all illegal transactions are viewed by the population in the same way. Some indeed are both habitual and strictly necessary for survival.[55]

However, if the boundaries of bribery, corruption, illicit market activity and so on vary considerably, the core definition of what is unacceptable public practice has remained remarkably stable across the centuries. In 1619 in England corruption was defined as the use of 'monies designed for the public service for private ends'.[56] In seventeenth-century Florence, corruption was described in similar terms, though it was considered not just a crime but also a sin. The great Florentine historian Guicciardini defended himself against such charges, arguing that he, like Pericles, was 'uncorrupted by money'.[57] Modern definitions of corruption, though more elaborate, boil down to much the same thing. Nepotism, too, has not changed its meaning over time.

As for justifications regarding the force of custom or circumstance, and the consequent creation of grey areas, it is as well to remember that, however plausible they sound, and understandable in dire circumstances, they stand at the beginning of a very slippery slope. Corrupt politicians all over the world have always used exactly such arguments to justify their conduct. In addition,

54. Anthony McFarlane, 'Political corruption and reform in Bourbon Spanish America', in W. Little and E. Posada-Carbó (eds), *Political Corruption in Europe and Latin America* (London: Macmillan, 1996), p. 61.

55. Caroline Humphrey, 'Rethinking bribery in contemporary Russia', in S. Lovell et al. (eds), *Bribery and Blat* (London: Macmillan, 2000), pp. 216–41.

56. Linda L. Peck, *Court, Patronage and Corruption in Early Stuart England* (London: Routledge, 1993), p. 161.

57. F. Guicciardini, *Consolatoria, Accusatoria, Defensoria. Autodifesa di un politico*, ed. U. Dotti (Rome: Laterza, 1993), p. 99. See the important work of J. C. Waquet, *Corruption: Ethics and Power in Florence, 1600–1770* (1984; University Park: Pennsylvania State University Press, 1992).

the global evidence that corrupt practices of all sorts both undermine faith in the state and damage economic performance is overwhelming.[58]

The best answer to them comes in Lord Nolan's famous *Report of the Committee on Standards in Public Life in Britain*, published in 1995:

> Frequently in our work we heard the expression 'grey area' used as a rationalisation of morally dubious behaviour. The ubiquity of the phrase, and the implication that some no longer seem to be certain of the difference of what is right and what is wrong in public life, concern us. When people in public life are in doubt about whether a particular action is consistent with standards expected of them, the only proper course is not to do it.[59]

There is a global fight going on against both a pervasive transnational illegal economy and against corrupt political practices. It is by no means clear who is winning – or, sometimes, who is on which side. Consequently, it is as well to be extremely clear, as Nolan's report was, about the boundaries and standards that we wish to establish.

Human consumption and environmental conservation

By the end of the twentieth century, for the first time in the ecological history of the planet, an acute awareness of the finite and fragile nature of global resources had come to predominate among expert opinion. The optimistic nineteenth-century view of the infinite availability of nature to humankind had given way to darker predictions. In early 1992, the US National Academy of Sciences and the Royal Society in London issued a joint report that began: 'If current predictions of population growth prove accurate and patterns of human activity on the planet remain unchanged, science and technology may not be able to prevent either irreversible degradation of the environment or continued poverty for much of the world.'[60]

58. R. Theobald, *Corruption, Development, and Underdevelopment* (Durham, N.C.: Duke University Press, 1990), pp. 125–32. For a convincing Asian overview see P. D. Hutchcroft, 'The politics of privilege: rents and corruption in Asia', in A. J. Heidenheimer and M. Johnston (eds), *Political Corruption: Concepts and Contexts* (New Brunswick, N.J.: Transaction, 2002), pp. 488–512.
59. *First Report of the Committee on Standards in Public Life*, vol. 1: *Report* (London: HMSO, 1995), p. 16.
60. US National Academy of Sciences and Royal Society, London, *Population Growth, Resource Consumption and a Sustainable World* (London and Washington DC, 1992), quoted in L. R. Brown and H. Kane, *Full House: Reassessing the Earth's Population Carrying Capacity* (London: Earthscan, 1995), p. 30.

It is as well to enumerate the various aspects of the problem that can be related back to two of the most basic of human functions: consumption and procreation.

Consumption

The twentieth century was unique for the extraordinary accleration that took place in the rhythms of human consumption. Between the 1890s and the 1990s the global economy increased approximately 14 times, world industrial output 40 times, energy use some 13 times, marine fish catch some 35 times. Incremental consumption, especially in the rich countries of the world and especially after 1945, was quite breathtaking: by 1998 24 trillion US dollars were being spent worldwide in private and public consumption, twice the figure for 1975, and six times that of 1950.[61] The overall effect on global ecology was bound to be startling. Few of the environmental changes of the twentieth century were entirely new (the human-induced thinning of the ozone layer was one), but the scale and intensity of pressure on the environment were quite unprecedented.[62]

All this created stress areas, some potentially more catastrophic than others. Non-renewable resources such as oil and minerals have been used up in great quantities, but the general consensus of expert opinion is cautiously optimistic with regard to their future. The ratio between production and reserves (not potential reserves but those that can be extracted at current prices) has actually increased in recent decades, and recycling and technological progress have increased the possibilities of substitution.

The same is not true with regard to what are sometimes called, with regrettable accuracy, 'natural sinks'. The atmosphere, one such 'natural sink', has been increasingly polluted in a number of ways, none more menacing than that of emissions of carbon dioxide (CO_2), which have quadrupled in the last fifty years. The connections between greenhouse gases, the thinning of the ozone layer, global warming and the possibility of profound climatic changes have generally if not unanimously been interpreted as a grave threat to life on the planet.[63] If temperatures do steadily increase, much of the world's population is in danger – though not all in the same danger. Some, especially

---

61. UNDP, *Human Development Report No. 9*, pp. 1 and 46.
62. John McNeill, *Something New under the Sun* (London: Allen Lane, 2000), p. 4; and p. 360, table 12.1, for increase factors, 1890s–1990s.
63. *Climate Change 2001: The Scientific Basis. Contribution of Working Group 1 to the Third Assessment Report of the Intergovernmental Panel on Climate Change* (Cambridge: Cambridge University Press, 2001).

in coastal areas, face floods and hurricanes; others, as in sub-Saharan Africa, droughts and famine. All are at risk.

The two other great 'natural sinks', the earth and the sea, have also suffered seriously from the polluting consequences of unrestrained consumption. Increasing mountains of refuse and of toxic waste are present in and upon the earth, and are regularly exported from the North to the South of the world. The sea and all that lives in it have had to contend with massive quantities of pollutants of all sorts, old and new, none more dramatic than the oil deposited regularly by the broken holds of ageing and uninspected tankers.

As with non-renewable resources, so with 'natural sinks', the human capacity to respond, modify and adapt is far from absent. The historian of the environment John McNeill has likened us to rats in our capacity to adapt our habits to changed circumstances. We are responsive to crises and can be flexible in our consumption. Thanks to the persistent tail waving of some far-seeing rats, the 'hole' in the ozone layer now appears to be diminishing in size. But in the environment, as we shall see in a moment, there are at work not only rats but sharks. The latter's interests and indeed survival are dependent on continuing to eat much of the same in unchanged circumstances. Their domi-nant presence cannot make us sanguine about the future.

Renewable resources are the third great environmental area affected by modern consumption (the first two being non-renewable resources and 'natural sinks'). Water, land, forests, fish, biodiversity are all, at least in theory, resources that can be renewed. However, the United Nations Development Programme informs us that the global availability of water has diminished by more than twice since 1950, that one-sixth of the earth's cultivated surface is suffering from severe degradation, that forest areas have declined since 1970 from 11.4 square kilometres per 1,000 inhabitants to 7.3 (1998 figures), and that many fish and animal species are at increasingly severe risk of extinction. Resources of these sorts may be renewable, but there is little indication that regeneration is actually what is happening.[64]

Furthermore, to return for a moment to earlier sections of this chapter, the great explosion of human consumption has been unequally distributed in the most dramatic of ways. The richest 20 per cent of the world's population are responsible for some 86 per cent of all private consumer spending while the poorest 20 per cent account for only 1.3 per cent. There are 1.4 billion people in the world who do not even have regular access to drinking water, let alone anything else. And, naturally enough, those who are richest and consume the

64. UNDP, *Human Development Report No. 9* (1998), pp. 60–90.

most, pollute the most. The United States alone is responsible for nearly one-quarter of all global CO_2 emissions.

Procreation

If modern consumption is the primary human activity in radical conflict with the preservation of the environment, procreation can be considered a second. In 1900 world population numbered 1.2 billion people, in 1950 2.5 billion, in 2000 just over 6 billion. By 2025 it is estimated to have increased to 7.8 billion.[65] Does the earth have sufficient carrying capacity for so vast a number of people?

The answer to that question appears to be a qualified 'yes'. The demographer Massimo Livi-Bacci has written recently, on the basis of a careful survey of existing evidence, that 'it seems realistic to think that the earth will be able to sustain 10 or 11 billion people during the coming century'.[66] However, his answer (and ours) does not stop there, for it is necessary to place patterns of procreation together with those of consumption in order to try and estimate their *combined* effects.

At first sight, the combination is anything but comforting. It is true that the most polluting part of the world population, in the rich countries, is also that marked by the slowest demographic growth. It is also true that in the North technological innovations are being intermittently employed to limit environmental damage. Even so, the North of the world will need a much more radical change in its consumption patterns to reduce significantly its contribution to world pollution. The search for alternative models and ways of putting them into operation constitutes one of the great challenges of the present era.[67]

However, the really unknown quantity comes not from the North but from the South, in particular from those poorer countries already characterised by high levels of fertility, and where population growth will be most marked in the future. Poverty and high fertility tend to go hand-in-hand not just because of ignorance or inaccessibility of contraceptive measures, but because in the absence of adequate health care and pension schemes, children act as some sort of family insurance against destitution and parental debility in old age. Over the next few decades it will be an essential task to improve the very

---

65. Massimo Livi-Bacci, *A Concise History of the World Population* (Oxford: Oxford University Press, 2001), p. 175.
66. Ibid., p. 193.
67. For an extended discussion, see below, esp. chapter 2, pp. 98–145.

meagre standards of living of these low- and middle-income countries – that 85 per cent of the world's population that, according to World Bank estimates, have an average annual income of only $1,250 dollars per head.[68] But to do so will entail dramatic increases in the use of resources: for agricultural production, resulting in pressure on arable land, forests, stocks of water and fish, as well as spiralling levels of pollution deriving from chemical fertilisers; for consumer goods, with a drastic increase in the use of non-renewable resources such as oil and minerals; for the development of land not previously built on, with consequent menaces to the fragile environmental balance of many parts of the world, especially densely inhabited coastal areas (two-thirds of the world's population live within 60 kilometres of coastlines).

It is thus crucial to understand that in the coming decades population growth in the South will be combined not just with increased standards of living, but ways of life based on current modes of consumption. The effects of this particular combination are quite unpredictable. Any forecast that denies the very heavy, perhaps intolerable, strain on global resources and ecological balance is short-sighted indeed. Yet the drive to adopt different modes of consumption, in both the South and the North, is as yet very weak. Nor can the South be expected to adopt more sober and sustainable models if the North continues on its wanton way. Indeed it cannot do so even if it wants to, because the North continues to export for all its worth its own consumer model, and its own waste, to the rest of the world.

Latife Tekin, in her memorable novel *Berji Kristin*, offered this description of immigration to Istanbul in the 1960s:

> When the garbage trucks had come and gone, the simit-sellers on the way to the garbage heard that eight huts had been built on the slopes [. . .] By noon people had begun to descend on the hillside like snow [. . .], people who had left their villages to move in with their families in the city, and others roaming the hills behind the city in the hope of building a hut. Men and women, young and old, spread in all directions. Kneeling and rising they measured with feet and outstretched arms. Then with their spades they scratched crooked plans in the earth [. . .] Next morning, by the garbage heaps – downhill from the factories which manufactured lightbulbs and chemicals, and facing the china factory – a complete

68. World Resources Institute, *World Resources 1998–1999* (Oxford: Oxford University Press, 1999), p. 345.

neighbourhood was fathered by mud and chemical waste, with roofs of plastic basins, doors from old rugs, oilcloth windows and walls of wet breezeblocks.[69]

By the year 2000 the city had a population of 9.5 million, expected to rise to 12.5 million by 2015. As such, it ranks as a medium-size metropolis among the urban conglomerations of the developing world. Mumbai (Bombay) is expected to have a population of more than 26 million by 2015, Lagos more than 23 million, Dhaka 21 million, São Paolo more than 20 million, Karachi and Mexico City 19 million each.[70]

In the chaos, spontaneity and desperation that characterises the massive flight of population to these mega-metropolises of Africa, Asia and Latin America, there is little that promises well in terms of alternative patterns of consumption. Spending on advertising in developing countries, much of it by transnational companies, has been in dynamic expansion, as has the number of television sets. From these and the billboards of the great cities come the forceful and unceasing invitations to traditional, unquestioning conspicuous consumption, much of it of dubious value for the welfare of the urban population (spiralling consumption of cars, fatty fast food and tobacco, for instance). However, little else is on offer. The languages of the media of different nations may be many and varied, but that of the advertisers is universal.

The nature of the great urban agglomerations, characterised by dis-economies of scale, absence of elementary services and lack of social integration, suggests strongly that the population explosion has taken a disastrous spatial form. More and more, the richer quarters of the city are fenced off in one way or another, protected by private guards and surveillance cameras. By contrast the extreme peripheries, the site of slums and shanty towns, are scarred by disease, malnutrition and the absence of basic services, in Nairobi as in Rio.[71] Nearly one-third of the global urban population of 3.2 billion people now live in slums; and at least half of the slum population is

69. Latife Tekin, *Berji Kristin. Tales from the Garbage Hills* (1983; London: Marion Boyars, 1993), p. 16.
70. UN Centre for Human Settlements (Habitat), *Cities in a Globalizing World: Global Report on Human Settlements, 2001* (London: Earthscan, 2001), table B.1, pp. 300–6; already in the year 2000, only three of the largest twenty cities in the world were in the global North – Tokyo, New York and Los Angeles.
71. UN Centre for Human Settlements, *The Challenge of the Slums: Global Report on Human Settlements, 2003* (London: Earthscan, 2003).

under the age of twenty. This constitutes a return to the world of Dickens on a massive, global scale, with an estimated 100 million children living on the streets, and with women improvising livelihoods as piece workers, street vendors, cleaners, ragpickers and prostitutes.[72] Urban dreams are rapidly replaced by the enduring squalor of daily life, from which rapid if risky escape is often only possible through membership of criminal bands.

There are, of course, other possible ways out, or alternatives to illegality. In the expanding Arab cities the absence of traditional forms of integration, together with the lack of services offered by the state (sanitary, educational or hygienic), have pushed their populations ineluctably towards those Islamic groups, both moderate and radical, offering solidarity and mutual aid. Poor housing in bidonvilles, unemployment, and high costs of living have done their work of disenchantment. As Bichara Khader has written, Islam appears 'as the last resource, an extreme refuge [. . .] the best response to unitary expectations (the return to the true *umma*, the community of believers), to the overcoming of inequalities and the levelling of differences, and the transcendence of clan, ethnic and intra-state divisions'.[73] In the slums of sub-Saharan Africa and much of Latin America, the counterpart of Islam is Pentecostal Christianity. Granting to women a significant role in the Church, insisting on the dignity of frugality and abstinence, and with a reputation for being colour-blind, Pentecostalism has grown into 'what is arguably the largest self-organised movement of urban poor people on the planet'.[74] Not all urban movements of the slum poor are so benign. Time and again, the patron–client relations which predominate in the slums lead their inhabitants to enrol in the bands of ethno-religious extremists, such as the anti-Muslim militias of the Oodua People's Congress in Lagos or the Shiv Shena movement in Mumbai.[75]

So what then can be done? The task appears to be a truly daunting one, in terms both of environmental conservation and of the terrible contrasts presented by modern metropolitan life, above all in the South of the world. Some steps have been taken to confront the first of these problems, almost

72. Mike Davis, 'Planet of slums', *New Left Review*, NS, 26 (Mar.–Apr. 2004), pp. 21–5.
73. Bichara Khader, 'La città araba di ieri e di oggi: alcune riflessioni introduttive', in Fondazione Giovanni Agnelli, *Città e società nel mondo arabo contemporaneo* (Turin: Fondazione Giovanni Agnelli, 1997), p. 17.
74. Davis, 'Planet of slums', p. 32.
75. Veena Das (ed.), *Mirrors of Violence: Communities, Riots and Survivors in South Asia* (New York: Oxford University Press, 1990).

none with regard to the second. From the 1972 United Nations conference in Stockholm onwards, there have been a number of significant international agreements regarding global environmental action. The International Convention for the Protection of the Ozone Layer (1985, brought into force in 1998) and the Montreal Protocol (1987, brought into force in 1989) took decisive steps to regulate the production and consumption of ozone-depleting substances, particularly chlorofluorocarbons (CFCs). The Kyoto Protocol of 1997, though considered by many to be insufficiently radical, sets out for the first time legally binding reduction targets for six key greenhouse gases. By February 2005, when the Protocol came into force, 141 countries, including China, India and most recently Russia, had signed it, but the United States of America had not.[76]

This sad fact constrains us to return to the distinction between rats and sharks. In environmental terms the United States is a shark. It has relied on a constant and plentiful supply of cheap fossil fuel throughout the twentieth century, and it shows few signs of changing its ways. Its standard of living embodies a level of material comfort and use of energy resources unprecedented in human history. In the four years between 1983 and 1987, Americans purchased 51 million microwaves, 44 million washers and dryers, 85 million colour televisions, 36 million refrigerators and freezers, 48 million video cassette recorders and 23 million cordless telephones – all for an adult population of only 180 million.[77] In 1992, at the UN conference in Rio de Janeiro on the Environment and Development, the then President of the US George Bush declared that 'the American way of life is not up for negotiation'. Given such a starting point, conflicts over increasingly rare global resources, such as oil, are liable to become the order of the day.

War and peace

The earliest evidence of war, in the modern sense of the term, derives from the frequent and lethal conflicts between hunter-gatherers of the Mesolithic period, some 10,000 to 5,000 years ago. In the late Palaeolithic cemetery at Gebel Sahaba in Egyptian Nubia, dating back to between 14,000 and 12,000 years ago, more than half of the fifty-nine men, women and children buried

76. With Russia accounting for 17 per cent of global emissions, its endorsement of the protocol was vital in order to reach the global 55 per cent threshold necessary to put the treaty into operation; Andrew Jack and Raphael Minder, 'Climate treaty passes last hurdle', *Financial Times*, 23 Oct. 2004.
77. Juliet Schor, *The Overworked American* (New York: Basic Books, 1991), p. 108.

there were found to have died violent deaths. Several adults had multiple wounds, some as many as twenty, and the wounds found on children were all in the head or neck. They had obviously been executed. The evidence from Gebel Sahaba and elsewhere offers, in the words of Lawrence Keeley, 'graphic testimony that prehistoric hunter-gatherers could be as ruthlessly violent as any of their more recent counterparts and that prehistoric warfare continued for long periods of time'.[78]

Are such histories the inevitable fate of humankind, destined to worsen as modern technology improves the capacity to kill, until such time as we all kill each other? There are many who have taken this to be the fundamental lesson of history. Men are 'natural born killers'. In 1932 Einstein wrote to Freud, asking him if it was possible for men to develop a greater capacity to resist the psychosis of hate and destruction.[79] Freud gave a half-hearted if cautiously optimistic reply, but others have preferred a darker, more determinist view. Human nature, so the argument goes, is what it is, and our destiny is not ours to control. Frequently such assertions are linked to neo-Darwinism. Man is a 'human animal', a highly inventive species but 'one of the most predatory and destructive'.[80] Or else, in the words of the military historian Robert O'Connell, he is 'an imperial beast, born with a weapon in his hand'.[81]

If all such assertions were true, then everyday politics would simply be a waste of time. The evolutionary dice are loaded against us, the weapons we have can easily destroy the earth many times over, and we may as well spend the little time left to us eating ice-cream or satisfying other sybaritic desires. However, the argument, given its importance, is worth unpicking a little

78. Lawrence H. Keeley, *War before Civilisation* (Oxford: Oxford University Press, 1996), p. 37. Only among those peoples who made use of stone- and bone-tipped weapons, which can survive embedded in or closely associated with human skeletons, can accidental injury or that inflicted by animals be clearly distinguished from wounds inflicted by humans. The use of such weapons has occurred in the last 40,000 years, and one of the earliest pieces of evidence of this sort is from Grimaldi in Italy where a projectile point was embedded in the spinal column of a child's skeleton dating back to the Aurignacian period (36,000–27,000 years ago).

79. The correspondence was published in 1933 under the title *Why War?*; for an interesting discussion of this exchange, see Daniel Pick, *War Machine: The Rationalisation of Slaughter in the Modern Age* (New Haven and London: Yale University Press, 1993), pp. 214-20.

80. See the highly polemical essay by the political philosopher John Gray, *Straw Dogs* (London: Granta, 2002), p. 4 and *passim*.

81. Robert L. O'Connell, *Of Arms and Men* (Oxford: Oxford University Press, 1989), p. 310.

more; fatalism, wearing the mask of realism and science, should not be allowed so easy a victory.

In the first place, if humans are animals, then they are animals of a very particular sort. As the biologist E. O. Wilson, no tender-hearted humanist, once commented: 'If hamadryas baboons had nuclear weapons, they would destroy the world in a week.'[82] Historical evidence would point to the conclusion that not all men, let alone all women, to whom we shall return in a moment, are unavoidably disposed to war. The human condition is more ambivalent than that. As every sergeant-major knows, 'ordinary' men have to be transformed into killers, and the process by which this takes place has been the subject, not by chance, of an endless stream of American feature films. If all men are genetically made for war, it is difficult to explain why so many of them shot or mutilated themselves to avoid the trenches of the First World War, why Napoleon's armies had to camp away from woods to avoid soldiers' nocturnal flight, or why nearly all men in all historical periods have gone into combat in an artificially induced state of inebriation.[83]

Of course, there are other narratives with regard to war, for men have always been deeply attracted to the emotions and passions that it arouses. One of these, which we try to suppress in our minds, is the delight in killing, the fascination with corpses, even the collecting – right up until the present time and among the most 'civilised' of soldiers – of the body parts of the killed. Another, easier to understand if not to approve, is the glory of war. Heroism, comradeship, the ideal of the ultimate sacrifice, all occupy a central place in what the anthropolgist Margaret Mead called 'the recurrent problem of civilisation':[84] that is, the need to define the male role in a passably acceptable fashion. In ancient as in modern history, war has been one of the dominant ways to do this, with virility and combat linked inextricably in a vicious circle. Men make war because war makes men.

Yet even here there exists a profound ambivalence. In the greatest novel ever written on this theme we find the young Count Rostov on the battlefield of Austerlitz, charging around on his horse. He is 'all a-quiver with excitement and hope', driven on by his image of himself as hero and messenger to

82. E. O. Wilson, *On Human Nature* (Cambridge, Mass.: Harvard University Press, 1978), p. 104. He continues: 'And alongside ants, which conduct assassinations, skirmishes, and pitched battles as routine business, men are all but tranquilised pacifists'.

83. These points are well made by Barbara Ehrenreich in her *Blood Rites: Origins and History of the Passions of War* (London: Virago, 1997), pp. 86ff.

84. Margaret Mead, *Male and Female* (London: Gollancz, 1950), p. 168.

the emperor. Unexpectedly, all ecstasy drains away from him. The Russians lose the great battle and he becomes 'afraid of losing not his life, but his pluck, which he needed so much [. . .] In Rostov's heart the sense of these fearful whizzing sounds, and of the dead bodies all around him melted into into a single impression of horror and pity for himself. He thought of his mother's last letter. "What would she be feeling now?" he thought, "if she could see me here now on this field with cannons aimed at me?" '[85]

So much for men. And women? Here, too, the argument can hardly be unequivocal, the mere mirror image of the human-nature argument advanced above, with women standing for peace just as men stand for war. It is not difficult to find in history examples of wives, mothers, sisters and fiancées who have encouraged their menfolk to go to war, who have shared their convictions and who have dedicated a great part of their energy to belligerent nationalist causes. There are increasing numbers of women soldiers in all the armies of the world. The hatred and dehumanising of the 'other' – a necessary prerequisite for his or her elimination – is not just a male characteristic.

However, it is worth trying to grasp an underlying historical difference in the attitudes of the two sexes to the question of war. Time and again, the caring and nurturing role of women, foremost with regard to their children and to their closest family, leads them to accord to life the highest of priorities. Among women, the strategies of non-violence often have the upper hand.[86] In nearly every societal structure in history, women have until very recently been excluded from the public sphere and relegated to the private one; but it as if this very relegation, demeaning on so many levels, has in the long term accentuated their impassioned defence of life, or at least that of their dearest ones, in the face of men's incessant public calls to war, sacrifice and death.

In the face of human-nature fatalism, that is the biological designation of the human species to self-destruction, we have thus far uncovered two important qualifying considerations: the ambivalence of men's emotions and attitudes

---

85. L. Tolstoy, *War and Peace* (1869; London: Pan, 1972), pp. 300, 305–6.
86. See the recent and beautiful study of a Minangkabau village by Peggy Reaves Sanday, *Women at the Center:Life in a Modern Matriarchy* (Ithaca, N.Y.: Cornell University Press, 2002). The Minangkabau of western Sumatra are the fourth largest ethnic group in Indonesia, numbering some 4 million people. In the village of Belubus customary law and a *matriarchaat*, as it is called by the villagers themselves, have come to prevail: 'although quiet and unobtrusive, gentle in its humility and politesse, the cultural order Minangkabau women uphold with the help of their brothers has had a remarkable staying power' (p. 240). Here as elsewhere, Aristotle's categories of male and female, and the values attributed to them, are reversed: wetness and softness become signifiers of fertility and growth, dryness and hardness of infertility and death.

with regard to war, and the overridingly peaceful and protective instincts of women, especially mothers, towards their loved ones. There is a third, more important still. If aggression of one sort or another is everywhere to be observed, in both males and females, the ways in which it is channelled or encapsulated vary greatly from society to society. As usual, it is anthropology which understands this best, for its analysis of other cultures has always been an invitation to reexamine critically our own. It was another distinguished woman American anthropologist, Ruth Benedict, who argued with great clarity and simplicity that it was the rules, culture and institutions that humans managed to create, *not* any biological need of human beings themselves, that decided the destiny both of 'primitive' and 'civilised' peoples: 'We wage the lethal variety of the genus War,' she wrote at the beginning of the Second World War, 'and the poisonousness of it comes not from what man is but from what society is.'[87]

She illustrated this fundamental distinction with reference to the histories of various tribes. The Iroquois Indians, who bear more than a passing resemblance to a certain present-day superpower (though Benedict could not have known that), behaved in the following tragic fashion:

> They were successful warriors who formed a confederacy 'to preserve the peace'. They talked of their peace aims in many touching metaphors and enshrined them in fine ritual poetry. Their confederacy made them the scourge of all the tribes within reach of their marches; 'to keep the peace' they ravaged the lesser tribes and disrupted their own economy. While the Iroquois warriors were away, tribes that had suffered at their hands banded together and fell upon their villages.[88]

On the other hand, Benedict continued, tribes in central Australia over a long period of time 'shared each other's ceremonies, came together in council, had safe conduct over vast distances, and established forms within which intertribal marriage was as orderly as marriage among blood relatives'. The suspension of war in central Australia was 'a response to warm ties of interdependence among widely separated tribes and these ties were reinforced by many rites and observances that seem to us bizarre'.[89]

---

87. R. Benedict, 'The natural history of war' (1939), in Benedict, *An Anthropologist at Work*, ed. Margaret Mead (London: Secker & Warburg, 1959), p. 377.
88. Ibid., p. 382.
89. Ibid., pp. 374–5. Benedict's article, unpublished in her lifetime, is to be compared with Margaret Mead's own short piece of the same period: 'Warfare is only an invention – not a biological necessity', *Asia*, 40 (1940): 402–5.

Benedict's emphasis on institutions (coming together in council), inter-mingling (intertribal marriage), and ritual (ceremonies, rites and observances) is of crucial importance. It restores to us the possibility – no more than that – of creating a social and cultural environment different from that which leads from aggression to war. It suggests an approach which is not fatalist but constructive: of a culture of peace that becomes natural over time.

The fact that democracies have never gone to war with each other is often taken as a modern ray of hope in this respect. The assertion should be handled with care. Democracies, at least in their limited present form (see below, chapter 5), do not necessarily have peace-loving general publics or enlightened leadership. In the past, they have often waged unforgivable colonialist wars, and at the time of writing are engaged, for dubious motives, in the occupation of Iraq. A democratic form of government is still only one of a number of domestic variables – not necessarily the determinant one – in making decisions on peace and war.[90] None the less, the theory and practice of democratic peace pushes in the right direction. However imperfect and insensitive to the impelling needs of the rest of humanity, the model of the European Union, based on peaceful cooperation between an ever widening number of democracies, is of great novelty and significance. So too is the fact that the democratic form of government, albeit often in very limited form, has spread to encompass – by the year 2000 – 120 out of the 197 nations of the UN. As Ulrich Beck has written, 'democracy is an intimate part of our modernity'.[91]

So too, though, are weapons of mass destruction. Humanity has been much better at inventing ideologies and institutions bent on war than on ones designed for peace, much better at dividing than uniting, much better at arms' races than at disarmament. Whereas forty years ago there were two nuclear powers, now there are eight, perhaps nine if North Korea's claims are to be believed. Nor is this all. Modern technology, as has often been pointed out, is advancing at such a rapid rate that sciences like genetics are opening up dramatically new possibilities of accidents and abuses, and these are, or soon will be, within the reach of individuals or small groups.[92] The diffusion of

90. Miriam Fendius Elman, 'Testing the democratic peace theory', in Elman (ed.), *Paths to Peace: Is Democracy the Answer?* (Cambridge, Mass.: MIT Press, 1997), pp.473–507.

91. Ulrich Beck, 'The democratisation of the family', in Beck, *Democracy without Enemies* (Cambridge: Polity, 1998), p. 65.

92. B. Joy, 'Why the future doesn't need us', *Wired*, Apr. 2000, quoted in Gray, *Straw Dogs*, p. 13.

knowledge, conceived of by the Enlightenment as the key to human progress, acquires a quite different and sinister meaning in this context. Both states and terrorist groups may make use of these possibilities. And while it is true, as an expert on terrorism has written, that 'there have always been enormous gaps between the potentiality of a weapon and the abilities and/or will to employ it',[93] there is very little to be sanguine about in the post-11 September world.

More than forty years ago, the Cuban crisis brought us to the brink of nuclear war, and the American poet Robert Lowell, in his 'Fall 1961', wrote:[94]

> All autumn, the chafe and jar
> of nuclear war;
> we have talked our extinction to death [. . .]
>
> A father's no shield
> for his child.
> We are like a lot of wild
> spiders crying together,
> but without tears.

We are back there now, with the same talk of imminent terror, the same desire to live, and the same feeling of helplessness. The dichotomies of the modern world, outlined briefly in this chapter, seem so insuperable and the source of so much conflict and hatred as to cast us down into the deepest despair. History, simply, does not seem to be on the side of reason or survival. Yet there may be ways out of this pit, if time will allow. These ways are not promissory notes of human redemption, but suggestions for linking everyday life to the wider problems of the world. They may not be enough, but at least they would allow us to make sense of the rhythms, choices, and purchases of our existence, day by day. Individual choice seems as nothing in a world of more than 6 billion people. Yet individual actions can have extraordinary cumulative effects.

93. David C. Rapoport, 'Terrorism and the weapons of the apocalypse', in H. Jokolski and J. M. Ludes (eds), *Twenty-First Century Weapons Proliferation: Are We Ready?* (London: Frank Cass, 2001), p. 16.
94. Robert Lowell, *Poems: A Selection*, ed. Jonathan Raban (London: Faber and Faber, 1974), p. 83.

2 Individuals, Choice and Consumer Capitalism

Freedom and self-interest

The contemporary world is characterised by ever greater affirmation of the individual and individualism. Historically, this process was said by the great mid nineteenth-century Swiss historian Jacob Burckhardt to derive from the early Italian Renaissance. Among the Italians of the fourteenth century 'not one of them was afraid of singularity, of being and seeming unlike his neighbours'. In Florence, by 1390, 'there was no longer any prevailing fashion or dress for men at Florence, each preferring to clothe himself in his own way'. It was this accentuated 'individuality', as Burckhardt called it, which made the Italians the first-born children of modern Europe.[1]

More usually, the twin revolutions – American and French – in the last decades of the eighteenth century have been seen as the crucial moment of passage from the ordered hierarchies of ancien régime Europe to societies based on individual liberty. Modern individualism was formed by the Declaration of Rights – on both sides of the Atlantic. Section 1 of the influential Bill of Rights of the state of Virginia of 12 June 1776 declares: 'All men are by nature equally free and independent and enjoy certain innate rights.'[2]

A strong if controversial case can also be made for seeing the growth in the autonomy and opportunity offered to individuals as one of the underlying characteristics of twentieth-century global history. At first sight, the twentieth

---

1. Jacob Burckhardt, *The Civilisation of the Renaissance in Italy* (1860; London: Phaidon, 1950), p. 82.
2. The French Declaration of the Rights of Man and of the Citizen, of 26 August 1789, begins in similar mode: 'Men are born and remain free and equal in rights.' See the classic comparison in G. Jellinek, *The Declaration of the Rights of Man and of Citizens: A Contribution to Modern Constitutional History* (Westport, Va.: Hyperion Press, 1979); originally *Die Erklärung der Menschen- und Bürgerrechte* (Leipzig, 1895).

century seems to be dominated not by individuals but by masses: mass production, massed rallies, ideologies based on mass action (whether of classes or nations, or both), mass armies, mass violence on an unprecedented scale. Yet the more distance we gain from that century, the more it becomes apparent how far its great authoritarian regimes were fighting rearguard actions, albeit on a major scale, against the constant pressure of individual desire for liberty, autonomy and self-expression. Louis Dumont's analysis of Hitler's *Mein Kampf* is revelatory in this context. For Hitler, the toxins undermining German families bore an individualist aspect – the assertion of women's rights and freedoms, the dissolution of traditional communities, the growth of democratic egalitarianism, the exploitation of the Aryan masses by a restricted plutocracy. All these trends were for him deeply negative and to be associated directly with the activities and interests of Jews.[3]

Sixty years later, in a quite different context, the internal collapse of the Soviet empire derived in no small part from the cumulative desire on the part of its inhabitants for individual freedom of movement, acquisition and self-expression. Even the last great mass regime mammoth of the century, the Chinese Communist Party, holding sway over 1.2 billion people, from 1978 onwards loosened the tight bonds with which it had bound Chinese society. If political individualism was battered to death in Tiananmen Square in 1989, economic individualism has been allowed ever freer rein.

The trend of contemporary history seems, then, firmly to point towards a steady, if contested assertion of global individualism. However, before proceeding further, some elementary distinctions need to be drawn. On the one hand, individualism can be seen as the growth of autonomy, rights, freedom of expression and opportunity. It is the very life-blood of liberty. On the other, it can and has been strongly associated with separation from society and a lack of solidarity with one's fellow human beings. De Tocqueville, in his *Democracy in America*, offered a famous early definition in this latter sense. For him individualism was certainly an expression of democracy; it was 'a mature and calm feeling', but it was also one 'which disposes each member of the community to sever himself from the mass of his fellows and to draw apart with his family and friends [. . .] it throws him back forever upon himself and

---

3. Louis Dumont, *Essays on Individualism* (Chicago: University of Chicago Press, 1986), pp. 149–79. Dumont notes (p. 176) that Hitler himself was 'infected' by the spirit of the age, believing profoundly in the struggle of all against all, and suggests that he projected on to the Jews the individualistic tendencies that he recognised also in himself.

threatens in the end to confine him entirely within the solitude of his own heart'.[4]

Can these two defining elements – the celebration of freedom and the triumph of solitude – be separated? Or does the one necessarily lead to the other? Much of modern reflection on individualism bears these strong negative and pessimistic connotations. The Catholic Church has always rendered the term synonymous with egoism, and has preferred to talk of 'persons' rather than 'individuals'. Most French thought in the nineteenth century, on both the right and the left, regarded *individualisme* as the equivalent of the separation and isolation of the individual from ideas of social purpose and solidarity.[5] Later on, the term became associated with social Darwinism: individuals were destined to engage in ruthless competition with each other, with only the fittest and best prepared expecting to survive. This ethos, so typical of a rugged Anglo-American individualism, of empire building and unmediated market relations, has echoed powerfully across time.[6] In the 1980s it received a new injection of life, with the political triumphs of Ronald Reagan and Margaret Thatcher, the worldwide spread of neoliberalism, and the development of a self-centred culture of rapid personal enrichment.

Yet it would be a grave mistake to reduce the affirmation of the individual only to these negative views of individualism. There are other traditions and interpretations. One of the most significant for our purposes is that of Romanticism. In Romantic thought the cult of the individual was strongly connected with the celebration of subjectivity and creativity, communion with and respect for nature, as well as restlessness and dissatisfaction with the contemporary world. Such states of mind could find many and contrasting expressions, even within a single lifespan. Sometimes they took the form of withdrawal from society, of an aching sense of pleasure lost, of nostalgia for a

---

4. Alexis de Tocqueville, *Democracy in America* (1835; London: Everyman, 1994), vol. 2, book 2, pp. 98–9. He distinguishes between individualism and *égoisme*, which was 'a passionate and exaggerated love of self', though he concludes that the one was 'absorbed' in the other. For de Tocqueville early American democracy had the power to combat these trends because 'the free institutions which the inhabitants of the United States possess, and the political rights of which they make so much use, remind every citizen, and in a thousand ways, that he lives in society' (p. 105). For an extended discussion of these last points, see below, chapters 4 and 5.

5. Michele Battini, *L'ordine della gerarchia. Contributi reazionari e progressisti alle crisi della democrazia in Francia, 1789–1914* (Turin: Bollati Boringhieri, 1995).

6. For a valuable introduction to the various interpretations of the term, see Stephen Lukes, *Individualism* (Oxford: Blackwell, 1973).

more chivalrous age. At other times, they expressed themselves through imaginative critique and revolutionary action.[7] As Shelley wrote, in memorable terms: 'A man, to be greatly good, must imagine intensely and comprehensively; he must put himself in the place of another and of many others; the pains and pleasures of his species must become his own.'[8] Here, as in much of early German Romanticism, there is a strong emphasis on individuality serving as the critical and creative conscience of a society, capable of overcoming conformity, constriction and repression. The poet, as in Shelley's 'Ode to Naples', becomes the link between nature and politics, the interpreter of a gathering wind:[9]

> Prophesyings which grew articulate –
> They seize me – I must speak them! – Be they fate!

An alternative, less pessimistic version of modern individualism can take this part of the Romantic tradition as its starting point, though hardly its point of arrival. In it the individual's self-realisation is intimately and imaginatively linked with a collective project; not, as in the regimes of the great dictators, by means of subordination to state control or the annihilation of individual will, but rather as the striving to place individual fulfilment and freedom in a wider and more socially responsible context. I shall return to Romanticism and its legacy later in this chapter, when discussing modern consumerism.

Choice and constraints

According to the *Human Development Report* of the United Nations in 1998, of the 4.4 billion people who live in the 'developing' countries of the world, one-third do not have adequate access to drinking water, one-quarter have no

---

7. 'One could say that from its origins Romanticism has been illuminated by the twin lights of the star of revolt and "the black sun of melancholy" (Nerval)'; M. Löwy and R. Sayre, *Révolte et mélancolie* (Paris: Payot, 1992), p. 30.
8. P. B. Shelley, 'A defence of poetry', in L. Winstanley (ed.), *Shelley's Defence of Poetry. Browning's Essay on Shelley* (Boston: D. C. Heath, 1911), pp. 18–19. And at the end of his essay he writes: '[Poets] measure the circumference and sound the depths of human nature with a comprehensive and all-penetrating spirit [. . .] Poets are the unacknowledged legislators of the world.'
9. P. B. Shelley, 'Ode to Naples', lines 49–50; see the discussion in L. M. Crisafulli Jones, 'Poetry and revolution: "Shelley's Ode to Naples"', in J. Cheyne and L. M. Crisafulli Jones (eds), *L'esilio romantico. Forme di un conflitto* (Bari: Adriatica, 1990), p. 206.

proper housing, and one-fifth do not have access to modern health services.[10] For them the very basics of individual survival, let alone fulfilment, are at risk. Their prime necessity is to reach a first plateau at which individual human capabilities can begin to be developed; to take the first steps in education, gender autonomy, mobility, and so on, affirming in this way 'the liberties and opportunities for each and every person, taken one by one, rather than simply as the agent or supporter of the ends of others'.[11]

However, it is also true that at the beginning of this century more individuals have attained possibilities for self-expression and choice than at any other time in modern history. Significant sections of global society, not only in the United States, Canada, Japan and western Europe, but also in eastern Europe and the Indian subcontinent, in South Korea as in Mexico, in Australia as in China and Brazil, now find themselves with more opportunity, freedom, mobility and economic resources than ever before. The urban, global middle classes are an increasingly powerful and numerous grouping. They are, naturally enough, a mixed bag, distinguished not only by income and place in production, but by education, culture and religion. They range from professionals, middle management and small entrepreneurs at one end of the scale, through large numbers of salaried workers and technicians in modern services and industry, both private and public, to the self-employed and artisans who have formed the traditional petite bourgeoisie of cities worldwide.

Their numbers are open to conjecture, their stability and political affiliations likewise.[12] In the Indian state of Gujarat it was lawyers and doctors who led the murderous Hindu gangs against their Muslim fellow citizens in 2002.

---

10. UNDP, *Human Development Report No. 9*, p. 14.
11. Nussbaum, *Women and Human Development*, p. 55.
12. There is little comparative literature on this theme. For some first indications from a global demographic point of view, N. Keyfitz, 'Consumption and population', in D. A. Crocker and T. Linden (eds), *Ethics of Consumption* (Lanham, Md.: Rowan & Littlefield, 1998), pp. 486ff. Keyfitz suggests a very broad estimate that between 1 and 1.2 billion people belong to a global middle class. On the fragile stability of the Japanese middle classes, from the early 1960s to the early 1990s, A. Gordon, 'The short happy life of the Japanese middle class', in Oliver Zunz et al. (eds), *Social Contracts under Stress* (New York: Russell Sage Foundation, 2002), pp. 108–29. For the role of the middle classes, both urban and rural, in different patterns of development, see the important recent study by Diane E. Davis, *Discipline and Development: Middle Classes and Prosperity in East Asia and Latin America* (Cambridge: Cambridge University Press, 2004). For a classic study of values and attitudes, Maria Ossouwska, *Bourgeois Morality* (1956; London: Routledge & Kegan Paul, 1986).

The historian Sunil Khilnani recounts how they 'roved in cars, punched mobile phones and used government-supplied computer print-outs of Muslim addresses to conduct their pogrom'.[13] But it was also a group of Hong Kong lawyers who on 1 July 2003, starting from an informal meeting in one of their homes, organised the Article 23 Concern Group which was to mobilise more than half a million people on civil human rights issues in Hong Kong.[14]

The global middle classes are thus a disparate force, with differing social attitudes and political sensibilities. However, they are united by the increased individual freedom and education they have obtained, their patterns of consumption, and the potential force of the choices they make at a day-to-day level. They could jump either way: towards consumption for its own sake and defensiveness and exclusiveness, the dominant patterns of the present time; or they could use their new freedoms to explore other directions, in which their individualism could become less isolationist and more responsive to their collective role and responsibilities in modernity. They are rich with choice. How are they to use it?

A first comment concerns the quality of that choice: it appears at times to be infinite, but there are more constraints on it than we are led to imagine. Choice is steered and constructed in the modern world, not necessarily in benign ways. It as well to examine some of these processes.

Time

The Victorians were the first to propagate systematically the idea that there is 'a time and a place for everything'. In the second half of the nineteenth century Western societies underwent a revolution in the concept of time which has aptly been called 'chronologisation' – the introduction and imposition of numerically standardised linear time.[15] In London, the metropolis at the centre of the world at that time, every morning steam trains running to precise timetables brought hundreds of thousands of commuters into the great central stations of the city. Punctuality became prime to modern social and economic relations. Later on 'time and motion' studies were introduced to control individual workers' productivity on the shopfloor of mass production factories. 'Overtime' began to be paid in a different way. Gradually, this process of chronologisation spread to the developing world and became one

13. Sunil Khilnani, *The Idea of India* (1992; London: Penguin, 2003), p. x.
14. For more details, www.margaretng.com. I am grateful to Mike Davis, one of the lawyers involved for telling me about the Article 23 and Article 24 Concern Groups.
15. J. R. Gillis, *A World of their Own Making* (Cambridge, Mass.: Harvard University Press, 1996), pp. 82ff.

of the essential elements of standardisation in late twentieth-century global modernity.

Time has come to matter almost as much as money, and over the last thirty years employed individuals have found that their time has become increasingly *congested*. There never appears to be enough time in a single day or week, and the list each of us makes at the beginning of each day is often only half completed by its end. Modern information technology has played a highly significant role in this process. The possibility of communication – fax, e-mail, internet – has been greatly increased, and the time that is necessary for each communication has been extraordinarily foreshortened, but the IT revolution has made individual lives not less complicated but more so. Every spare minute seems no longer spare but occupied.

Juliet Schor's 1991 study of the 'overworked American' is illuminating in this respect. In the United States, as the working day has grown longer and more people take work home, signs of stress have grown. There has been a marked increase in hypertension, gastric problems, heart disease, depression, exhaustion and so on. The number of people having recourse to sleep disorder clinics has spiralled, with shiftwork, the 24-hour business culture, and the accelerating pace of life all being held responsible.[16] There are also increasing complaints of not having enough time to spend with one's family. The problem appears to be particularly acute among working women; in one study, half of all employed mothers reported that trying to reconcile work and home caused either 'a lot' or an 'extreme' level of stress. 'Time poverty', concludes Schor, 'is straining the social fabric.'[17]

Not all expressions of this strain are pathological ones. They are also present, revealingly, in the small decisions of everyday life. It is lunchtime in New York. Manhattan office workers consider joining the queue for a popular, sandwich-making deli. They see that the waiting time is too long, glance at their watches and move on. The English sandwich chain with the French name, Prêt à Manger, has tried to cash in on the logic behind this minute sequence of actions. Its sandwiches are ready made, no one is asking for more cheese, and the queues move much faster. The English company's successful entry into a fiercely competitive market derives from what has been called the 'time trade-off': control over the quality of your sandwich is relinquished in order to have a little more time to eat it, or sit for two minutes in the spring sun, or cram into the lunch break one more thing that is on the daily list.[18]

16. Schor, *The Overworked American*, p.11.
17. Ibid., p.15.
18. I. Parker, 'An English sandwich in New York', *Guardian*, 9 Aug. 2002.

Imprisonment in an invisible cage of constrained time is not just an American malaise. A recent study of families in the central Italian region of Emilia-Romagna – where the *tempi* are hardly those of Manhattan – revealed extraordinarily long hours of work for men: 45.2 per cent of them spent between 41 and 55 hours each week working outside the home; another 30 per cent more than 55 hours per week. These were not high-powered business-men, but production workers and clerks, artisans and small entrepreneurs.[19] Work creates its own logic and rhythms, not necessarily imposed but internalised. So too, as we shall see, does shopping.

It is often only at moments of very grave crisis that the subaltern nature of such choices come to be questioned by individuals. The regrets of one small entrepreneur, this time in Tuscany, were recounted by his daughter to the sociologist Francesco Ramella:

'Both my parents went out to work. In fact in the first part of my childhood, up to the age of ten, I spent really very little time with them [. . .] The most time I spent with my father was when he was gravely ill. He died of a tumour and was ill in the three years previously [. . .] if he hadn't had that illness, I doubt if he would ever have really understood the meaning of having children [. . .] He always said at that time: "If I could turn the clock back, I would have spent Saturday and Sunday with my children while they were still little, I wouldn't have gone to work or to a Fiera." Do you see what I mean?!'[20]

Father Ernesto Balducci was well known in Tuscany as a priest of rare culture and openness to the problems of the world. In one of his works he talks of two types of time, distinguishing between an apparently 'useless' time, that of Being (il tempo dell'Essere), a time 'which dances and turns upon itself', and the time of 'Existence', which is ours, that of everyday life. It is a fundamental distinction which little in the contemporary world helps us to realise:

19. G. Bursi, 'Dalla parte della famiglia: "fare casa"', in Istituto Regionale Emiliano-Romagnolo per i Servzi e Sanitari (IRESS) (ed.), *Famiglia e territorio. Azioni e servizi a sostegno della famiglia nei Comuni della provincia di Modena* (Milan: Franco Angeli, 2000), pp. 16–17.
20. Francesco Ramella (ed.), *Under 36. Giovani adulti a Poggibonsi* (Poggibonsi: Nencini, 1998), pp.137–8.

The room in which I slept when I was a child had a window with a view over a rocky precipice [. . .] beyond which there rose the outline of a group of hills. On one side of the precipice I could see the long, distant shape of an ancient convent of the nuns of the Order of Poor Clare. During the night, the bells of the convent called the nuns at regular intervals to 'mattinar lo sposo'. From time to time, with the sound of the bells I used to get out of bed, to gaze at the spectacle of the lights first going on and then off, one after the other, in the minute windows of the nuns' cells. Now I have come to understand the fascination of that nightly scene, which I enjoyed all by myself, almost clandestinely. It was as if I came face to face with the other side of Life, where time has different rhythms from ours, a time that is 'useless', that of Being, a time which dances and turns upon itself, and which does not pay heed to our time, which is that of Existence. I could say that in the course of my life I have never really strayed from that window.[21]

Individualisation, 'flexibility', risk

Not only is choice constrained and contorted by our habitual version of time, it is also rendered more complicated by modern society. Freedom of choice, superficially so appealing and liberating, is often extremely difficult to manage in real life. Both Ulrich Beck and Anthony Giddens have emphasised how in modern developed societies the individual no longer has the certainties, routines and sense of belonging that were so typical of the age of mass production. In the golden era of postwar world trade, which lasted from the 1950s through to the early 1970s, the great Fordist factories produced standardised goods for ever widening circles of consumers. Since then capitalism has become more unstable and the degree of fluidity in individual lives has greatly increased. In the postwar North of the world there were often 'standard' biographies – the male factory worker employed in the same place for thirty years or more, his wife a housewife, perhaps with a part-time job, caring primarily for a 'normal' family with two children, owning one car, one telephone and one television, and taking two-week summer holidays. Now 'standard' biographies have given way to 'chosen' ones – a construction which is a significant part of what Beck has called 'individualisation'. People have to make up their own routes through life, improvising and experimenting.

21. E. Balducci, *Il cerchio che si chiude*, ed. L. Martini (Genoa: Marietti, 1986), pp. 153–4, quoted in Bruna Bocchini Camaiani, *Ernesto Balducci. La Chiesa e la modernità* (Rome: Laterza, 2002), p. xi.

They have become, in Beck's words, 'tinkerers with themselves'.[22]

At first sight this may appear highly attractive, infinitely preferable and richer in choice than the repetitive routines of Fordism or the ordered hierarchies of premodern society. But 'individualisation' takes place in a context of greatly increased flexibility, uncertainty and precariousness. In its original meaning, flexibility referred to the movement of a tree first bending in the wind and then recovering its original position. It named a tensile strength, the property of a plant. However, in the neoliberal world of today, as Richard Sennett has pointed out, 'the practices of flexibility [. . .] focus mostly on the forces bending people'.[23]

Global neoliberalism, which enshrines that social Darwinist version of individualism so prominent in the 1980s and 1990s, has been signified by the growth of deregulation, the dispersal of collective solidarities and the exposure of the 'naked' individual to the forces of the market. In the workplace, choice in these circumstances tends to be translated into short-term contracts, lack of social insurance, an absence of trade unions, and the consequent arbitrary power of supervisors and bosses. There is always the possibility of saying 'no' and walking out. The system does not force you, as feudalism did, to be a serf for life. But the problem is that if you do walk out there is nowhere much else to go.

In many parts of the South of the world, as is by now well documented, these trends often wear a very savage face: sweatshops, child labour, and total vulnerability to market forces. Better sweatshops and child labour than no work at all, say the defenders of the economic transformations of the last thirty years. Probably so, but the choice between the two hardly does credit to an international economic system of such immense resources and wealth. Here we return to the problem of profits and ethics.[24]

In the lifespan of a single individual in the North of the world, flexibility in its modern sense makes itself most felt at two moments: at the beginning of the work cycle, where young people are the most willing to accept temporary jobs, and when they are most ruthlessly exploited in the name of 'learning experiences'; and at what is often a premature end to the cycle, when at forty

---

22. Ulrich Beck, 'The reinvention of politics', in U. Beck, A. Giddens and S. Lash, *Reflexive Modernisation: Politics, Tradition and Aesthetics in the Modern Social Order* (Cambridge: Polity, 1994), pp. 15–16. For Beck's original and compelling treatment of this theme see his *Risk Society* (1986; London: Sage, 1992).

23. R. Sennett, *The Corrosion of Character* (New York: Norton, 1998), p. 46.

24. Klein, *No Logo*, ch. 9, pp. 215–53.

or fifty years old manual workers, clerks, managers and so on are unexpectedly thrown out of their jobs, and thereafter have the greatest difficulty in 'reinventing' themselves, and in holding on to their sense of self.

Risk and vulnerability are thus the name of the neoliberal game. But the degree of risk is unevenly distributed. At its highest levels present-day capitalism encourages risk-taking and speculation, but also offers enormous compensations and safeguards to its operators. The growth of unregulated global financial markets has meant the endorsement of speculation and accumulation at hitherto unheard-of levels. Daimler-Chrysler now earns half of its profits not from the sale of cars, but from foreign currency trading. As Alan Greenspan, chairman of the Federal Reserve Board, commented in July 2002, in his testimony before the United States' Senate Banking Committee, 'It is not that humans have become any more greedy than in generations past. It is that the avenues to express greed have grown so enormously.'[25] This is the 'casino capitalism' which Susan Strange analysed so well.[26] It is not a systemic mode of operation that encourages a sense of limit or of individual responsibility.

Choice and consumer capitalism

The Western model

Nowhere is choice more important than in what we consume on a daily level. In everyday life, from the moment we wake up (that too, like the New York sandwich is a time trade-off choice) we are making decisions about consumption: toothpaste, shampoo, conditioner, shaving cream, razor blades, toilet paper, make-up, perfume, clothes and shoes for the day, beverages, types of yoghurt and cereals, bread, spreads, jams, bicycle or car, train or bus. And all that is just to get the day started.

The world of goods and services is as important a part of capitalism as are financial markets, and an equally dynamic one – but it is infinitely more

25. Cited as opening quote to Frank Partnoy, *Infectious Greed: How Deceit and Risk Corrupted the Financial Markets* (London: Profile, 2003).

26. Strange, *Casino Capitalism*. See also, by way of an example, the sober and revealing article on derivatives by L. van Liedekerkee and D. Cassimon, 'Derivatives: power without accountability', in L. van Liedekerkee et al. (eds), *Explorations in Financial Ethics* (Louvain: Peeters, 2000). The authors write: 'An accountable company should be aware of the potential impact its has on its surroundings. A culture of accountability is careful in its operations; it breeds safety and security. We shall argue hereafter that at the personal, the company and the systemic levels there is hardly a culture of accountability, but rather a culture of unaccountable striving for fast fortune' (pp.135–6).

attractive. The states of financial markets are regularly presented with great solemnity on television news bulletins all over the world, but for most of us they are just a list of figures that go up and down, in largely inexplicable ways, on a daily basis. By contrast, goods and services glitter beyond compare. The richness of choice on offer is the main pillar and justification of the present economic system. Often such a choice is presented as synonymous with freedom itself. No one should underestimate its allure, for modern consumption is for nearly all of us a source of irresistible attraction and self-definition. It is indeed, apart from our own faces, probably the most important defining element of individuality in the modern world.

Yet modern consumption is deeply flawed. As we have seen in chapter 1, its cumulative effect now seriously threatens environmental survival on a world scale. Consumer capitalism knows no limits – except people's continuing capacity to purchase – and in order to flourish it has constantly to invent new desires. Its motor runs on a repetitive cyclical action: desire–acquisition–use–disillusionment–discarding–desire again. It is quite a simple mechanism and it appears to be foolproof, but it is actually making global fools of us all. Its functioning is based on two fundamental premises: insatiability and incremental growth. Nearly everything we possess has to be replaced, and our possessions are destined to grow in size and number. Constant rejection and constant accumulation therefore go hand-in-hand. This is a recipe for disaster.

If we return for a moment to an individual human capabilities approach, then it becomes immediately clear how crucial basic elements of modern consumption are for individual self-realisation; not just sufficient water and food, a decent dwelling and clothes, but also access to medical care, an adequate level of education, a television and a computer. Mao Zedong once said that as far as material consumption was concerned, the bicycle, the radio, the wrist watch and the sewing machine were the only possessions necessary.[27] Perhaps they were, in China before and during the Cultural Revolution, but they are not now, for every age invents its own essentials. A fundamentalist attitude to consumption is thus not the answer at all.

However, the incremental and insatiable nature of modern consumption is far from exclusively concerned with essentials, however each age wishes to define them. A few examples from key elements in our present-day material culture will illustrate this point.

Homes are one. In Australia, in the outer suburbs of Sydney and

27. In March 1949 Mao wrote: 'The comrades must be taught to preserve the style of plain living and hard struggle'; Stuart S. Schram, *The Political Thought of Mao Tse-Tung* (New York: Praeger, 1969), p. 320.

Melbourne, there is a new rage for what have come to be called 'McMansions'. The term was coined in the United States, of course, and describes huge new double-storey project houses with porticos and columns, big front doors with vaulted entries, and triple garages. They have been put up in record time and occupy almost the whole of the 400-600 square metres of the individual family's suburban plot. Gone is the traditional backyard with its trees, garden, vegetable patch, and room for the children to run around or build tree houses. Instead the children are taken by their parents in cars to organised sports activities. Above all, they find their entertainment inside, for in the McMansions there are not only bedrooms, multiple bathrooms, an open-plan kitchen/family room/dining room/lounge, but also a games room and a big-screen media room. All this, while the average number of persons in Australian households, as everywhere in the developed world, is constantly shrinking – from 3.7 persons in 1981 to 2.7 in 2001. Environmentally, the McMansions are anything but sustainable: there is no shade from trees, the houses cook in the afternoon sun, and air-conditioners churn endlessly on.[28]

Cars are another. By 1998 the United States had more cars than drivers: 184,980,187 licensed drivers compared to 207,048,193 licensed motor vehicles. In the year 2000, *Ad Age* magazine estimated that in America the seven largest automobile manufacturers spent over $11.9 billion on advertising new cars, while the federal government itself invested only $7 billion on mass transit systems.[29] Each day every American adult spends an average of more than 70 minutes behind the wheel. Furthermore, two-thirds of all car journeys in the United States are made by one person on their own, giving a new and eerie dimension to individualism. Robert Putnam has commented: 'One inevitable consequence of how we have come to organise our lives spatially is that we spend more of every day shuttling alone in metal boxes among the vertices of our private lives.'[30] Commuters all over the world often describe this time alone as restful and as an opportunity for reflection. However, it is a strange modern habit, to say the least, and to be caught up in

28. J. Hawley, 'Be it ever so humungous', *The Australian*, Good Weekend Supplement, 23 Aug. 2003. Builders of Australian McMansions offer individual variations, such as nine different façades that can be fitted to the same interior: French Provincial, Tuscan, Georgian, Federation, Victoriana, Colonial, American Colonial, and Australian Traditional or Modern.

29. H. Dittmar, 'Sprawl: the automobile and affording the American dream', in Juliet B. Schor and B. Taylor (eds), *Sustainable Planet: Solutions for the Twenty-First Century* (Boston: Beacon Press, 2002), p. 109.

30. Robert Putnam, *Bowling Alone: The Collapse and Revival of American Community* (New York: Simon & Schuster, 2000), p. 212.

ever more frequent traffic jams is not at all likely to be restful: as the minutes tick away, the prospects of being late increase, and modern time stress gnaws away again at our insides. In the United States, annual congestion-related delay per driver rose steadily from 16 hours in 1982 to 45 hours per driver in 1997.[31] In environmental terms, the constant increase all over the world in the production and use of private motor cars, and the recent pernicious trend to purchase light trucks and so-called 'sports utility vehicles' are best described, without fear of exaggeration, as catastrophic. They are a menace for humanity, but no single government has yet had the courage or good sense to stick an irremoveable 'this can kill' sign on the bonnet of a single car.[32]

Toys are a third. The multiplicity, discarding and waste inherent in modern consumption in this area are memorably captured by Jonathan Franzen in his novel *The Corrections*. Gary Lambert is an upwardly mobile financial wizard, father of three boys, unhappily married, resident in a very considerable American McMansion:

> The old playroom in the basement, still dehumidified and carpeted and pine-paneled, still *nice*, was afflicted with the necrosis of clutter that sooner or later kills a living space: stereo boxes, Styrofoam packing solids, outdated ski and beach gear in random drifts. Aaron and Caleb's old toys were in five big tins and a dozen smaller bins [. . .] in the face of such a glut even Jonah, alone or with a playdate pal, took an essentially archaeological approach. He might devote an afternoon to unpacking half of one large bin, patiently sorting out action figures and related props, vehicles, and model buildings by scale and manufacturer (toys that matched nothing he flung behind the sofa), but he rarely reached the bottom of even one bin before his playdate ended or dinner was served and he reburied everything he'd excavated.[33]

Finally, food. The upward spiral of obesity in all the developed countries tells its own tragic story. To be part of the global middle classes means to eat

31. These figures are based on a study of sixty-eight urban areas in the United States, ranging from Los Angeles to Corpus Christi to Cleveland to Providence; ibid., p. 213.
32. At the global level, the United States consumes more than one-third of the world's gasoline; more than one-third of US carbon dioxide emissions and 40 per cent of nitrous oxide emissions come from the transportation sector. In recent years, significant improvements in tailpipe emissions of ground-level pollutants, the direct result of clean-air regulations, have been offset by increases in average driving time. Over 41,000 Americans die each year on the highways, and cars are the leading killer of the nation's teenagers; Dittmar, 'Sprawl', pp. 111–12.
33. Jonathan Franzen, *The Corrections* (New York: Farrar, Straus & Giroux, 2001), p. 168.

too much, throw too much away and to suffer from weight-connected illnesses. Britain is the country experiencing the most rapid rise in obesity in Europe, with 22 per cent of its population now obese and the problem tripling among children in the past twenty years. A recent report published by the health select committee of the House of Commons warned that if present trends continue there is a real danger of children dying before their parents because of weight-related diseases.[34]

If we go back to Franzen's Gary for a moment, we find that he is not fat, but obsessed with cooking mixed grills on the family barbecue:

He did partridge breasts, chicken livers, filets mignons, and Mexican flavored turkey sausage. He did zucchini and red peppers. He did eggplant, yellow peppers, baby lamb chops, Italian sausage. He came up with a wonderful bratwurst-rib eye-bok choy combo. He loved it and loved it and loved it and then all at once he didn't.[35]

In order to have more goods and services, people work harder, earn more, spend more, and increase their debts. Even if both partners earn well, somehow they often can hardly make ends meet. There is clearly something wrong here. To quote Juliet Schor again: 'Work-and-spend has become a mutually reinforcing and powerful syndrome – a seamless web we somehow keep choosing, without even meaning to.'[36]

A significant part of that web has been woven by the retail structure of modern consumption. All over the developed world, individuals – housewives above all – have become accustomed to shopping in ever larger spaces which offer ever greater numbers of things to buy. The incremental logic of consumerism is at work here too, in spectacular spatial fashion. By the early 1990s 4 billion square feet of the United States had been converted into shopping centres – 16 square feet for every American man, woman, and child. The trend in the last fifteen years has been ever upward, and not only in the United States. Wal-Mart is now the largest single employer in the United States, and the Walton family the wealthiest.[37]

---

34. J. Mason, 'Ministerial effort on child obesity crisis "inadequate"', *Financial Times*, 27 May 2004. See also the renowned work by E. Schlosser, *Fast Food Nation: The Dark Side of the All-American Meal* (New York: Houghton Mifflin, 2001).
35. Franzen, *The Corrections*, p. 164.
36. Schor, *The Overworked American*, p. 112.
37. Ibid., p. 107. For a devastating exposé of Wal-Mart, see B. Ortega, *In Sam We Trust* (New York: Times Books, 1998).

Shopping in malls and hypermarkets can be a contested gender terrain, hated by some men and the origin of bitter disputes. It is a European metropolitan legend about IKEA, the Scandinavian superstore for lifestyles, that more marriages have broken up in it than anywhere else. Certainly, work-and-spend offers no guarantees of being a harmonious way to conduct our lives. But going to Wal-Mart or IKEA or their like is not just, nor even primarily, a negative experience. It is very widely considered a family outing, a new form of sociality, which includes the possibility of stopping for a coffee or a meal, sometimes exotically Swedish as in the case of IKEA. The great spaces and high roofs of these modern temples make a profound impression on all visitors. Goethe's appreciation of the remains of the temples of Paestum in southern Italy comes to mind, with his advice to the visitor that 'it is only by walking through them and round them that one can attune one's life to theirs'.[38] The great halls of modern consumption are far from ruined. They are jampacked with goods, there is the offer of exceptional prices and discounts, and the possibility of having *more* for the same price (3 for 2). We walk through them and round them, their goods smile at us from the shelves, we fill up our trolleys obediently and at the end, unlike Goethe in the Campanian countryside, we pay at the cash tills.

Even where the spaces are more modest, the supermarket or hypermarket often serves as a focus for a modern urban neighbourhood. On the Florentine periphery, 'le Piagge' constitutes one of the most difficult parts of the city, with modern but highly unsatisfactory public and private housing serving some 10,000 inhabitants. Many of the latter are not Florentine in origin and have been transferred there, so that the area has become a sort of deposit for 'problem' families. Unemployment, drugs and criminal networks are wide-spread. Apart from an exceptional Catholic Comunità di Base, under the guidance of a radical priest, Don Alessandro Santoro, there are no clubs, shops or social services, and no gathering points that might bring people together. In the autumn of 2002 the Coop, the Italian consumer cooperative chain of super- and hypermarkets, opened a new commercial centre at le Piagge, and its piazza and walkways became a new neighbourhood meeting place. But it is a centre which is private, not public and it is entirely consumption oriented. Francesca Manuelli, who has studied the quarter, has commented:

The piazza-galleria at le Piagge, though its has the physiognomy of a public piazza and is always crowded, is in fact private property and when

38. J. W. Goethe, *Italian Journey* (1786–8; Harmondsworth: Penguin, 1970), p. 218.

the shops are shut access to it is prevented by rolling shutters. As a consequence social relations [. . .] have to follow a commercial timetable, and the inhabitants continue to feel themselves *guests* in a space which, even if it is welcoming and looked after, none the less does not belong to them and is structurally functional only to consumption.[39]

Malls and hypermarkets, then, are the temples and palaces of the modern world, replacing the great sheds of the Fordist factories and the spacious halls of the banks, now largely superfluous at a local level. The new consumption temples have many downsides. One is that they are often lethal for the environment in terms of traffic congestion, the use of concrete, huge car parks, urban sprawl and the absence of any planned integration between purchasing, residence and community. Secondly, and closely connected, they destroy small shops like wildfire. Independent retailers cannot compete in terms of prices, and transnational chains like McDonalds and Starbucks eat up local enterprise. The big-box operations (Wal-Mart and company) and the clusterers (Starbuck and friends) transform retail landscapes. This is Naomi Klein territory. Of course, some local shops continue to thrive, but as she has written, 'these are [usually] high-end specialty retailers in gentrified neighbor-hoods, while the suburbs, small towns and working-class neighborhoods get blanketed in – and blasted by – the self-replicating clones'.[40]

The spread

As must be apparent by now, this is a disconcerting model of consumption. What makes it worse is that it is being exported worldwide, uncritically, on the wings of extremely powerful transnational companies, usually of American origin. Seen from its point of departure, the process is cause for celebration. As the *Boston Sunday Globe* declared in May 2004:

American movies, fast foods and brand names dominate the global marketplace not because of any sinister snuffing out of competition but because people almost everywhere – from Soweto to Shanghai – are genuinely enraptured by Hollywood's latest and really do enjoy eating Kentucky Fried Chicken or wearing fashions from The Gap.[41]

39. Francesca Manuelli, 'Le Piagge. Storia di un quartiere senza storia, 1979–2003', M.A. diss. University of Florence, 2003, p. 115.
40. Klein, *No Logo*, p. 155.
41. C. Nickerson, 'On world stage, critics of US grow louder', *Boston Sunday Globe*, 2 May 2004.

There is undoubted truth in this bald assertion, and considerable enthusiasm for the new global consumer culture at its point of arrival. But the argument concerning its merits can hardly be said to end there. Let me take the case of contemporary China to illustrate the pros and cons of what is happening on a world scale. In doing so, I would like to avoid an oversimplistic model which emphasises exclusively the destruction of previous autochthonous cultures and the uncritical acceptance of the new. Certainly that is a part, probably a major part, of what is happening, but the process is more complicated. The anthropologist Daniel Miller has urged us, rightly, to look not just at '*a priori* culture' (what existed before global invasion and standardisation), but also '*a posteriori* culture', the 'subsequent localisation of global forms', the integration and elaboration in original ways of the massive influx from outside.[42]

Under the Communist regime of Mao Zedong, individual and family consumption was fiercely compressed and controlled. In what was still a very poor society, with memories still fresh of the dreadful years of famine that had followed the failure of the 'Great Leap Forward' (1958–60), state-controlled workplaces, in both city and countryside, distributed goods and services. Today few adults have forgotten the monotony of diets in the 1960s and 1970s. At home, standard furniture included workplace-issued desks, tables and chairs, though each family had a few personal possessions. In the cities, blue- and white-collar workers lived in similar homes, took bicycles and buses to work, and made the same limited choices in terms of leisure activities and personal clothing. Individualism was regarded as a crime, a betrayal of the collective values of a Communist society. Only the high-ranking cadres of the party, closeted in their special compounds, enjoyed a different lifestyle, cashing in on their wide discretionary powers to obtain favourable treatment for themselves and their clientele. Overall, the Chinese consumer system of these years could be described as one of 'involuntary simplicity', the antithesis of the 'voluntary simplicity' which the Western model's most acute critics advocate as an alternative to consumerism, and to which we shall return below.[43]

42. D. Miller, 'The poverty of morality', *Journal of Consumer Culture*, I, 2 (2001): 239. Although Daniel Miller's work has served as a beacon for us all, I am less convinced by other parts of his argument in this particular essay, for his denunciation of the dangerous 'moralism' of his colleagues' approach is not accompanied by any real discussion of the implications of the historical direction of consumption, or any proper engagement with reasoned critiques of these global trends.
43. Deborah S. Davis (ed.), *The Consumer Revolution in Urban China* (Berkeley: University of California Press, 2000); K. Gerth, *China Made: Consumer Culture and the Creation of the Nation* (Cambridge, Mass.: Harvard University Press, 2003); M. Meisner, *Mao's China and After* (New York: Free Press, 1999).

From 1978 onwards, with the triumph of Deng Xiaoping, this model changed dramatically. Decollectivisation, the revival of private entrepreneurship in both countryside and city, the state's decision to separate places of production from those of consumption, the opening up of the country's vast home market to foreign companies, the extraordinary rate of annual growth of China's GDP – all these led to a consumer revolution of breathtaking proportions. Its velocity and mass diffusion have no parallel in the history of Western consumption. A few indications will have to suffice to describe it here. Diets changed and diversified, clothes and footwear likewise, the range of urban leisure-time entertainments grew exponentially (dancing, bowling, cinema, concerts); homes not only grew in size and offered more privacy (in urban areas fewer families had to share kitchens and toilets with other families), but were put up for sale. An advertisement in a Shanghai newspaper of May 1994 exhorted its readers: 'buy a home and become a boss!'[44]

In the earlier decades of the Communist regime, the most important rites of passage in an individual's life had been observed with great frugality. The Bureau of Civil Affairs issued marriage licences and newly married couples celebrated with simple tea parties or meals in their homes. Funerals followed a similar sober pattern. Cremation was widely practised, and memorial services were often held at workplaces. Twenty-five years later, marriage ceremonies for the rapidly growing and dynamic Chinese middle classes had come to have the material and symbolic importance of southern Italian ones: lavish and long-lasting banquets for a considerable number of guests, with a great show of luxury goods. The Western-style wedding gown of the bride has assumed particular importance as a status symbol.[45]

At one very important level, the explosion of individual choice can only be welcomed, for it marks the passage from a very poor, repressed and controlled society to one with ever growing access to the benefits and delights of modern consumption. Standards of living and health have greatly improved, as have the possibilities to choose.[46] Individuals have been able to take their distance

44. Deborah S. Davis, 'A revolution in consumption', in Davis, *The Consumer Revolution*, p. 9.
45. M. Gillette, 'What's in a dress? Brides in the Hui quarter of Xi'an', in Davis, *The Consumer Revolution*, pp. 80–106.
46. Peter Nolan, *China and the Global Business Revolution* (New York: Palgrave, 2001), p. 914, table 14.6. Betwen 1980 and 1997, private consumption had more than trebled, infant mortality had decreased from 42 to 32 per 1,000 births, and the numbers of those in absolute poverty had decreased from 262 million (1978) to 74 million (1996).

from the authoritarian state in a key area of their lives. In the cities, new social networks have been created around consumption, as in the case of bowling and dancing. Some authors suggest that even though, since 4 June 1989 and the massacre in Tiananmen Square, the one-party state maintains its political grip with an iron glove, the consumer revolution is undermining the regime on a daily basis. Consumption and freedom, so it is suggested, once again go hand-in-hand.

Yet this is very far from the whole story. The same elements of insatiability and incremental growth which characterise the Western model of consumption are at work every day in China as well. When Deng Xiaoping introduced his new policies, he defined their success as the creation of a 'relatively comfortable' (*xiaokang*) society, with a target of $800 per capita annual income by the year 2000.[47] But new market relations do not lead to even growth and level targeting. Inequalities of every sort have become rife – between city and countryside, between regions, between the coastal cities and the rest of China, between classes and generations. Consumer fever has its own logics and pattern of uneven accumulation. It also has its own motor, impossible to change unless there is a collective will to do so. China, like America, is in the grip of a 'work and spend' tornado.

Sometimes, we can catch glimpses of the autonomous filtering, integration and elaboration of the new wealth – the creation of that '*a posteriori* culture' which Miller has in mind. The high priority given to pianos and piano lessons in middle-class Chinese homes is just one example of spending that is by no means a simple imitation of a Western model. However, the degree to which most choice is directed from outside and made to conform to a global model seems to be very great. In the 1990s, China was the second largest recipient of foreign direct investment in the world.[48] What did this mean for patterns of consumption?

Let us return to toys. In the major urban centres of the country, the Communist Party's long campaign for population control has resulted in a predominantly one-child family structure. By 1992, of the 49 million births in the urban districts of Shanghai, 97 per cent were first births. These single children of Shanghai are the first generation in Chinese history to be mass consumers of toys. Previously, parents had no money for toys, and in any case

---

47. H. Lu, 'To be relatively comfortable in an egalitarian society', in Davis, *The Consumer Revolution*, p. 124.
48. For an exhaustive analysis of this investment see Y. Huang, *Selling China: Foreign Direct Investment during the Reform Era* (Cambridge: Cambridge University Press, 2003).

regarded them as an unnecessary indulgence for children beyond the age of eight. Now they are willing, sometimes under protest when their children press them, to spend a significant part of their rising incomes on their children's pleasure.

The pattern and cultural models of this spending are dominated by major companies in the West, Taiwan and Japan. As the sociologists Davis and Sensenbrenner have noted, it was in the mid-1980s, with the advent of advertising on Chinese television, that Shanghai viewers first caught a glimpse of Heinz baby foods and Johnson and Johnson baby lotions through the rosy haze of Hong Kong commercial landscapes.[49] Since then, advertising and spending on children have proceeded by leaps and bounds. In the summer of 1996, some of the most frequent purchases were Ultraman action figures, Micky and Minnie T-shirts, Disney character watches, special meals for birthdays at Kentucky Fried Chicken or McDonald's, and Chicago Bull tank tops – worn by several hundred thousand Shanghai boys between the ages of eight and eighteen. Purchases were often clearly gendered. For girls there was new, heavy spending on dolls and hair ornaments, but also on a studio photography session, advertised in English as well as Chinese for 'glamour kids' in the Parkson department store in the centre of Shanghai. Girls were photographed with a favourite cartoon character or a huge white rabbit. The basic cost was 300 rmb, rather more than half an average monthly wage. Of course, more expensive versions were on offer. A glossy portrait 4 foot square cost 800 rmb or $100 at 1996 prices.

As must already be apparent from this account, American cartoons and their spin-offs play a very large part in the purchases and desires of Shanghai children. In 1996, *Toy Story* (first issued in 1995) hit the Shanghai cinemas and shops. It is of a certain relevance to our argument that this intelligent animation tells the story of how a boy rejects an old toy (Woody) in favour of a new one (Buzz). Davis and Sensebrenner recount the fascinating exchange between a forty-year-old father and his ten-year-old daughter in the No. 2 Department Store on Huaihai Road. The daughter ran first to the collection of plastic Ultraman figures:

Father: You want this? (pointing at the Ultraman)
(Daughter nods and picks up a boxed set of two smaller figures to compare with the larger single one hanging on a wall display)

49. Deborah S. Davis and J. S. Sensenbrenner, 'Commercialising childhood: parental purchases for Shanghai's only child', in Davis, *The Consumer Revolution*, p. 54. I am heavily indebted to this splendid article for the paragraphs that follow.

Father: What does it do? It is meaningless, and besides you are too old to buy toys. It is just a strange toy to play with. What do you need it for?

They then went together to look at the *Toy Story* watches. The daughter wanted one of these, but the father once again refused. Finally, they settled on a clearly utilitarian object, a pencil case, of which the father bought two, both bearing the Taiwanese Bon-Bon cat motif. The daughter was reported as seeming to be 'reasonably satisfied'.[50]

This captured moment in a Shanghai apartment store in 1996 tells us many things. It reveals how much of a tussle is going on over goods, with young consumers heading obediently the way the global media and advertising have pointed them (to the Ultraman figures, to the *Toy Story* watches), with parents resisting in the name of the utility of things, and with the two generations reaching a compromise (useful pencil boxes, but at least with a Taiwan logo). Yet all this was eight years ago, and the incoming tide of consumption is an inexorable one. How long will it be before the Shanghai equivalent of Gary Lambert, hard at work in the new city stock exchange, returns home to gaze at a similar accumulated debris of toys, though without a third child to attempt heroic excavation? Perhaps that moment has already come, but there has been no one around to record it.

Imaginative hedonism

Up to this point I have been mainly concerned with choice in material culture, and objects in particular. But there is a whole area of modern consumption which has more to do with the immaterial than the material, and which Colin Campbell, in a ground-breaking work of 1987, named 'modern autonomous imaginative hedonism'.[51] Central to this concept is the place of longing, day-dreaming and self-invention. Faced with the extraordinary proliferation of modern 'dream machines' – video games and cassettes, Walkmans and DVDs, endless surfing on the internet and multiple TV channels – individuals now have an unparalleled opportunity to invent and inhabit their own imaginary worlds. Their point of departure is usually a room in a home, but their point of arrival has no necessary contours. The journeying is not tied to the world of goods but is based on the reception of images and a consequent fantasizing, often about one's self. It is usually a confused journey, punctuated by zapping

50. Ibid., p. 69.
51. Colin Campbell, *The Romantic Ethic and the Spirit of Modern Consumerism* (Oxford: Blackwell, 1987), pp. 77–95.

between television channels and the searching late at night for images empathetic to one's own state of mind,

Of course, such a process of dreaming and self-imagining has always taken place in relation to the world of goods. Virginia Woolf, in her short story 'The new dress', recounts the thought patterns of a woman in front of a mirror, trying on a dress for the first time:

> Suffused with light, she sprang into existence. Rid of cares and wrinkles, what she had dreamed of herself was there – a beautiful woman. Just for a second [. . .] there looked at her, framed in the scalloping mahogany, a grey-white, mysteriously charming girl, the core of herself, the soul of herself; and it was not vanity only, not only self-love that made her think it good, tender, and true.[52]

Modern imaginative hedonism shares many of the properties of the illusory experience which Woolf describes. It differs from it, I would suggest, in three distinct ways. The first is, of course, its intangibility. Woolf's Mabel adjusts the shoulder of her new dress; the player of a video game sees but cannot touch. Both make reference to Baudrillard's sign world, but one is part of the material world and the other is not.[53]

Secondly, and closely linked, there is a different relationship at play between senses and emotions. If the senses dominated traditional consumption, it is the emotions which prevail in the modern. The imaginative world of modern hedonism – in its films and games – plays to strong situations and emotions: of triumph and defeat, love and hate, fear and courage. It would be foolish to maintain that such emotions were absent from an earlier consumerism, or that the senses are absent from a later one. Viewing – the essential activity of modern imaginative hedonism – is sensory; so, too, is the sexual release that men derive, in their millions, from images on internet sites. But there can be little doubt that in modern hedonism the balance between experiencing and imagining has shifted towards the latter.

The fleeting mention of masturbation is directly connected to the last and most important distinction. Modern consumption, and its imaginative part in

---

52. Virginia Woolf, 'The new dress', in Woolf, *The Haunted House and Other Stories* (1944; London: Hogarth Press, 1962), pp. 51–2. I am grateful to Colin Campbell for this example.
53. J. Baudrillard, 'Consumer society', in *Jean Baudrillard: Selected Writings*, ed. M.Poster (Cambridge: Polity, 1988).

particular, is ever more a *solitary* experience. De Tocqueville's warning with regard to the consequences of individualism, quoted at the beginning of the chapter, returns to haunt us here: 'it throws him back forever upon himself and threatens in the end to confine him entirely within the solitude of his own heart'.[54] We have already encountered solitary Americans spending ever longer each day in their cars. This is not an exceptional situation in modern life but a recurring one.

A very good example of the connection between modern imaginative consumption and the increasing isolation of the individual is to be found in the widespread use of Walkmans. Such usage is of particular interest because for once it is aural, not visual, consumption that is being analysed. The positive aspects of the practice are immediately apparent – principally the chance to select and listen to one's own choice of music in practically any situation – travelling, lying on the beach, jogging, commuting to work, and so on. It is an extraordinary modern privilege. Yet its negative effects are highly relevant to this discussion. Walkmans can isolate their users from the world around them. They encourage people to block out the soundscapes of everyday life – the complex mixture of the train clicking over the rails, people turning the pages of their newspapers, the doors opening at the next stop – in favour of a single overwhelming sound, which can be heard by those around the Walkman user only as a tinny and disturbing tinkle. Walkmans also lead their users to aestheticise and transform their surroundings. Powerful music transmitted directly into the ears makes one look at one's surroundings and one's neighbours in a different, removed way. *They* are here, but *I* am somewhere else. Or, as one London girl told a researcher of this subject in the mid-1990s: 'It's like looking through a one-way mirror. I'm looking at them but they can't see me.'[55] There is nothing inherently wrong, or even new, about such 'cocooning'; often we all need to be separate, to enjoy privacy, to be partially removed from our surroundings. But the trend towards withdrawing from social situations in favour of contact through screen or phone, or no contact at all, seems to be an inexorable one. Each of us is a modern-day Odysseus bewitched by the Sirens, but where are the oarsmen with their ears blocked with wax pulling us to safety?

54. See above, pp. 51–2.
55. See the suggestive article of Michael Bull, 'The seduction of sound in consumer culture: investigating Walkman desires', *Journal of Consumer Culture*, 2 (2002): 88.

Romance and advertising

At this point it is worth returning for a moment to the Romantic concept of the individual. I suggested earlier in this chapter that the Romantics' attention to individual feelings and their search for self-fulfilment led the movement in the first half of the nineteenth century in contradictory directions: either towards solitary withdrawal, and a harking back to a lost and unrecoverable past; or else to a fierce and creative engagement with the world, often in a self-sacrificing way. Sometimes, in the course of a single lifespan, we can find both tendencies. The effects of modern autonomous imaginative hedonism are not so ambidirectional. The day-dreaming it inspires, the instruments it has put at our disposal, the richness of the imaginative dreams it produces, all seem to lead to the separateness of the individual, not to her or his critical engagement. The history of individualism in the developed world since 1968 points strongly in this direction. Or, to put it in Luc Boltanski and Eve Chiapello's terms, modern capitalism has successfully integrated the 'creative critique' of the '68ers, transforming the idealism of the student revolutionaries into a new Romantic individualism expressed through the world of consumption, both material and imaginative.[56]

Once again, the role of suggested, perhaps even constrained, choice in this process is a vital one. Modern advertising exercises a very strong hold over individual imaginative hedonism. Once, in its earlier days, advertising was primarily concerned with goods. The English poet Philip Larkin wrote in 1964:[57]

> In frames as large as rooms that face all ways
> And block the ends of streets with giant loaves,
> Screen graves with custard, cover slums with praise
> Of motor-oil and cuts of salmon, shine
> Perpetually these sharply-pictured groves
> Of how life should be.

Gradually, though, with the exact dating varying sharply from country to country, advertising has become less concerned with the inherent quality of

---

56. Luc Boltanski and Eve Chiapello, *Le Nouvel Esprit du capitalisme* (Paris: Gallimard, 1999); see also Peter Wagner, 'The project of emancipation and the possibility of politics, or, what's wrong with post-1968 individualism?', *Thesis Eleven*, 68 (2002): 31–45.
57. P. Larkin, 'Essential beauty', in Larkin, *The Whitsun Weddings* (New York: Random House, 1964), p. 42.

'motor-oil' or 'cuts of salmon', and more with how certain goods offer a romantic lifestyle, or emotional realisation, or even a philosophy of life. The dreaming of a single individual is often captured by these omnipresent advertisements, which play to the emotions more than to the senses, more to how life 'could be' than to the 'should be' of Larkin's poem. The consumer is encouraged to cut loose, to imagine herself or himself as another. Cigarettes, fizzy soft drinks, makes of jeans, types of beer, and most recently and obsessively cars, all offer lifestyle advertising of this kind, in which romantic love, far-away places, haunting melodies and sexual fulfilment are combined. All the products in this list, with the exception of jeans, damage one's health; only in the case of cigarettes is this made explicit. These are the 'branded lifestyle bubbles'. They are the 'romance' of the Starbucks coffee experience, the smooth, conquering style of the Audi car, the 'way of life' of Diesel jeans. As Diesel's proprietor, Renzo Rosso, said, 'The Diesel concept is everything. It's the way to live, it's the way to wear, it's the way to do something.' And Starbucks, according to its marketing director, 'wants to align ourselves with one of the greatest movements towards finding a connection with your soul'.[58] This may appear gobbledy-gook from the outside, but no one should underestimate its possible effect. Advertising slots are the syringes of consumer capitalism, the products of immense expenditure and ingenuity, intent on injecting into our heads in the course of thirty seconds aspirations and desires, and the dream of being an enhanced self, with a different prowess.

Advertisers who are not entirely cynical about their work, and there are a few, would reply that all this is bunkum. They maintain, using the favourite image of the industry, that advertising merely mirrors society. It responds to needs rather than creating them, and it has no scientific capacity to turn us into Pavlovian dogs, jumping up obediently in response to the right emotional stimuli. Consumers, they argue, are so unpredictable, and the world so complex, that even the most expensive and best-laid marketing strategies can go badly wrong. The British-born David Ogilvy, one of America's most renowned advertising figures, was adamant in 1962 that advertising 'follows *mores* but never leads them. The public is *bored* by most advertisements, and has acquired a genius for ignoring them.'[59]

Some of us, it is true, are bored by adverts, as well as appalled by their invasiveness, but a general defence of this sort is weak and unconvincing. If

58. Klein, No Logo, pp. 25, 64, 153.
59. S. Fox, *The Mirror Makers: A History of American Advertising and its Creators* (New York: William Morrow, 1984), p. 329, and for Ogilvy's career, pp. 225–39.

advertising is really so ineffective and so widely ignored, it is difficult to understand the economic rationale for continuing to spend billions of dollars on it. Nor is it true that marketing merely mirrors society. Advertisers' ideas of society are narrowly limited to those people who can afford to buy advertised products. The rest of society (that is, the majority of the world's population) does not count, indeed does not exist, because it has no purchasing possibilities to speak of.[60] If advertising really reflected society, then at least three-quarters of it would be 'social' advertising, intent on highlighting the great majority of the world's population living in poverty, and on drawing people's attention to their position in global chains of consumption. In Italy more than twenty years passed before Silvio Berlusconi's Mediaset company, which effortlessly dominates commercial television in that country, began producing a minimum of 'socially responsible advertising' among the tens of thousands of advertising spots that it broadcasts regularly.[61] These are the fig leaves which poorly cover habitual practice.

Advertisers, then, are powerful and proactive in their propositions, but they are not all-powerful and theirs need not be, though they often are, the only propositions. Through the instruments and content of modern consumption, individuals are drawn ever more into journeys that are solitary, imaginative, hedonistic and romantic. But they cannot escape forever. In each of their lives, there comes a moment of *verification*, when 'non-places' are not enough. It may be a fleeting moment, or it may be much longer lasting, if an alternative and coherent viewpoint is readily available in the real world. For, sooner or later, individuals need to measure themselves against reality, to obtain external proof, to try and decide on forms of conduct.[62] With regard to critical individualism and consumer capitalism, we need to enquire what sort of conduct that might be.

Alternative readings and passages of everyday life

Michel de Certeau, in the introduction to his famous work *The Practice of Everyday Life*, wrote of consumers being 'immigrants in a system too vast to be

---

60. For these and other points, Michael Schudson, *Advertising, the Uneasy Persuasion* (New York: Basic Books, 1984), pp. 235–8: 'In short, the consumers the marketers listen to are not persons, not citizens, but thin voices choosing from among a set of pre-determined options' (p. 236).

61. Paul Ginsborg, *Silvio Berlusconi: Television, Power and Patrimony* (London: Verso, 2004), p. 21.

62. Campbell, *The Romantic Ethic*, p. 214.

their own, too tightly woven for them to escape from it'.[63] In the face of such a system he identifies a way of looking at everyday life that is highly germane to our purposes. De Certeau did not believe that open confrontation was either advisable or likely to be successful. Instead he advocated a constant *deflection* of power, and made reference to a whole number of actions to which he gave suggestive names: murmurings, ruses, joyful discoveries, polymorphic simulations, and systems of operational combination (*les combinations d'opérations*). Potentially, these could all be elements of 'resistance'. For him tactics were more important than strategy, and tactics meant being on the watch for 'spaces within which to manoeuvre', as well as opportunities that were to be 'seized on the wing'. Politics was to be a form of daily bricolage, the assembling of minute acts of autonomy which would distance the individual from the controls of a 'disciplinary' society.

One highly unlikely but evocative example of these practices is walking in the city. For de Certeau footsteps constitute 'an innumerable collection of singularities', and his section on them begins with a quotation from the *Aeneid*: 'The Goddess can be recognised by her step.' Where we walk, how we establish a 'here' and a 'there', what resonances street names have for each of us, what routes we choose to take, all these constitute 'a modern art of everyday expression': 'The long poem of walking manipulates spatial organisations, no matter how panoptic they may be: it is neither foreign to them (it can take place only within them) nor in conformity with them (it does not receive its identity from them). It creates shadows and ambiguities within them.'[64]

It is in the micro-actions and interstices of everyday life that alternatives are to be sought. If television advertisements constitute the daily infiltrating mechanisms for the dominant consumer society, then there are other counter-actions by which their messages can be deflected and even be made to rebound on their creators. 'Pushed to their ideal limits,' wrote de Certeau, 'these procedures and ruses of consumers compose the network of an anti-discipline.'[65]

De Certeau never developed his insights into a coherent theory of everyday politics. Indeed, to do so would have been to negate the nature of his enterprise, constructed as it is as much on the unconscious, the spontaneous and

63. Michel de Certeau, *The Practice of Everyday Life* (Berkeley: University of California Press, 1988), p. xx, and the whole of the 'General introduction', pp. xi–xxiv; originally *L'Invention du quotidien*, vol. 1: *Arts de faire* (Paris: Union Générale des Éditions, 1980).
64. Ibid., p. 101, and more generally ch. 7, pp. 91–110.
65. Ibid., p. xv.

the instinctive as on any ordered or coordinated pattern of action. Yet his method is invaluable, for it poses in the most delicate of forms the central question: what each individual can do in the actions of daily life to reverse the highly damaging model of consumption outlined above.

The bonfire of the vanities

In Florence, on the last day of Carnival in 1497, and again on the same day a year later, a great ceremony took place in the Piazza della Signoria. It had been ordered by the radical Dominican friar Girolamo Savonarola, who at that time exercised considerable moral force within the Florentine Republic. Savonarola was fiercely opposed to what he considered the vanity and wanton consumption of the Florentines, and he gave instructions that a sample of their possessions, which had been collected more or less voluntarily, be burnt in the central piazza of the city. A high pyramidal structure was constructed, composed of several tiers. On the lowest were placed false beards, masks and carnival disguises; next came precious editions of the Latin and Italian poets, among them Boccaccio; then women's ornaments and toilet articles, scents, mirrors, veils and wigs; higher up, lutes, harps, chessboards and playing cards; finally, right at the top, paintings, especially of female beauty. In 1497 a Venetian merchant who happened to be present at this remarkable ceremony offered the Florentine government 22,000 gold florins for the objects about to be burnt. The only answer he received, according to the chronicles of the time, was that his portrait, too, was painted and burned along with the rest.[66]

Savonarola's is not the approach that is being advocated here, though a modern day re-enactment would certainly cause a sensation. One might indeed have some sympathy for his denunciation of the excesses of Florentine consumption, for it is enough today to take a winter stroll in the heart of the city to behold what a wasteland of fashion shops it has become. But Savonarola's solution was nothing more nor less than religious funda-

66. Burckhardt, *The Civilisation of the Renaissance*, pp. 295–6. For a contemporary account of the second occasion, L. Landucci, *Diario fiorentino dal 1450 al 1516* (Florence: Sansoni, 1883), p. 163, 27 Feb. 1498; also Lorenzo Polizzotto, *The Elect Nation: The Savonarolan Movement in Florence, 1494–1545* (Oxford: Clarendon Press, 1994), pp. 38ff., who stresses the participation of a centralised children's movement in campaigns to rid the city of 'vanities' and other incitements to sin. Such campaigns were not an invention of Savonarola; the followers of San Bernardino had organised similar bonfires in other Italian cities at earlier dates. For further discussion of beauty, misogyny and gender relations with respect to this event, see Elisabeth Cropper, 'Introduction', in F. Ames-Lewis and M. Rogers (eds), *Concepts of Beauty in Renaissance Art* (Aldershot: Ashgate, 1998), pp. 1–11.

mentalism, the attempt to create a theocracy. His was a lost cause, because in modern history the battle between restrictive authoritarianism and the freedom of individual choice has always, sooner or later, been resolved in favour of the latter.

Instead, I think it is essential to stress the powerful cumulative effects of individual actions, taken freely on a daily basis. If a collective idea and general shape of an alternative model of consumption could be created and become widely shared, then each of us could contribute to it in one way or another, and in so doing make more sense of our daily lives. I have in mind here the sort of 'molecular action' to which Antonio Gramsci made passing reference in his *Prison Notebooks*. For him, the constant, cumulative, individual defections from Mazzini's democratic Action Party in the middle of the nineteenth century towards the monarchists of Piedmont both undermined the chances of a progressive solution to the Risorgimento, and changed the composition and policies of the new nation's ruling elites. Gramsci likened the process to 'molecular changes which in fact progressively modify the pre-existing composition of forces, and hence become the matrix of new changes'.[67] Naturally, molecular actions of this sort need not work only in the direction of reinforcing dominant elites in society. They can also function in an opposite way, bringing together de Certeau's 'murmurings' and 'ruses' with daily actions that assume a self-multiplying force. They can be motors of change.

Nature

In this 'reverse' process Romanticism has a crucial role to play. We have seen, in the company of Colin Campbell, how important Romantic ideas were in legitimating individual pleasure as a good in itself, in fostering the restless and continuous consumption of modernity, and in populating and even defining the dreams of individuals' imaginative hedonism. But the force of Romantic imagining does not stop there. In the quest for verification, to bring dreams back to earth, so to speak, and at the same time to ennoble them, Romanticism has a crucial role to play. Nowhere is this truer than in our relationship to nature. William Wordsworth wrote, with extraordinary prescience some two hundred years ago:[68]

67. Antonio Gramsci, *Selections from the Prison Notebooks*, ed. Q. Hoare and G. Nowell Smith (London: Lawrence & Wishart, 1971), p. 109.
68. William Wordsworth, 'The world is too much with us', in H. Gardner (ed.), *The New Oxford Book of English Verse* (Oxford: Clarendon Press, 1975), p. 507.

The world is too much with us; late and soon
Getting and spending, we lay waste our powers:
Little we see in Nature that is ours;
We have given our hearts away, a sordid boon!

Yet it is possible to reverse this long tide, and to do so by using our imaginations. 'Green' consumerism already has a discreet history. It aims to choose products that privilege ecological sustainability, that do us good and that respect the delicate balances of nature, rather than destroying them. The debate over how to make such products more widely available, and the precise form they should take, is an intense and complicated one. But for our purposes the most important thing is to begin somewhere; to take daily actions, even of a minimal nature, which place us on the side of the outgoing tide of conservation and reclamation, rather than the incoming one of destruction. To make choices of this sort is to turn one's back on the prevailing suggestions (to put it no stronger) of advertising, and to imagine oneself, perhaps with some glee, as part of de Certeau's murmurings, ruses and 'joyful discoveries'.

Of extraordinary importance is our daily attitude to water. The present fad, all over the developed world, for buying expensive little plastic bottles of mineral water is attractive – and mistaken. It is attractive because the constant imbibing of water is good for our organisms, and it also cools us off in an ever warming planet. But the waste and expense involved is stunning. Each of us needs to insist that at our place of work there is a water fountain attached to the public drinking water supply, from which we can fill up a single container free of charge. Water is one of the most precious of natural resources, the one we most take for granted but whose scarcity is the source of growing conflict.

The list of the possible linkages of our daily life with a different approach to nature is a long one, and water is but one example.[69] What is vital, though, is to reawaken in ourselves the connection between consumption and nature, and to reinterpret romantic longing not in terms of publicity for automobiles but, to go back to Wordsworth again, so as to feel the wind upon our faces, and so as to safeguard what is beautiful and innocent on our planet. We cannot do that unless we incorporate into our daily lives elements which contribute, in molecular terms, to an alternative model of consumption.

69. I. Ivoi, 'Un bicchiere d'acqua', in Ivoi, *Fare con meno* (Florence: Arpat, 2001), pp. 81–6; Vandana SHIVIA, *Water Wars: Privatisation, Pollution and Profit* (London: Pluto Press, 2002).

Shopping: producer and consumer alliances

In a striking passage, the Church of England's approved prayer book for the year 2000 and for the new millennium addresses the question of shopping:

> Where we shop, how we shop and what we buy is a living statement of what we believe [. . .] If we take our roles as God's stewards seriously, shoppers collectively are a very powerful group [. . .] If, when we ourselves are not on the poverty line, we always go for the cheapest price, without considering that this price is achieved through ethically unacceptable working conditions somewhere in the world, we are making a statement about our understanding of the word neighbour.[70]

It is not necessary to be a Christian (let alone to be of the Church of England) in order to underwrite the above statement. Daily, individual acts of shopping are of extraordinary importance in determining terms of trade, social conditions and human capabilities on an international level. The anthropologist Daniel Miller, in one of his many writings on consumption, maintained that the housewife was the 'global dictator' of the modern world, even if 'the exercise of power which derives from consumption is not experienced as empowerment in the daily lives of those who wield it'.[71] Up until now, daily choice has rarely included the consideration of where goods come from, how they are produced, in what sorts of conditions they are made or grown, who chooses what is put before us. Slowly, though, increasing numbers of shoppers throughout the developed world are asking these questions and drawing their own conclusions on how best to consume. This is a subterranean movement, not heralded by any political party except the Greens, still of modest proportions and influence, but of enormous potential.

A first element of choice is that signalled by the Church of England – the decision not to buy goods whose production is based on gross exploitation, often of children. It is an area of intervention where there have been some spectacular successes – the campaigns against Nike, Gap and so on. In 1996 Wal-Mart's Kathee Lee collection of clothing was personally sponsored by a favourite American television chat-show host, Kathee Lee Gifford, who was being paid a mere 5 million dollars for the use of her name. It then emerged

70. *New Start Worship* (London: New Start, 2000), quoted in Hertz, *The Silent Takeover*, pp. 149–50.
71. Daniel Miller, 'Consumption as the vanguard of history', in Miller (ed.), *Acknowledging Consumption* (London: Routledge, 1995), pp. 34 and 36.

that the clothing was being stitched by teams of Honduran children, working enormously long hours for wages as low as 31 cents an hour. Gifford burst into tears on television, and rapidly became an active campaigner against sweatshops.[72] However, a very great deal remains to be done. An accurate survey published in Great Britain in 2002 revealed that most clothing retailers have no published codes of comprehensive conduct which guard against gross malpractices.[73] And there are other difficulties to which I shall return below.

A first step, then, is the refusal to buy certain goods or use services which have been signalled with precision as being based on gross exploitation, or as damaging to the environment. This is already a very important and unusual choice, but it is essentially a negative one. There is a second category, that of positive choice, which is both more challenging and more imaginative. At its heart lies the idea of alliances between consumers and producers. Consumers, if they so wish, can refuse to accept the logic of prevailing commodity chains, and choose instead to create their own links with certain types of producers.

Such alliances can be created at local, national and international levels. Locally, consumers who make such choices tend to privilege small producers and artisans, who otherwise risk extinction. They also tend to try and buy in-season local fruit and vegetables, rather than exotic, out-of-season produce which has been frozen and transported by transnational companies from all over the world. One of the most renowned and ingenious of these consumer movements is an Italian one, that of Slow Food. Here, the prevailing modes of modernity are attacked on two fronts: that of time, for the consumption of food is to be slowed down rather than accelerated, enjoyed rather than stuffed rapidly down; and secondly that of commodity chains, for the Slow Food movement searches out and patronises small producers of local delicacies, whose skills and secrets risk oblivion if not carefully supported.[74]

On an international level, the Fair Trade movement is slowly gathering force. At its heart is the idea of building specific links between producers from

72. Hertz, *The Silent Takeover*, p. 150.
73. W. Young and R. Welford, *Ethical Shopping* (London: Fusion Press, 2002), pp. 83–9. The authors gave ratings from half a star to a best of five stars. The highest rated company was C&A with three stars. Most companies, including Armani, Austin Reed, Benetton, Bon Marché, Diesel, French Connection, Gucci, Hugo Boss, Jaeger, Laura Ashley, Mothercare, Tie Rack, Viyella, Yves St Laurent, and so on, scored only half a star or no star at all.
74. Carlo Petrini, 'Il cibo e l'impegno', *Micromega*, quaderno supplemento al n.4 (2004), pp. 7–16.

the South of the world and consumers from the North.[75] Coffee has been one of the vanguard products for this sort of alliance. It was in 1973 that a Dutch group first imported directly a small quantity of coffee from a Guatamalan cooperative. Today, one of the most successful Guatamalan cooperatives is the Chajul one, high up in the Sierra de los Cuchumatanes in the north-west of the country, with 3,000 members representing 20,000 people and forty-eight small communities. The local population belongs mainly to the Maya-Ixil and Quiché ethnic groups. The coffee they produce, using traditional native methods, is 100 per cent Arabica and is among the best in the world. The link with Northern consumers has been highly beneficial for an isolated mountain area in a country which has recently known thirty-seven years of civil war, with over 150,000 people killed. Civic development in Chajul – improved health care, bursaries for students to finish schooling, a pharmacy and a little museum – is in strident contrast with conditions in the central Magdalena valley in Colombia, which I briefly described in chapter 1. If one is an extreme example of occupied space, of space lost to any semblance of legality and overrun by terrorist gangs, the other is of space reclaimed and hope restored.[76] There can be few better examples of the way in which the individual consumer choices of a minute section of the global middle classes (in this case mainly Dutch and Italian) have built bridges to a very distant rural population. There is an indication here, no more than that, of a 'verification' process, of an alternative journeying which is not pure escapism, which does not content itself with 'non-places'.

Not all Fair Trade is between producers in 'developing' countries and consumers in 'developed' ones. Exchange between and within 'developing' countries, with wealthier middle-class sections of the population rethinking their consumer practices, is at its first stages. In the year 2000 in Dhaka, capital of Bangladesh, the Fair Trade movement organised a highly successful exhibition, with its goods on sale. Mexico has introduced its own national

75. For the growth of the movement in Holland, see N. Roozen and F. van der Hoff, *L'Aventure du commerce équitable* (Paris: Lattès, 2002); for Italy, Francesco Gesualdi, *Manuale per un consumo responsabile* (Milan: Feltrinelli, 2002), with a useful list of Italian and international addresses in the appendix; for a basic introduction, D. Ransom, *The No-Nonsense Guide to Fair Trade* (London: New Internationalist and Verso, 2001). The International Federation for Alternative Trade (IFAT) is a global network of 143 fair trade organisations in forty-seven countries, many of them Southern producers; see its website, www.ifat.org.
76. For Chajul, see L. Guadagnucci and F. Gavelli, *La crisi di crescita. Le prospettive del commercio equo e solidale* (Milan: Feltrinelli, 2004), pp. 17–18. For the central Magdalena valley, see above, pp. 33–4.

'Transfair' label. In India, the Sasha association, which coordinates fifty women's groups, has opened a retail outlet in Calcutta, which sells 30 per cent of its products.[77]

Very often the language of these initiatives is a female one. The staff who work in and manage the retail outlets for the Fair Trade movement in Europe, are 80 per cent women. The suffocating patriarchal cultures of much of the South are potentially vulnerable to the dynamics of long-range producer and consumer alliances across the world. In chapter 1, I briefly described the synergies produced by the encounter between powerless female members of a society and a democratic and enabling group such as the Bangladesh Rural Advancement Committee, which has brought work, benefits and emancipation to groups of very poor rural women.[78] Many Fair Trade initiatives move in the same direction.

Another form of action, closely linked to the 'positive' choice of buying Fair Trade products, is that of placing one's money in an ethical bank or ethical funds. These latter have been among the fastest growing elements in financial services; in Britain by the year 2000 their value was more than £3.7 billion. Most banks, like clothes retailers, do not have any general ethical policy governing loans and investments, and in Britain four such banks (Lloyds TSB, Barclays, NatWest and HSBC) control 65 per cent of the market for current accounts. But there are exceptions, such as the Co-operative Bank, Triodos Bank and the Ecology Building Society. The Ethical Investment Research Service now charts the development of alternative investment strategies of this sort.[79]

Ethical funds can be used to screen off negative investments, such as those in arms trading or in the tobacco companies, but they also have the potential to reach the most distant and poorest members of the world's population. If we go back to rural Bangladesh, the Grameen Bank, founded by Muhammad Yunus, is present in some 36,000 villages. It has granted credit to hundreds of thousands of people, enabled them to avoid usurers, and to take microeconomic choices of their own.

All these examples, and there could be very many more, are just drops in the ocean of the world's economy and its population's consumer habits. But they are highly significant for two fundamental reasons. The first is that they are tied to transformative processes at the point of production. The Fair Trade

77. Ibid., p. 30.
78. See above, pp. 21–2.
79. For further details, see www.eiris.org. For British banks, Young and Welford, *Ethical Shopping*, pp. 108ff.

mark is only granted to products where certain conditions are met, the most important being that small-scale farmers can participate in democratic organisations of their own, that plantation or factory workers have the right to join trade unions and are assured of decent wages as well as decent working conditions and housing, that there is no child labour or forced labour, and that there is a clear strategy for environmental sustainability. Furthermore, buyers agree to pay producers a social 'premium', to be used to improve their local living, educational and working conditions. The Chajul pharmacy, museum and school bursaries are the results of just such a premium.

These requirements are of special significance because they have the potential to link world trade and commodity chains in a virtuous circle of security, self-organisation and social benefits, in strident contrast to the neoliberal experience of low wages, health and safety dangers, absolute insecurity on the job and grotesque profits for distant companies. It is an alternative model of distinct fascination. Ideally, it gives to North and South common goals and values – a common quest for democracy, for horizontal not vertical social relations, for autonomous choices.

The second and still wider significance lies with the question of peace and war. Instead of a privileged and arrogant North of the world being viewed with hatred and resentment by major sections of the global population, the long flows of Fair Trade principles might allow us to go back to the bases of peaceful and prosperous coexistence suggested by the American anthropologist Ruth Benedict. The suspension of war among the aborigines of central Australia was, we may remember, 'a response to warm ties of interdependence among widely separated tribes, and these ties were reinforced by many rites and observances that seem to us bizarre'.[80] Fair Trade alliances between producers and consumers are indeed highly bizzare, if not downright subversive, at least when viewed from the board rooms of the major transnational companies or from the great halls of the hypermarkets. But they allow imaginative and direct contacts to be made between everyday shopping choices and the production of goods in the poor and poorest parts of the world. They respond, in a minimalist but potent way, to Shelley's invocation to make 'the pains and pleasures of the species' become our own.

Difficulties

The above account has been purposely idealistic. There are obstacles, limitations and difficulties which must now be brought to the fore. From the point

80. See above, p. 47.

of view of producers, more than one voice has been raised to suggest, not without foundation, that the relationship between 'Southern' producers and 'Northern' consumers is a highly unequal one, almost a disguised neocolonialism. Producers have demanded more say on the international and national bodies that regulate Fair Trade practices, more understanding of local conditions, and more flexibility with regard to the enforcement of Fair Trade codes. Hardly surprisingly, some producers, in their impatience to gain access to ever wider markets, tend to stress economic expansion over all else.[81]

These growing pains are as nothing compared to the structural restrictions on the range and supply of goods (let alone services) that the Fair Trade movement offers at the moment. Although an estimated 7,000 different products are now available, two-thirds of the overall turnover is taken up by coffee, chocolate and tea. Not that these are small employers at a global level. Between 20 and 25 million people throughout the world depend on coffee for their livelihood, with small producers and family farms dominating production in Latin America, Asia and Africa.[82] Under the normal terms of trade they can expect 10 per cent of the final price, compared to 55 per cent for the shippers and roasters and 25 per cent for the retailers. The giants Kraft, Nestlé, Procter & Gamble, and Sara Lee dominate world coffee markets. If literally hundreds of experiences like that of Chajul in Guatamala were to flourish, then the dynamics and relations of production in the coffee market would no longer be the same. But how many products and services in our daily lives remain out of the reach of Fair Trade!

It is enough to go back to the list I made of commodities used to get the day started, in order to realise how few of them are available through alternative networks. As for 'normal' retailers, perhaps only a body lotion or a cream from the Body Shop would fit our bill early in the morning, for the Body Shop is one of the very few major companies to have launched its own, respected International Community Trade Scheme.[83] Perhaps, too, a cotton shirt from a women's cooperative in Kerala in southern India, if you happen to live in central Italy and your local Cooperative supermarket chain has continued its link-up with producers there. Perhaps Fair Trade tea or coffee if you've really made a point of looking for them on the shelves of the supermarket, at the health food store, or in a Fair Trade shop. But the majority of our habitual

81. Guadagnucci and Gavelli, *La crisi di crescita*, pp. 30–2.
82. S. Zadek et al., *Purchasing Power: Civil Action for Sustainable Consumption* (London: New Economics Foundation, 1998), p. 29.
83. Young and Welford, *Ethical Shopping*, pp. 137–41. The Body Shop is one of only six retailers of all types to earn a four-star ranking in their survey.

consumer needs are simply not covered by Fair Trade whether at the beginning, during, or at the end of the day.

The difficulties and reticences of consumers themselves are manifold. At first sight, the situation seems to be encouraging. Many opinion polls relate that consumers in the developed world declare that they are willing to pay higher prices for products and services that are not the result of gross exploitation, or do not damage the environment. However, the limited evidence we have from anthropological fieldwork suggests otherwise. When Daniel Miller accompanied some fifty shopping expeditions in a street in north London in 1998, on only one occasion did a shopper take materials back for recycling, and on only two did a shopper purchase 'ethical goods'. Miller concluded, 'Overall, the evidence from my work and from others is that pure "Red" shopping based on the selection of goods primarily in consideration of benefiting others is extremely rare.'[84] We need to ask why this is so.

In trying to construct an answer, Miller suggests a distinction between the 'morality' and the 'ethics' of shopping. He sees the act of shopping as centrally related to a 'desire to express love implicitly through a material practice'.[85] *Moral* shopping, for him, is usually concerned with thrift and with making a loving choice for one's family, oneself or one's friends. A child's favourite cereals or drink, an elegant bargain for the house, good quality products at advantageous prices, these are expressions of moral shopping, of ascribing pre-eminence to care at home. I shall return to this conception of morality and of home life in my next chapter. *Ethical* shopping, on the other hand, is according to Miller a means by which the immediate interests of the household are intermingled with concern for others, with a sensibility to wider questions of equity and justice. Shopping of this sort was seen by many during his fieldwork as a kind of 'cold' shopping in contrast to the 'warm' variety, which is generally an expression of love for people for whom one feels immediately responsible.[86]

These are suggestive distinctions, but I wonder if they are the whole story. The strong existing disincentives to Fair Trade shopping should be laid

---

84. D. Miller, *The Dialectics of Shopping* (Chicago: University of Chicago Press, 2001), p. 119. Whether 'red' is the correct colour to attribute to this kind of shopping is a very open question.

85. Ibid., p. 136.

86. Ibid., p. 137. Miller is at pains to make it clear that the people in his chosen street (a mixture of working-class and lower middle-class households) could not be considered mean, and were altruistic in many ways, from the helping of the elderly and disabled with their shopping (often by doing it for them), to the giving of money to charity. The block came with shopping.

alongside Miller's explanation, and perhaps help to explain the situation more fully. Lack of information is paramount. Whereas the presentation, publicity and promise of 'normal' goods are insidiously and incessantly part of our lives, the limited range of alternatives usually receives no publicity at all. In the supermarket there may be Fair Trade tea, but the supermarket management will not usually waste one dollar, pound or euro on explaining why on earth we should buy it. Then the marketeers will tell us that the product has been withdrawn through lack of demand.[87] Most people at the moment simply regard shopping of this sort as quirky.

Another disincentive regards quality and preference. I will offer two stories in lieu of ethnography. Both concern friends who certainly cannot be considered narrowly closed off in their own worlds. One, in London, offered me a Nescafé at his home. I asked him why he of all people did not drink Fair Trade coffee. 'I did,' he replied, 'but the last batch was of really poor quality, and so I went back to Nescafé.' A second friend, this time in Providence, Rhode Island, took me to one of his favourite coffee bars. Fair Trade coffee was on offer, and I asked for one. 'Don't make me feel guilty,' said my friend, laughingly, 'but I can't give up my favourite cappuccino.' I assured him that I didn't want to make him feel guilty at all; the problem of long-standing preferences is not an easy one to overcome.

Finally, there are the disincentives of convenience and price. Fair Trade goods, especially if they are not tea or coffee, have usually to be sought out in special shops. As yet, it is a very small clientele who does so. Furthermore, the question of price, touched on by Miller, is far from secondary. Few, indeed, are the shoppers who are going to look for a carpet with the Rugmark label, which guarantees the working conditions under which it has been produced. Rugmark has worked for more than a decade in India and Pakistan against the forced labour of children, who have often been *sold* by desperate parents to carpet factory owners. Bonded children of this sort cannot, of course, form unions, they are easily intimidated, and they are often abused and beaten.[88] How much easier for all of us not to think – or more often not to know – about

---

87. At the British Library in London (May 2004) there are large signs in the coffee bar and restaurant advertising Fair Trade coffee. But when I asked for one, the French worker on a short-term contract replied that it was 'temporarily' unavailable. There had not been much demand, he said, and we agreed that this was a shame.

88. See www.rugmark.org. for many details and individual cases. In spite of all the difficulties, more than 2 million carpets carrying the Rugmark label were sold in Europe and North America in the period 1995–2002.

such things, and settle instead for one of the beautiful, accessible and relatively cheap carpets available at IKEA or elsewhere.

And yet so-called 'moral' shopping is hardly a solution, nowadays, for the long or even medium term. Perhaps we express a certain familial morality by making certain habitual choices, though I have my doubts. More likely, either from ignorance, or lack of money, or time, as a response to advertising or to a 'special' offer, we as individuals often make the wrong choice. It is wrong because it fails to establish the potential of a single, everyday consumer act in the building of bridges between two worlds, in linking the love of oneself with a love of humanity. It fails to see that our actions and the conditions of others are inextricably and urgently intertwined. To pretend otherwise is not only to harm those we do not know, but those we do.

Conclusion

Sometimes in the history of consumption a rapid expansion in the world of goods and in the outward trappings of luxury has been met with forms of rejection, even of revulsion. Albert Hirschman, in his renowned reflection of 1982, *Shifting Involvements*, wrote: 'Along with appreciation, infatuation and even addiction, affluence seems to produce its own backlash, almost regardless of what *kinds* of goods are newly and more abundantly marketed.'[89] He had in mind principally the years of 1968 and after, when students all over the world briefly rejected many aspects of consumer capitalism. If we go back in time, then Savonarola's fierce reaction to the fifteenth-century Florentine assertion of possessive individualism and the human vanities associated with it also seems to fit the bill. After these brief backlashes, though, consumption has always continued its forward march.

Rather than a moralistic, brief and often hypocritical revulsion, we need to try and rethink what might constitute the acceptable terms of consumption in a gravely threatened world. The continuous assertion of individualism lies at the very heart of modernity, but there is no necessary reason why it should translate automatically into blind self-interest. It is certainly true that among the reasonably well-off sections of the population in the developed, and above all in the developing world, there is a constant and avid desire to consume goods and services, and an equally constant invitation from nearly all sources to upscale one's desires. But it is equally true that there is a growing unease

---

89. A. Hirschman, *Shifting Involvements* (Princeton: Princeton University Press, 1982), p. 46.

about all this, about the waste involved, the environmental damage caused, and the dissatisfaction aroused.

An alternative approach, starting from the individual, would stress the need for a 'reappropriation' of the material world, which would entail a reflection on personal needs and desires. To separate the two is always very tricky, but in present circumstances a sense of limit, and of the preciousness of things, is absolutely essential. Some critics of present models of consumerism call for a new 'voluntary simplicity' in our attitudes to the material world. Others talk of a sobriety which can lead to contentment.[90] These are precious indications, as long as we hold in mind that our end aim is not to destroy or deny the desire to consume, but to set it in an acceptable social context. Vital to this enterprise is the recognition that an individual act of consumption is linked to commodity chains all over the world, and that a single purchase is charged with significance and potential. There is a consumer from the North who wants to buy a carpet for her home. There is a little girl in India who has been bought out of captivity and given the chance to go to school and to fulfil her human capabilities. Is it really so impossible to link the two, not in a patronising or evangelical way, but in terms of mutual respect and common goals?

90. See, for example, Schor and Taylor, *Sustainable Planet, passim.*

3 Families

Families are the principal institutions which form individuals in the modern world. All contemporary political discourse has to face them full on, not just take them for granted or assume they merely lurk in the background. Families are, rather, *agents* of everyday politics, pre-eminent sites not only of emotions and affections, intimacy and dependency, but also of education, socialisation and the construction of opinion. To a large extent they shape the way in which individuals connect to the wider world. What sort of agents and institutions they are is therefore of paramount importance. John Stuart Mill was one of the few modern political thinkers who recognised this clearly; Lenin, for instance, certainly did not. Nor did Rawls. Mill wrote in 1869:

> The family is a school of despotism, in which the virtues of despotism, but also its vices, are largely nourished. Citizenship, in free countries, is partly a school of society in equality; but citizenship fills only a small place in modern life, and does not come near the daily habits or inmost sentiments. The family, justly constituted, would be the real school of the virtues of freedom.[1]

He is right, but those who have wished to 'constitute justly' the family – churches, social reformers, dictators and so on – have often been disappointed. Families have a noticeable habit of going their own way. They have their own secrets, memories and language. The opinions expressed around the kitchen table, the last words of the day whispered to a child at night-time, the attitudes passed from one generation to another, by gestures as much as

1. J. S. Mill, 'The subjection of women', in Mill, *On Liberty and Other Essays* (1869; Oxford: Oxford University Press, 1991), p. 510.

words, all these shape profoundly the way in which family members look at the world outside them and respond to its orders or suggestions. Even states that were extremely invasive of familes, such as those of the great European dictators in the middle of the last century – had difficulty in getting families to do exactly what they wanted.[2] Families are certainly influenced by the laws and norms of states and churches, especially over long periods of time, but they are far from being merely passive and absorbent.[3]

I do not want to suggest that they are impervious to change, or that individuals are unfree, incapable of breaking away from certain family paradigms. If family formation simply *determined* an individual's destiny, then it would be difficult to explain what the old-Etonian Eric Blair (George Orwell to the world) was up to, washing plates in Paris in the late 1920s and then going off to fight for the Republicans in the Spanish Civil War. But even the rebels bear with them the imprint of the deep psychological patterns of early childhood. 'The family – that dear octopus', wrote the English author Dodie Smith in 1938, 'from whose tentacles we never quite escape nor, in our innermost hearts, ever quite wish to.'[4] Families deserve this chapter to themselves.

In the pages that follow I begin by discussing a number of distinctions: between home and family, between different types of family, between the families in which we live and those of which we dream. But above all I concentrate on two contrasting versions of family life: one which is mainly self-regarding and inward-looking, insulated from the wider world and concerned above all with itself; the other which is porous rather than impermeable, open not closed, curious and willing to intermingle. Consumer capitalism pushes us towards the first, in which a certain sort of individualism finds a potent family form; but the urgency of global politics presses us towards the second.

2. P. Ginsborg, 'The family politics of the Great Dictators', in D. Kertzer and M. Barbagli (eds), *The History of the European Family*, vol. 3: *Family Life in the Twentieth Century* (New Haven and London: Yale University Press, 2003), pp. 174–97. Increased birth rates under Hitler and Stalin were modest in a long-term perspective; Hitler failed to mobilise many German women for his war; Franco, one of the most terrible of the dictators, could not even get families to Mass on a Sunday in significant parts of post-Civil War Spain.

3. A point excellently made by Ferdinand Mount in his *The Subversive Family* (London: Jonathan Cape, 1982).

4. D. Smith, *Dear Octopus* (London: Heinemann, 1938), p. 120.

Home, sweet home

At the end of the day, most of us go home to eat, and then to sleep. This is far from a universal pattern, even in the North of the world. Mihail Rusu, thirty-one years old, was a Romanian immigrant to Florence in June 2004. Having nowhere to eat or sleep, he climbed into one of the big rubbish containers that line the streets of the city. Late at night, the containers are hitched up to the dustmen's lorries, which are equipped with heavy cutting blades to churn the rubbish as it pours out. Fast asleep, Mihail Rusu was thrown with the rubbish onto the lorry's blades, and died a terrible death. He had nothing with him except his passport in a plastic container, some change, a piece of paper with a few telephone numbers on it, one of which was his mother's, and a packet of Pall Mall cigarettes.[5]

Most of us go home at night, but home does not necessarily coincide with family. The household has often included within its walls beings who are not relatives: slaves in the ancient Greek *oikos*; servants of one sort or another in wealthier families all over the world; animals – not only domestic ones, but farm animals in peasant households, or toads and lizards in India, coming and going even in middle-class homes.

'Family', on the other hand, can certainly refer to those with whom we do not live, and to whom we do not go home at night. The term includes our parents, or more broadly, those to whom we are related, either by blood or marriage. Yet although each of us has a fairly precise idea of whom we have in mind when we talk of our family, our criteria of inclusion and exclusion vary enormously. Many people think the dog is more important than a cousin. Family is thus not a precise analytical category. A useful preliminary distinction can be drawn between the 'family of origin', from which we have come, and the 'family of procreation', which we will make. But not all individuals 'make' families. In the developed world, for instance, increasing numbers of people are choosing to live together but not to have children.

Home and family are thus not necessarily the same thing, but common usage often elides them. Prevailing American and western European discourse still holds firmly, though perhaps with increasing desperation, to an ideal of a domestic group made up of a man, his wife and their children. We can rejoin for a moment Gary Lambert in *The Corrections*, preparing one of his barbecues: 'And so here he was, still grilling. Through the kitchen windows he

---

5. L. Montanari, 'Urla disperate, poi è schiacciato', *la Repubblica*, Florence edition, 2 June 2004; also C. Riconda, 'Uomini topo braccati e affamati', ibid.

could see Caroline thumb-wrestling Jonah. He could see her taking Aaron's headphones to listen to music, could see her nodding to the beat. It sure *looked* like family life. Was there really anything amiss here but the clinical depression of the man peering in?'[6]

Family is nearly always 'not what it once was'. Each generation, as it grows older, tends to denounce its successor and complain of the decline of family life. Throughout the nineteenth and the twentieth centuries we can hear a constant lament for the decline, if not the imminent demise of the family. This lament is not specific to the Catholic Church. Christopher Lasch, for instance, began his well-known book *Haven in a Heartless World* (1968) with the bald statement that 'the family has been slowly coming apart for more than a hundred years'.[7] It may look that way to contemporaries, but family life, for all its loosening and destructuring, is also enduring. That, too, seems to be a lesson of the twentieth century. Marriage has declined as a great historical institution, but society has not dissolved into a network of individuals. Instead, the family has shown itself to have a remarkable *plasticity*, constantly changing in form and numbers, but remaining the primary focus of loyalty for individuals, for love and nurturing as well as for other, less worthy emotions and modes of behaviour.

Modern families have taken on a bewildering variety of forms. Let me mention just a few. There are so-called 'postmodern' families, like those analysed by Judith Stacey in Silicon Valley, California. These are families in great trouble, the product of 'the devastating economic effects on women and children of endemic marital instability'.[8] Here, in the 1980s, men soaked up a fast-track individualist culture, heavily oriented towards enrichment and social mobility. They became 'workaholics', with 60–80 hour weeks, their family voices reduced to little more than whispers. Women, especially working-class women, struggled. They aspired to autonomy, but the market gave them few opportunities to realise it, and the frequency of divorce left them and their children disoriented and economically insecure. Today, mothers fight to defend their children from a rampant narcotics economy, and often reinvent kinship ties in an extended and imaginative way.

There are, by contrast, the close-knit families of the villages and towns of the 'industrialised countryside' of central and northern Italy. Here too, as we have

---

6. Franzen, *The Corrections*, p. 166.
7. C. Lasch, *Haven in a Heartless World* (New York: Basic Books, 1977), p. xx.
8. J. Stacey, *Brave New Families: Stories of Domestic Upheaval in Late Twentieth Century America* (New York: Basic Books, 1990), p. 13.

seen,[9] men often overwork and spend little time with their children, but solidarities frequently extend across three generations, with grandparents looking after their grandchildren on a daily basis, and then themselves being cared for in advanced old age. Spatially and emotionally, proximity is the rule of the day. Children rarely move far away from their family of origin, and 'pop in' on a daily basis. Grown-up sons see their mothers with almost alarming regularity. These 'long', loyal, generationally extended families do not all live together under the same roof, but they form a single unit with regard to strategy and ambitions. They are important sites of saving, entrepreneurship and investment.[10]

Then there are 'reconstituted' families, a very modern phenomenon, increasingly common in major urban conglomerations. These are highly complex groupings, often spatially spread, which try and put together pieces of families deriving from previous unions, sometimes successfully, often less so. Time is often a complicated business here. The routine of everyday life – the sort of family time that is repetitive and appears, deceptively, to be infinite – is punctuated by children having two homes, visiting at holidays, having to deal with parents in different geographical locations and cope with step-parents who may well not be welcoming.[11]

In the North of the world, as birth rates decline, the overwhelming tendency is for households to have an ever smaller number of members. There are heterosexual couples who live together without having children, and single-sex household groups, like gay and lesbian domestic couples. There are also increasing numbers of people, especially old people, who live alone, and are sometimes referred to in the statistics as 'single-member families', a truly contradictory label. These are often widows who have lived through the whole cycle of their 'families of procreation', have witnessed the departure of their children from the family home, and have then mourned the loss of their husbands. For them, family is memory.

In very many parts of the South of the world, though by no means all, the majority of families are threatened by a single, great enemy – deprivation. In the fluid milieu of the Latin American popular classes, it needs little to tip a

9. See above, ch. 2, p. 57.
10. G. De Rita, 'L'impresa familiare', in P. Melograni and L. Scaraffia (eds), *La famiglia italiana dall'Ottocento ad oggi* (Bari: Laterza, 1998), pp. 383–416. For a case study, P. Ginsborg, 'I cambiamenti della famiglia in un distretto industriale italiano, 1965–1997', in P. Ginsborg and F. Ramella (eds), *Un'Italia minore. Famiglia, istruzione e tradizioni civiche in Valdelsa* (Florence: Giunti, 1999), pp. 109–54.
11. See Marzio Barbagli, *Provando e riprovando* (Bologna: il Mulino, 1990).

family over the abyss. The extended family often acts as a buffer in older, more established urban communities and in rural areas. But even there the cohesion of families is a fragile thing. A Peruvian priest in Cuzco explained to Duncan Green: 'Peruvian society is very authoritarian, and when you live in poverty any mistake or accident becomes a disaster and is severely punished. If a kid loses a sheep, he heads for the hills and won't come back. The responsibility is too great.'[12] It is in the shanty towns on the edges of the great metropolises that the stresses on families, especially those with numerous small children, are greatest. Physical abuse is very common. The worst beatings are usually handed out by step-parents rather than parents, with battering by stepfathers the commonest reason given for street children to have left home.

Deprivation in the poorest parts of the world also takes the form of brutal gender-based restrictions, which cripple the life possibilities of female family members. In chapter 1 we saw briefly how men in the northern Indian and Bangladeshi villages studied by Martha Chen have historically confined their women. Female space is only that of the household, with markets, roads and towns forbidden to them. But female deprivation is not only spatial. The patriarchal system, enshrined by law, makes sure that marriage contracts are decided by male family members, with sisters or daughters disposed of for as little as a colour television or a wristwatch. Here 'the family' amounts overwhelmingly to neglect, abuse and degradation.[13]

The different demographic patterns of much of the South – high fertility and low resources, rather than low fertility and high resources, as in the North – make their weight felt. The loss of a job, the illness of the main breadwinner, involvement in petty crime, alcoholism or imprisonment – these can quickly lead to breakdown of the family and irreparable damage to its members. Anita Desai's beautiful novel for children, *The Village by the Sea* (1982), tells just such a story, through the eyes of the elder children of a poor family in Thul, on the Indian coastline south of Bombay. The family is afflicted by the father's drunkenness and the mother's chronic ill-health. The twelve-year-old son, Bari, returns at night to the hut that serves them as a home:

> Lila, Bela and Kamal. He seldom thought about them, or their lives, because they lived so close together in that small hut, sharing the same kind of life. It was the hard life that occupied him, entirely, so that he

12. D. Green, *Hidden Lives: Voices of Children in Latin America and the Caribbean* (London: Cassell, 1998), p. 25.
13. A point forcibly made by Martha Nussbaum, *Women and Human Development*, p. 243.

could not see them separated from it, as people, as individuals. Lila, Bela and Kamal – his three sisters, one older and two younger than him. Here they were, with nothing but a small smoking fire to light their hut or give them comfort while he was away.

What were they waiting for? What were they hoping for? They could never look forward to working on a fishing boat or in a factory, as he did. They would have to marry, one day, and he would have to see to it since his father would not [. . .] He must have a job if he was to find his sisters a way out of the dark, gloomy house and the illness and drunkenness and hopelessness that surrounded them like the shadows of the night.

He knew he could never earn enough in Thul to help the whole family. He would have to go to Bombay. [. . .] He went into the hut, Pinto bounding ahead of him. They looked up at him. Their sad, frightened faces made him cry out, 'What has happened?'[14]

Families depend on constancy, care for individual members, and reliability over time. They need a steady income, health care, and education for the children. All too often this set of values and necessities is in strident contrast with those of global neoliberal economics. Poor families may be scooped up by capitalism's onward drive, but the ruthlessness and 'flexibility' of labour markets all over the world can cast them out again with terrible and unpredictable ease.

Privacy, everydayness and dreaming

Family and home, taken together but not taken for granted, denote intimate space, a necessary claim to separation of an *inside* from an *outside*. Life where there is no such separation, where community incessantly pokes in its inquisitive nose or the state its eagle eye, is life without an essential dimension. However modest, an 'inside' is essential, as a place of domestic sociality, of freely expressed beliefs and conscience, of intimate sexual acts. The undeniable fact that such an *Intimsphäre*, as the Germans call it, is also often the place of individual oppression and acts of daily, repetitive cruelty should not lead us to the conclusion that the space itself should be abandoned. Rather, the need is to elaborate the possible connections between inside and outside, and to seek ways in which oppressed family members can find

14. A. Desai, *The Village by the Sea: An Indian Family Story* (London: Puffin Books, 1984), pp. 45–6.

succour and recourse from the outside against the daily source of their oppression. Time and again, those who suffer in families none the less cling to them, for often they are all they have.

Privacy is essential and should be jealously guarded, as liberals have been at pains to point out. In the past it was sometimes dismissed as a mere piece of bourgeois ideology. Certainly, the modern 'intimate' family has its origins in middle- and upper-class aspirations at the end of the eighteenth and the beginning of the nineteenth centuries, but the desire for the privacy of a home, as Barrington Moore Jr has noted, is also to be found very strongly among German factory workers before the First World War, and American automobile workers after the Second. When Italian peasants flocked to the Milanese hinterland during the 'economic miracle' of the 1950s, one of the things they most celebrated was a private apartment, even in a peripheral urban wasteland, far from the prying eyes of the rural courtyards from which they had come.[15]

Privacy, as Julie Innes has pointed out, has essentially to do with possessing control over a realm of intimacy.[16] In that realm, families or domestic groups create their own daily patterns. They will sit down to meals together, watch television, plan holidays, express opinions, argue. Everyday life within four walls is dependent on complex coordination, on an ongoing system of exchanges, at its best on a gift economy, where family members willingly give of their time and energy to others – to get up in the middle of the night to give the baby a feed, to sit with a child over homework, to care for an ill member of the family.[17] Time and again it is the central female figure, most often the mother (but in Desai's tale it is Lila, the thirteen-year-old daughter) who shoulders these responsibilities, who makes the most gifts to the others.

Ideally, privacy is not only collective but individual. One of the greatest achievements of modernity is the creation of more space for individuals *within* homes a sort of 'inside of the inside', enabling families, as in modern Shanghai, not to share toilet facilities with others, parents to be able to make love in a room separate from that of their sleeping children, teenage boys and girls to have spaces of their own. Most families, in most of the world, have still a very long way to go in this respect.

15. For the town of Rho in the Milanese hinterland, see A. Pizzorno, *Comunità e razionalizzazione* (Turin: Einaudi, 1960), pp. 184–5. For the German and American examples, Barrington Moore Jr, *Privacy: Studies in Social and Cultural History* (Armonk, N.Y.: M. E. Sharpe, 1983), p. 285.
16. J. C. Innes, *Privacy, Intimacy and Isolation* (Oxford: Oxford University Press, 1992), p. 69.
17. M. Douglas, 'The idea of a home: a kind of space', *Social Research*, 58, 1 (1991): 18.

Finally, privacy is crucial because it marks, as Jürgen Habermas has written, the confines of 'an invulnerable zone of personal integrity and independent judgement'.[18] Often in history the privacy, or semi-privacy, of domestic space has been the place of resistance to external oppression. The contemporary African American activist bell hooks has underlined 'the subversive value of homeplace, of having access to private space where we do not encounter white racist aggression'.[19] Domestic, closed space has always been vital in the organisation of political solidarities. Very often, as we shall see, it is the first moment of civil society, with a meeting in a living room or a *salotto* or a *salon* giving rise to an association or local movement.

Each of us belongs to a family, of one sort or another, and often we are prepared to do for it more on a daily basis than we do for any other social group. Family *matters*, as Juliet Finch pointed out, in one of the most sensitive recent studies of family loyalties and sense of obligation.[20] Yet many of us compare our families to an ideal discourse of what *the* family should be like, and dream, in one way or another, of the circumstances and indeed the members of our family life being different. As John Gillis writes perceptively: 'We all have two families, one that we live *with* and another we live *by*. We would like the two to be the same, but they are not.'[21]

In the Christian world, no other moment brings home better this tension than Christmas. In an article with the memorable title, 'The Great Christmas Quarrel and other Swedish traditions', Orvar Löfgren collected a large body of interview material on Swedish Christmas celebrations, past and present. As he surveyed this material, he realised 'that all these recollections really were about something else, something more important: dreams of family togetherness or frustrations over generation conflicts, hope for the future or longing for a nostalgic past, reflections on how life has turned out and what it could have been'.[22]

Authenticity is at the heart of the annual ritual which constitutes a Swedish Christmas, with constant reference being made to the austere and supposedly genuine traditions of a rural past. Sweden is now a very secularised society, but at Christmas its families emphasise the sacred and the restrained: real candles,

---

18. J. Habermas, *Between Facts and Norms* (Cambridge, Mass.: MIT Press, 1996), p. 368.
19. b. hooks, 'Homeplace as site of resistance', in hooks, *Yearning. Race, Gender and Cultural Politics* (Boston: South End Press, 1990) p. 47.
20. J. Finch, *Family Obligations and Social Change* (Cambridge: Polity, 1989).
21. Gillis, *A World of their Own Making* p. xv.
22. O. Löfgren, 'The Great Christmas Quarrel and other Swedish traditions', in D. Miller (ed.), *Unwrapping Christmas* (Oxford: Clarendon Press, 1993), p. 217.

matching colours and natural materials. Preparations are long and minute. Every morning children open a window in the advent calendar; on 13 December there are Lucia celebrations at school, at work and at home. Houses are cleaned and carpets are rolled up in preparation for the magical moment of Christmas Eve morning, when at least one room of the house has been transformed and is reopened, complete with red curtains, candlelight, decorated gingerbread houses, skating gnomes on pieces of reflecting glass and, of course, the Christmas tree and its presents.[23]

In this highly charged atmosphere of expectation, the family often cannot cope. At the very moment of its consecration, it implodes, for it cannot live up to the ideal it has set itself in its collective head. Mothers are on the verge of tears from overworking, grandparents are wistful and condescending ('I think [my daughter's] is a slightly *shallow* Christmas Eve'[24]), children are impatient and hyperactive. All adults overeat and overspend. The Swedish bilateral kinship system, the balancing of the maternal and paternal sides of the family – is put to its hardest test. So too are 'reconstituted' families, of which there are growing numbers in Sweden, which simply do not fit into Christmas. To which parent are the children to go? No question is surrounded with greater tension. Thus, the higher the expectations and the more conformist the ritual occasion, the greater the difficulty for modern families to accept themselves for what they are.

A world apart

Familism

Privacy is sacrosanct, but it has its dark side, and not only at Christmas. Dominant versions of modernity accentuate the privatisation of family life, its separation from the public sphere, its dedication to home-centred consumption. Rachel Whiteread's notable piece of sculpture, *House* (see below, p. 198), which in 1993 won the high-profile Turner Prize for Contemporary Art in Britain, potently suggests this sort of family life. It is a cast of the interior of a house that has been demolished, 'negative space' solidified into concrete and preserving the 'memory of a presence'. The concrete cast can be

23. Ibid., pp. 220–1. The Americans, much more religious than the Swedes, are denounced for celebrating a Christmas which is far too loud and glittery, too commercial and synthetic. Yet since the 1960s the most popular television programme of the year in Sweden has been an hour of Walt Disney cartoons on the afternoon of Christmas Eve.
24. Ibid., p. 225.

seen as a home which is not just inward-looking but is absolutely shuttered up against the outside world. It is a perfect fortress, without even those spy-holes which characterise medieval castles, and from which defenders could size up the oncoming enemy. There is no chance of looking in, let alone 'popping in', and no way of getting out, let alone 'popping out'. Perhaps it is a refuge, but it looks more like a prison, a family prison, a site of neurosis and disfunction, perhaps even of violence.[25]

In brutal fashion, Whiteread has captured one of the essentials of modern family life – its enclosedness, introspection, and preoccupation with itself. In 1967 the British anthropologist Edmund Leach provoked widespread discussion by stating in his Reith lectures on the radio that 'today the domestic household is isolated [. . .] The family with all its tawdry secrets and narrow privacy is the source of all discontents.'[26] Many listeners objected and Leach had to apologise, reassuring them that he had not wished to speak out against the family.

The home as an inviolable space and the family as an inward-looking unit have a very long modern history, which it is worth examining at least in part. No single author extolled the virtues of the self-reliant family with more eloquence than the fifteenth-century Florentine Leon Battista Alberti. His famous *Libri della famiglia*, written in the 1430s as a series of fictional conversations between family members, emphasised that family and state were analogous in both structure and hierarchy, but that the microcosm of the family was to be considered superior to the macrocosm of the republic.[27] The family derived its existence from nature, the city state from convenience or necessity. Alberti's view of human nature and of *virtù* is of great interest for our general argument. For him love was an almost exclusive prerogative of the extended family. It was there that human nature gave of its best. Outside the household lay a hostile world in which diffidence and calculation were the necessary guidelines. In his blunt and vivid dialogues, home was a rural refuge from an untrustworthy humanity, a space in which the family deliberately turned its collective back on the misdeeds and problems of the world:

Hidden away in your villa [in the countryside], you can avoid being witness to the thefts, villainy and vast numbers of the worst sorts of

25. Commentary on, and photographs of Whiteread's work are to be found in J. Lingwood (ed.), *House* (London: Phaidon Press, 1995). The sculpture itself was demolished by the local authorities after only a few months.
26. E. Leach, *A Runaway World?* (London: BBC Publications, 1968), p. 44.
27. L. B. Alberti, *I libri della famiglia* (1433–40); (Turin: Einaudi, 1972).

humanity, who in the city flit continuously before your eyes, and never cease to fill your ears with their chatter. Hour after hour they bellow and screech in the streets below, like the most furious and repellent of beasts.[28]

The state was also to be regarded with suspicion because of its interfering nature and the natural tendency of those who held political power to use it for their own purposes. For Alberti, the two collectives – family and republic – were thus counterposed, and it was above all in the family that the values of 'amore' and 'pietà' found their highest expression.[29] His dialogues anticipate (by a very long way) the sort of discussions that we encountered in chapter 2, where Daniel Miller contrasted moral and ethical shopping. Alberti would very much have approved of the first, based on family care and love, and have had little time for the second, with its subordination of immediate family interests to a wider sense of justice.

Across the centuries, the self-enclosed family, defensive and suspicious of the outside world, has found more critics than supporters. The most striking condemnation that I have found of it comes in a collection of Chartist literature. The long pamphlet *America Compared to England* was written in 1849 not by a British Chartist but by a radical American, the Cincinatti lawyer Robert W. Russell. In his chapter entitled 'The mischiefs of families living separately', Russell pursues a quite different view of human nature from that of Alberti. What, asks Russell are the consequences of the actions of those who stress separation before all else?

28. Ibid., p. 247. My translation. For a complete version in English, see L. B. Alberti, *The Family in Renaissance Florence*, ed. Renée Neu Watkins (Columbia, S.C.: University of South Carolina Press, 1969).
29. Ibid., p. 218. Much of Alberti's diffidence in this respect can be derived from the fact that his family had been exiled from Florence. However, more than one Renaissance scholar has pointed out that Florentine family diaries and chronicles, of which there were a considerable number in these decades, nearly always tended to express considerable mistrust of government and of those who held public office. For a sensitive comparison between this Florentine tradition and the contemporary Venetian one – which operated no such caesura between family and state – and between the writings of Alberti and those of the Venetian Giovanni Caldiera, see M. King, 'Caldiera and the Barbaros on marriage and the family', *Journal of Medieval and Renaissance Studies*, 6 (1976): 19–50. For the concept of *virtù* in Alberti's second dialogue on The Family, see the important comments of Q. R. D. Skinner, *The Foundations of Modern Political Thought* (Cambridge: Cambridge University Press, 1978), vol. 1, p. 92. For the influence of Alberti's family model on Italian history, C. Tullio-Altan, *La nostra Italia* (Milan: Feltrinelli, 1986), esp. pp. 22–4.

Windows are carefully blinded to exclude the public gaze from without. An insignificant garden is carefully walled-in from mere jealous privacy, leaving a public eyesore in a dead wall. The houses are prisons in appearance, and the inmates are prisoners in reality. It is a just observation of Lord Bacon's that there is in man's nature a secret inclination and motion towards love of others, which, if it be not spent upon some one or a few, doth naturally spread itself towards many; thus the living in separate families necessarily confines our regard from the whole human race. We are shut up within four walls, and anything beyond them concerns us very slightly. We see society as through a microscope, for it is all comprehended in the small circle of our family and acquaintance. Thus it is that our charity begins at home, for there it tells best [. . .] All are individualised, cold and forbidding; each being compelled to take a hundredfold more care of himself than would otherwise be necessary.[30]

In the twentieth century it was an American sociologist, Edward Banfield, writing in 1958 about the villagers of Chiaromonte in the southern Italian region of Basilicata, who developed an analytical framework for these sorts of family attitudes. He coined the term 'amoral familism' to describe the ethos of southern Italian rural life. The extreme backwardness of Chiaromonte and similar villages was caused, according to him, by 'the inability of the villagers to act together for their common good, or indeed, for any good transcending the immediate, material interest of the nuclear family'.[31] This was 'amoral familism', and Banfield claimed that such crippling and exclusive concentration on the nuclear family was intimately linked with underdevelopment. To drive home his point, he contrasted the desolation of collective life in Chiaromonte with the vibrant associationism of a similar sized but far more prosperous village in the United States, St George, Utah. If only southern Italian families would take a page out of an American cooperative book, they would soon climb out of poverty.

30. W. R. Russell, 'America compared to England', in G. Claeys (ed.), *The Chartist Movement in Britain, 1838–50* (London: Pickering & Chatto, 2001), vol. 5, pp. 363–4. The whole pamphlet is to be found on pp. 137–408.
31. E. Banfield, *The Moral Basis of a Backward Society* (Glencoe, Ill.: Free Press, 1958), p. 10. Banfield's 'predictive hypothesis' was that the villagers 'acted as if they were following this rule: "Maximise the material, short-run advantage of the nuclear family; assume that all others will do likewise"' (p. 83).

Banfield's theses were heavily, and in part justly criticised,[32] but the term 'familism' stuck, at least in an Italian context. It probably did so because it is intimately connected not just with the past but with the present. Familism is not just Italian, rural and archaic; it is also, as we shall see in a moment, exquisitely urban and modern.[33]

However, the term itself needs to be better defined for the realities of the contemporary world. I would suggest that it should be viewed in relational terms. Modern familism is a particular *relationship* between family, civil society and the state; particular in that the values and interests of the family are counterposed to the other two principal moments of human associationism.[34] In this definition, the respective weight of all three elements in the relationship – family, civil society and state – have to be taken into consideration. It is not enough, as in Banfield's case, to make the ethos of the family do all the explanatory work. In Italy's case, the solidity of family units, when linked to the relative weakness of civil society especially in the south, and to an absentee but often punitive state, has promoted familism in its modern form. Other countries exhibit a different mix of these elements, and different grades of integration of families into a wider societal discourse.

Though space does not permit an extended treatment here, it is possible to suggest that in China and many Middle-Eastern countries similar elements of familism prevail. In China the influence of Confucianism, with its strong emphasis on father–son relations and on filial piety, when combined with the declining power of the Imperial state, meant that in historical terms the family became the central point of reference in Chinese society. Nepotism was rife at all levels.[35] After taking power in 1949, the Chinese Communist Party waged

32. See the excellent collection of articles in the appendix to D. De Masi's Italian edition of Banfield, *Le basi morali di una società arretrata* (Bologna: Il Mulino, 1976), and in particular A. Pizzorno, 'Familismo amorale e marginalità storica, ovvero perché non c'è niente da fare a Montegrano', at pp. 237–53.
33. See Laura Balbo, *Stato di famiglia* (Milan: Etas Libri, 1976), pp. 132–3. In Britain the concept of 'privatism' is that most akin to 'familism'. For its use, see the renowned study of Luton workers by J. Goldthorpe et al., *The Affluent Worker* (3 vols, Cambridge: Cambridge University Press, 1968–9). A revisiting of Luton and a contesting of the privatism thesis is to be found in F. Devine, *Affluent Workers Revisited* (Edinburgh: Edinburgh University Press, 1992).
34. For an extended discussion of the term civil society, see ch. 4, pp. 132–5.
35. The situation in 1935–37 is carefully described in the work of Olga Lang, *Chinese Family and Society* (New Haven and London: Yale University Press, 1946), esp. pp. 54–6 and 181–92 on nepotism. Francis Fukuyama has also noted the important link between familism and Confucianism in his *Trust: the Social Virtues and the Creation of Prosperity* (London: Penguin, 1996), pp. 85ff. His definition of familism – 'too strong

war on these habits and attitudes, but in the wake of the 1978 reforms the power of the family has forcefully reasserted itself.[36]

As for the Arab Middle East, the traditions of the endogamous community family, characterised by frequent marriage between first cousins, the cohabitation of married sons with their parents and equal inheritance between brothers, has had a fundamental influence upon social formations. No family could be more 'closed' than one in which marriage partners of the next generation are chosen from within its midst. The influence of families and family clans, even when traditional family forms have broken down in more recent times, has been of fundamental importance for the realities and the possibilities of politics in the region.[37]

The American model

In the very same year, 1958, that Banfield pointed his accusing finger at the 'amoral familism' of the Italian south, J. K. Galbraith, in a renowned passage in *The Affluent Society*, described something eerily similar for the United States, though based on quite different economic circumstances. No one at the time or since, as far as I am aware, has thought of making the connection:

> The family which takes its mauve and cerise, air-conditioned, power-steered and power-braked automobile out for a tour passes through cities that are badly paved, made hideous by litter, blighted buildings, billboards and posts for wires that should long since have been put underground. They pass on into a countryside that has been rendered largely invisible by commercial art. (The goods which the latter advertise

an insistence by society on maintaining family ties at the expense of other kinds of social relationships' (ibid., p. 65) – is slightly more generic than mine.

36. For a detailed account of the first decades of the Communist experience, N. J. Diamant, *Revolutionising the Family: Politics, Love and Divorce in Urban and Rural China, 1949–68* (Berkeley: University of California Press, 2000).

37. For further discussion, see below, chapter 4, pp. 151–3. See also Emanuel Todd, *The Explanation of Ideology: Family Structures and Social Systems* (Oxford: Blackwell, 1985), pp. 133–45; Beshara Doumani (ed.), *Family History in the Middle East: Household, Property and Gender* (Albany, N.Y.: State University of New York Press, 2003). It is worth noting that in Turkey, in contrast to the Muslim Arab countries of the Middle East, a different relationship has existed historically between family and state, with both the Ottoman and the Kemalist state maintaining a clearly autonomous sphere of power and primacy. The family in Turkey, although strong and important in society, has never become a determining political force. Except in very rare cases, families have not exercised a continuity of public power which has extended beyond two, or at most three, generations; H. Gerber, *State, Society and Law in Islam* (Albany, N.Y.: State University of New York Press, 1994), p. 149.

have an absolute priority in our value system. Such aesthetic considerations as a view of the countryside accordingly come second. On such matters, we are consistent.) They picnic on exquisitely packaged food from a portable icebox by a polluted stream and go on to spend the night at a park which is a menace to public health and morals. Just before dozing off on an air mattress, beneath a nylon tent, amid the stench of decaying refuse, they may reflect vaguely upon the curious unevenness of their blessings. Is this, indeed, the American genius?[38]

Galbraith was exaggerating, of course. In the 1950s American families were not so hermetically sealed inside their limousines, and nor were all cityscapes, let alone landscapes, wastelands. Associationism was at its height and families were often heavily involved in religious groups, parent–teacher associations, and a host of other activities. Classic studies of American suburban life at that time record the constant intermingling of families. Not all parks were blighted with the stench of decaying refuse. Yet there was a glaring contrast between private affluence and public squalor, white residential opulence and black urban slums, even if it was still mediated in part by that *connectedness* that de Tocqueville had identified as one of the essences of American democracy.

The decline of that connectedness in the ensuing half-century has been dramatically and meticulously charted by Robert Putnam in his recent *Bowling Alone* (2000). I will discuss his findings on associationism and social capital in more detail in my next chapter. Here instead I would like to underline how in the three key areas of family, civil society and state there have been significant shifts in the American case over the last half-century: families have increasingly withdrawn into the private sphere, civil society has declined in numbers and quality, and public services and public spaces have shrunk dramatically, especially in the last two decades. Taken together these form the bedrock for a new, modern American familism.

It is the first of these three trends, the privatisation of American family life, which most concerns us here. When the anthropologist M. P. Baumgartner did her fieldwork in a suburban New Jersey community in the mid-1980s, she discovered a culture of isolation, self-restraint and what she termed 'moral minimalism': 'Weak social ties breed a general indifference and coldness, and a lack of conflict is accompanied by a lack of caring'.[39] Neighbours kept

38. J. K. Galbraith, *The Affluent Society* (1958; London: André Deutsch, 1977), p. 192.
39. M. P. Baumgartner, *The Moral Order of a Suburb* (New York: Oxford University Press, 1988), p. 134.

themselves to themselves, expecting little from each other, and offering little in return. All over America there has been a dramatic increase in the amount of time spent *inside* the house. Putnam records, for instance, that the greatest increases in sports-related consumption in the 1990s involved 'in-home' activities, like treadmills and workout equipment. One of the few areas of associationsim to grow in that decade was the security-oriented 'Neighborhood Watch' groups. However, a 1998 Department of Justice survey of twelve cities found that only 11 per cent of all residents had ever attended a neighbourhood watch meeting, as compared to 14 per cent who kept a weapon at home, 15 per cent who owned a guard dog, and 41 per cent who installed extra locks.[40] 'Gated communities', which boast physical barriers, security guards and surveillance cameras to keep the unwanted out, have spread rapidly.

The effects of television

At the centre of an increasingly privatised and home-centred lifestyle, not just in the United States, stands the television. Where once there was the hearth in peasant homes, now there is a television, occupying the key symbolic space in the family home. All over the world, from Borneo to Brazil, ethnographers have reported the placing of cherished family pictures, of children and of ancestors, as well as of relatives who have emigrated, on the top of the television.[41] No single object commands more everyday attention. By 2001 average adult daily viewing time in the United States had reached 4 hours 22 minutes. The equivalent figure for Italy was 3 hours 58 minutes, for Turkey 3 hours 49 minutes, for Japan 3 hours 45 minutes, and for Brazil 3 hours 19 minutes.[42] That constitutes a pretty large chunk of every day, a larger proportion than for any other activity except sleeping; and the graphs for annual viewing, even in countries where the number of televisions per household has reached saturation point, still show steady increases. In 2002, Rupert Murdoch, the world's most powerful television magnate, predicted that in five years the number of homes hooked up to interactive TV would increase

40. R.D. Putnam, *Bowling Alone*, p. 107.
41. D. Morley, *Home Territories: Media, Mobility and Identity* (London: Routledge, 2000), pp. 87f. Morley comments: 'For the purposes of official surveys in the UK, a household is often defined as those who eat together. It seems, however, that in some cases a household may perhaps be better defined as those who view together' (p. 89).
42. For these comparative statistics, see www.csm.com.cn/content/news_events/20021012 (IP data 2000/01).

fifteen-fold.[43] 'Hooked up' is indeed the right verb, and it is given added resonance by the rapid spread of computer games.

The debate over the effects of television is fascinating and complex. One school of thought has chosen to underline, with differing tonalities, the beneficial effects of the constant presence of the small domestic screen. Rachel Whiteread's *House* may not have any windows, but it is very likely to be in contact by aerial with the outside world. The family inside may be physically isolated, but it receives any amount of stimuli and information all the same. It can stay put but still 'visit' other places and situations. This was what Raymond Williams called 'mobile privatisation'.[44]

Television helps families as nothing else can to be part of a national, or even international, community. Family members can watch news programmes and debates, form opinions, be part of a very wide viewing public that shares the same culture and programmes. Commentators who underline these aspects write of television's 'horizontal' or even 'democratic' qualities. Joshua Meyrowitz, for instance, argues that television as a *medium* is at least as important as its content, for it leads to a new 'situational geography' of social life. Hierarchical senses of place and position are broken down, leading to the creation of new and more universal spaces of communication: 'through television rich and poor, young and old, scholars and illiterates, males and females, and peoples of all ages, professions, classes and religions often share the same or very similar information at the same moment.'[45] Even well-worn television stereotypes, like the intrepid policewoman in an American soap, can have an extraordinary effect in another viewing world, such as that of rural and patriarchal India or Bangladesh.

However, such arguments have to be balanced against the 'vertical' hierarchies of television ownership. Television is not a medium which lends itself easily to any form of democratic control. In general, mass media markets are not made for minnows. They require huge injections of capital, and over the past twenty years they have witnessed a dramatic process of concentration. While public broadcasting appears an ever more beleaguered outpost, global commercial television ownership is concentrated in the hands of a restricted oligarchy.[46] Its members have a number of traits in common: fierce attention

43. W. Goldman Rohm, *The Murdoch Mission* (New York: Wiley, 2002), p. xiv.
44. R. Williams, *Television, Technology and Cultural Form* (London: Fontana, 1974), p. 26.
45. J. Meyrowitz, *No Sense of Place* (Oxford: Oxford University Press, 1985), p. 90.
46. Informative of this world is R. V. Bettig and J. L. Hall, *Big Media, Big Money: Cultural Texts and Political Economics* (Lanham, Md.: Rowan & Littlefield, 2003); see also below, pp. 172–3.

to levels of audience share, on which their life-blood, advertisements, depends; insatiable acquisitive tendencies; limited and conformist cultural frameworks. All this means that the medium is not safe in their hands. They may experiment occasionally and leave some editorial independence to their subordinates, but by and large they play safe, aim for high profits and produce television of a repetitive and unedifying quality, permeated by advertisements and selling techniques of every sort.[47]

Sometimes television is used overtly for the purposes of political control and indoctrination. This is the case, spectacularly so, of Silvio Berlusconi's Italy, where both public and private television are in the premier's hands, and also the case of his friend Vladimir Putin, the Russian premier, who was reported in 2003 by the OECD Office for the Protection of Freedom of Expression in the Mass Media for 'exercising direct or indirect control over many newspapers and the totality of the electronic means of information'.[48] It was also the case of Indian television under the control of the BJP (Bharatiya Janata Party), which attempted to 'reshape' the Indian viewing public through Hindu television soap operas and propaganda, as well as the advertising of a range of consumer objects, known as 'Retail Hindutva'.[49]

Yet it would be a mistake to think that families merely lap up, in an uncritical fashion, the messages, political or otherwise, that are being projected at them from the small screen. Research into family viewing shows the degree to which television is filtered through family culture, and how much translation, criticism and rejection, or simple lack of attention, is involved in the watching of television programmes. The caustic comments, pet names and jokes which constitute a family's private language often confront and in some ways transform the images that are being presented to them.

One of the best examples of these processes comes not from sociological research, but from a famous piece of television fiction. *The Simpsons* gather at the beginning of their cartoon in front of the television, behaving very much as a passively receptive family of middle America should behave. Yet their

47. As one American reader wrote recently to the *Financial Times*: 'Despite the 50 or more channels available to the typical American cable TV viewer, the fare is mostly the same stultifying and mind-numbing drivel'; B. Myers, 'Dissent that drowns in the din of TV drivel', *Financial Times*, 22 Feb. 2003.
48. See the report of the Head of the Office, Freimut Duve, on www.ocse.org., 11 Dec. 2003.
49. A. Rajagopal, *Politics after Television* (Cambridge: Cambridge University Press, 2001), p. 279.

viewing and daily life are made up of constant disagreements, different ideological positions, battles over what should or should not be done. Homer, the father, when he is not entirely dominated by selfish short-term material interests (in one episode he sells his soul to the devil for a donut) is most certainly a classic familist figure, believing fervently in the credo 'my family right and wrong'. His son Bart is well on the road to hyper-individualism. But his wife, Marge, saves her husband again and again, and their passionate daughter Lisa is environmentalist, vegetarian and feminist rolled into one. Theirs is a family always on the brink of the abyss or beyond, but in its ravaged, atomised way it still constitutes a collective with its own independence of judgement.[50]

The debate about television continues, but two features stand out clearly, both of them highly damaging to the possibilities of creating an alternative everyday politics. The first is that television is *the* medium for long-term, incessantly repeated advertising suggestions. As I suggested in the previous chapter, these are the syringes of modern consumer capitalism, highly tuned and expensive products designed to inject specific aspirations and desires into our heads. It would be foolish indeed to underestimate their influence over time. Television advertising may appear innocuous enough, to be admired for its ingenuity, or else useful as a break to get something to eat from the kitchen, but its function is clear enough: to establish at the heart of family life a certain vision of 'normality'.

In this normal world, the family lives its daily life surrounded by a multiplicity of commodities – cars, cell phones, televisions, video cameras, computers, and so on. It is asked to enjoy them for a period and then to reject them in favour of newer ones. It is to spend much of its time and energy discussing, working to earn money for and shopping to meet these cyclical commodity needs. It does not need to think much about the world around it, except to be depressed from time to time about the barbarity of 'human nature'. It need know nothing about civil society. Family life in television advertising is not that of *The Simpsons*, of losers adrift in a competitive world. Rather it is that of winners, opulently celebrating products and romances with relatives and friends, in cars, on beaches, inside sparkling homes. Advertised

---

50. For an acute analysis see P. Cantor, '*The Simpsons*: atomist politics and the nuclear family', *Political Theory*, 27, 6 (1999): 734–49. Not by chance the series became Rupert Murdoch's greatest seller all over the world, a fact that encapsulates the many contradictions of modern television; W. Shawcross, *Murdoch: The Making of a Media Empire*, 2nd rev. edn (New York: Touchstone, 1997), pp. 280–8.

families are the incarnation of 'negative' freedom, in the sense of getting on with their own lives without risk of interference.[51]

The second, highly damaging effect of television is closely linked to the first. Television has an extraordinary power to tie people to their homes. In their classic study of family and kinship in east London in the 1950s, Michael Young and Peter Willmott reported the effects of recently introduced television on working-class families on a new council estate:

The family sits night by night around the magic screen in its place of honour in the Parlour. In one household the parents and five children of all ages were paraded around it in a half circle at 9 p.m. when one of us called; the two-month-old baby was stationed in its pram in front of the set. The scene had the air of a strange ritual. The father said proudly: 'The tellie keeps the family together. None of us ever has to go out now.'[52]

Fifty years later, in his exhaustive study on the United States, Robert Putnam found that television watching was *the* single most important factor in explaining the decline of American civic life: 'Nothing – not low education, not full-time work, not long commutes in urban agglomerations, not poverty or financial distress – is more broadly associated with civic disengagement and social disconnection than is dependence on television for entertainment.'[53] He found that selective viewers – those who watch specific programmes and then turn the television off – were significantly more involved in community life than habitual viewers – those who turn the television on and leave it on. Habitual viewing was directly co-related to civic disengagement.[54] Furthermore, television viewing is an increasingly solitary occupation. Among American children aged eight to eighteen, less than 5 per cent of their viewing was done with their parents, and more than one-third was done entirely alone. In 1996, of the 76 per cent of American children who had their own bedrooms, 59 per cent had their own television.[55] Behind the wealth of Putnam's statistics lies a particular model of modern family life, in which solitude, privacy, consumption and enclosedness combine.

51. On negative and positive freedom the classic text is I. Berlin, 'Two concepts of liberty' in Berlin, *Four Essays on Liberty* (1958; Oxford: Oxford University Press, 1969), pp. 118–72.
52. M. Young and P. Willmott, *Family and Kinship in East London* (1957; London: Penguin, 1990), p. 143.
53. Putnam, *Bowling Alone*, p. 231.
54. Ibid., pp. 224–5.
55. Ibid., p. 480 n.17.

'Only connect'

Mario Merz's *Igloo* offers a rather different perspective. For Merz the *Igloo* is a home and a refuge, but unlike Rachel Whiteread's *House* it is not sealed up against the outside world. On the contrary, his igloos in one way or another are open; some of them are transparent. You can see inside them and from the inside you can see out. 'This little construction, the mistress of space,' wrote Merz, 'creates the inside by its definition of itself, as the measure of an anthropological space, and creates the outside by that same definition. IGLOO = HOME.'[56] This home is of modest proportions, based one might say on 'voluntary simplicity', and its very modesty and openness define its relation to the spaces outside it. Of course, taken literally, a transparent home would be a nightmare, permanent domestic 'reality show' in which all privacy disappears. Nor are the dimensions of the *Igloo* reassuring. But I think the openness and sobriety that Merz has in mind are not of the literal sort, but are rather an invitation, much as Whiteread's is, to rethink the nature of home and the relationship between internal and external.

How complex Merz considered such a relationship to be can be gleaned from the *Igloo* (see below, p. 199) housed in the Tate Modern in London. It is of 1985 and bears the pertinent if enigmatic title, 'Do we revolve around houses or do houses revolve around us?' I find it of particular significance for the themes of this book because it has an illuminated walkway (perhaps 'crawlway' would describe it better) that connects the *Igloo* to the outside world. Connectedness is possible, Merz suggests, but it is not going to be easy. And as if to underline this point he has placed shards of glass along the passage connecting the *Igloo* to the external world. Through the glass you can see the outside, but can you get there?

If we look around, as well as backwards in time, we can get glimpses of different sorts of relationship between families, and between the inside and the outside. Modernity's dominant version of these relationships is neither ubiquitous nor inevitable. In the second half of the nineteenth century and the first half of the twentieth, traditional working-class quarters in major European cities, like the Barriera San Paolo of Turin or London's Bethnal Green, offered a different texture of everyday family life.[57] The memory and sometimes the history of these quarters are prey to idealisation, but there are

56. M. Merz, *I Want to Write a Book Right Now* (Florence: Hopfulmunster, 1986), p. 139.
57. For Turin, see G. Levi et al., 'Cultura operaia e vita quotidiana in Borgo San Paolo', in *Torino tra le due guerre* (Turin: Musei civici, 1978), pp. 2–45.

also clear recurring themes: the doors of houses left open, the constant 'popping in', the internal crampedness that made for external sociability, the kids playing in the street.

Or else we can follow Martha Nussbaum in her exploration of the differences between the daily rhythms of family life in India and those in the United States. For Nussbaum the Indian home, among all classes, 'is simply more porous'. Even in upper middle-class families, writes Nussbaum, 'visitors drop in unannounced and there is a constant ebb and flow of people through the house'.[58] The out-of-doors is in some sort of balanced relationship with the indoors. The Indian family itself is less centred than the American on romantic love for a single other person, with all the narrow concentration and attendant disappointments that that often entails. Instead, partly from the necessity deriving from arranged marriages, Indian women put much of their energy into forming mutual support groups among themselves.

Or else, as another variant, there is the anthropologist Stefano De Matteis's description of families in the alleys of contemporary Naples, and the links between artisan and shopkeeping families and the world that surrounds them, even up to the present day. Here families are drawn out of their shells: 'It is as if the central family, that of the workshop or shop, is subject to a series of centripetal forces which, while they do not threaten the family's unity, extend it, push it out of its habitual shape, confer upon it a variable rhythm.'[59]

Of course, in all these examples there are some important lines of distinction to be drawn. Connection can easily become intrusion. The vital questions of privacy, and of the safeguarding of private space and individual choice, are not to be sacrificed to some nostalgic idea of lost community. Nor is it sensible to propose as an alternative model of modernity the back streets of Naples or the now largely defunct working-class communities of urban Europe.[60] The challenge is different: to accept and indeed to celebrate some basic defining elements of modern family life – intimacy, privacy, love of

58. Nussbaum, *Women and Human Development*, p. 259. For the variety and complexity of Indian families, see P. K. Roy (ed.), *The Indian Family: Change and Persistence* (New Delhi: Gyan, 2000), and Roy (ed.), *Family Diversity in India* (New Delhi: Gyan, 2003).
59. S. De Matteis, 'Storie di famiglia. Appunti e ipotesi antropologiche sulla famiglia a Napoli', *Meridiana*, no. 17 (1993): 142.
60. It is important to remember that both in the past, and in some parts of the developing world now, economic necessity and spatial proximity have often pushed families towards cooperation and solidarity, and not just to Banfield's 'amoral familism'. The whole history of the working-class movement testifies to the achievements, as well as the difficulties, of this other path. For the tensions between these two possible

home – but to place them in a radically different social and cultural context. That search is precisely for a different quality of family life, open and disposed to intermingle with other families, not excessively self-enclosed and self-referential, based on a 'variable rhythm' which could take its place alongside de Certeau's ruses, murmurings and joyful discoveries.

Gender (and other) relations

The old rhythms, those of traditional family life, have been profoundly disturbed by changing gender relations. Patriarchy has ruled supreme for many centuries, and it still exercises an absolute power in very many parts of the world. As I mentioned in chapter 1, patriarchy takes many forms and its modes of working are highly complex and differentiated across time. But fundamentally male power of this sort is exercised on both an internal and external level: inside the house, with the habitual right to command, to punish and reward, to love women but also to hold them in little regard; outside it, with the exclusive authority to represent the family, to decide on its economic interests and indeed its destiny. If we return to our Florentine example of the 1430s, Leon Battista Alberti had very clear ideas about the necessary, and indeed natural, properties of these gender and family relations:

> Just as little honour would accrue to us if our women were to take part in the daily transactions of the *piazze*, mixing with men in the public eye, so it seems to me even less honourable to shut myself up in the house surrounded by women, when instead I desire to do manly things among men [. . .] Women are almost all timid by nature, soft and slow, and therefore most useful as sedentary guardians of our goods. It is almost as if nature itself provided for our living together, decreeing that the man returns to his house, and the woman is there, ready to serve him. But there can be no doubt, Giannozzo, about our judgement of those idlers who spend the whole day in the company of the little women of the household, or fill their heads with silly women's gossip. They have hearts that are neither male nor magnificent, and the more they seem content to be feminine rather than masculine, the more they are to be condemned.[61]

directions, with reference to modern urban Brazil, see E. P. Reiss, 'Banfield's amoral familism revisited: implications of high inequality structures for civil society', in J. C. Alexander (ed.), *Real Civil Societies* (London: Sage, 1998), pp. 21–39.

61. Alberti, *I libri della famiglia*, pp. 266–7. My translation.

Little by little, these very deeply rooted attitudes have changed, though at different speeds in different cultures. In modern democracies, a major shift took place during the second half of the twentieth century. The assertion of individual choice, rights and autonomy permeated families, radically trans-forming their power relations, dynamics and everyday life. Women gained increasing parity with men, increased rights and protection under the law, and increased freedom to study and enter the labour market.[62] Children, too, have gained more freedom and rights than ever before.

The images of men in families have also been transformed. In European family photograph albums of the late nineteenth and early twentieth centuries, the male head of the household stands upright and apart, striking a particular pose in which authority and virility are combined. His wife is seated, with their children clustered around her, while she gazes at her husband or at the camera. By contrast, a hundred years later similar albums show fathers holding the baby (as they do, increasingly, in everyday life), or even on all fours, with children on their backs.[63] Gender relations, and relations between parents and children, have become less formal, more egalitarian and more physically intimate. Leon Battista Alberti would be simply appalled.

This great transformation of the last sixty years has led some commentators to theorise optimistically about the problem that most taxes us here – that of the connection of homes and families to the problems of the wider world. A more democratic and egalitarian family, so the argument runs, intertwines with and contributes to a more democratic society; the greater the equality and sense of justice in the family, the more these values will extend to society. As Anthony Giddens wrote in *The Third Way*: 'There is only one story to tell about the family today, and that is of democracy. The family is becoming democratised, in ways which track processes of public democracy; and such democratisation suggests how family life might combine individual choice and social solidarity.'[64]

---

62. A. Janssens, 'Economic transformation, women's work and family life', in Kertzer and Barbagli, *The History of the European Family*, pp. 79–80. If we limit our gaze only to Europe, female labour-force participation rates have shown constant increases from 1960 onwards, reaching more than 50 per cent in twelve countries by the end of the century. Female activity rates are highest in Scandinavia and eastern Europe, lowest in southern Europe, Austria and Ireland.

63. F. de Singly and V. Cicchelli, 'Contemporary families: social reproduction and personal fulfillment', in Kertzer and Barbagli, *Family Life in the Twentieth Century*, p. 343.

64. A. Giddens, *The Third Way: the Renewal of Social Democracy* (Cambridge: Polity, 2000), p. 93.

It is a seductive and hopeful argument, but it must be treated with care. The problem is that there is no neat relationship between behaviour in the domestic sphere and the shape of what happens outside of it. Nor are there concentric circles of human associationism, each of which derives its mode of behaviour from the smallest and most central, which is that of the family. Or, to put it in another way, the oak tree of the state does not grow from the acorn of the family; nor does state policy determine the nature and attitudes of the family.

My argument is rather that each of the linkages examined in this book – between individuals, families, civil society and the state – is complicated and often fragile. Indeed some, such as that between families and civil society, may be disjointed, or not exist at all. To return to Merz for a moment, there can be no guarantees that the shards of glass blocking the passageway from the *Igloo* are surmountable, or that once outside we will have enough energy and time to make a difference.

If we look a little closer at modern 'democratic' families, the lack of any automatic connection between their interior life and the external world becomes immediately apparent. Such families may indeed behave in a loving, joyful and egalitarian way *within* themselves, but there is nothing that stops them from being entirely indifferent to what is happening *around* them. Indeed, the worse things become at a global level, the more they may wish to blank out what is happening in order to maintain their sense of internal security and love. The human capacity for denial is extraordinarily strong. In addition, changes wrought by modernity within families have not *necessarily* helped their collective sense of connection. On the contrary, much in the modern world – 'work and spend', lack of time, television, advertising – forcefully invites families to be more passive and detached, more concerned above all with themselves.

A realistic view would also question how profound the changes in gender relations really are, and examine the very many problems which these changes have thrown up. Let me look first at women. Women's emancipation has been only partial, and nearly always it has led to the greater complication of their everyday life. Work outside the home, as has been noted time and again, is a double-edged sword. There is more opportunity, but less time. Women active in civil society find themselves having to combine going to meetings in the evenings, carrying out their family work of care and sustenance, and doing regular paid work outside their home. In societies like Italy and Spain, where the older generation is more rarely placed in old people's homes than in north-western Europe or the United States, the needs of ageing parents constitute a grave problem of daily responsibility for the central female figure of the family. Sometimes she has to look after not just her parents but those of her husband, as well as her own nuclear family. Daily life becomes an almost impossible balancing act. At the end of a day a woman in this sort of situation has very little energy left indeed.

One habitual response is for women to limit the number of children they bear, or not to bear any at all. By the end of the twentieth century childlessness in women had reached about 20 per cent in Britain, Australia, the US and Germany.[65] This marked decline in fertility rates in the North of the world raises a structural and methodological problem of primary importance. During the course of their life history (which is often called the 'family life cycle'), families have varying amounts of time available and disposition to interact with the outside world. With the arrival of a baby, and oft-interrupted nights, a couple is bound to retreat into the family unit, preserving energy for essentials. At the other end of the family life cycle lie (or sit) elderly grandparents whose mobility and energy have greatly declined. Between these two moments there are many others, with far greater potential.

Many studies show that one of the moments when families are most likely to open out is when they have young school-age children, and that it is women not men who take the initiative. Mothers go to parks, meet other mothers, start chatting. Children sleep over, friendships are made between parents at nursery and primary school, and civil society battles are often waged around schools and the public services connected to them. However, the major decline in fertility rates reduces the frequency of such moments, and their relative weight in society. Another possible aperture of time and availability comes for women when their children (or child) have reached the age of autonomy. As we shall see in the next chapter, women between the ages of 45 and 60 are some of the most active members of present-day civil society.

What of men? The overall impression is of men (including myself) who nearly always put work first, and who often dedicate to it very long hours, from necessity or choice, or both. Consequently, they have little time left either to support the women who are closest to them, or to look after children in the home when their partners are active outside it, or to participate regularly in civil society themselves. Attempted redefinitions of gender roles and arguments over individuals' time and availability remain sites of enormous tension. Everything is in flux. There can be little doubt that there are a growing number of so-called 'new fathers', especially in north-western

65. C. Hakim, 'Models of the family, women's role and social policy', *European Societies*, 1, 1 (1999): 36.

Europe and north America, fathers who assume much more responsibility for children, and who develop sensitivities that have been assumed to come with being a mother.[66] But in southern European societies like Italy, official statistics show that in terms of daily time women are definitely better off without husbands or male partners, because the little those do to help is far outweighed by the amount of female care they both require and demand.[67] And in developing societies like India, men resent women who deprive them of caring time and energy, devoting it instead to their own education or work. It is as if they have been deprived of an ancestral right.[68]

I do not want to end this section on too negative a note, or on one which simply castigates men. A great transformation is taking place in very many countries of the world. In it, women are gaining education, opportunity and choice more than ever before. At many levels this transformation is imperfect and partial, but it is of very great significance and propulsive power none the less. Simultaneously, men and women in innumerable homes are treating each other with a greater degree of equality than ever before. The potential of all this is very great, but so far it has not been brought to bear in a focused way on the questions being raised here.

Sharing

One possible way forward lies in developing the concept and practice of sharing. This is not a new concept; indeed it was furiously debated in ancient Greek political theory, and the terms of that discussion resonate over time. In *The Republic* Plato regarded 'mineness' as anathema. So much so that both the family and private property were to be abolished for the guardians of the Republic. 'Only in this way', Plato argued, 'will they [the guardians] keep to their true character [. . .] They will not rend the community asunder by each applying that word "mine" to different things and dragging off whatever he can get for himself into a private home, where he will have his separate family, forming a centre of exclusive joys and sorrows.'[69]

66. S. Coltrane, 'The future of fatherhood: social, demographic and economic influences on men's family involvements', in W. Marsiglio (ed.), *Fatherhood: Contemporary Theory, Research and Social Policy* (London: Sage, 1995), pp. 255–74; A. Herlth, 'The new fathers: what does it mean for children, marriage and for family policy?', in F.-X. Kaufmann et al. (eds), *Family Life and Family Policies in Europe*, vol. 2 (Oxford: Oxford University Press, 2002), pp. 299–320.
67. ISTAT (Instituto nazionale di statistica), *Indagine multiscopo sulle famiglie. L'uso del tempo in Italia* (Rome: ISTAT, 1993).
68. Nussbaum, *Women and Human Development*, p. 248.
69. F. M. Cornford (ed.), *The Republic of Plato* (Oxford: Oxford University Press, 1941), p. 162.

For Aristotle, on the other hand, 'mineness', as expressed in the individual family and household property, was the social basis on which the polity rested. In *The Politics* he argues fiercely against Plato's ideas, maintaining that they would involve both the destruction of the state and of those affective kinship ties on which the fostering of future generations depends. 'The nature of the state', he writes, 'is to be a plurality',[70] and as such it depends on individual families, each with their own households and property. Real kinship, based on individual families, is for Aristotle infinitely preferable to communal ties, as we can tell from his impassioned cry, 'how much better it is to be the real cousin of somebody than to be a son after Plato's fashion!'[71]

However, it is crucial for our purposes to note that Aristotle did not just stop there. He was far from simply ready to accept the status quo of Athenian households as he found them. On the contrary, in *The Politics* he advocates a whole series of measures to transform them: communal eating for men and boys was to be encouraged by the establishment of public meal-tables (*syssitia*), not just for certain categories of citizens such as magistrates and priests, but for the whole citizenry.[72] No citizen was to hold too much or too little property, for 'a city ought to be composed, as far as possible of equals and similars'.[73] Education above the age of seven was to be the responsibility of the state, not the household, and in commenting upon this proposal Aristotle moves back in Plato's direction (at least the Plato of *The Laws*, if not of *The Republic*):

And since the whole city has one end, it is manifest that education should be one and the same for all, and that it should be public, and not private – not as at present, when everyone looks after his own children separately, and gives them separate instruction of the sort which he thinks best.[74]

70. Aristotle, *The Politics*, ed. S. Everson (Cambridge: Cambridge University Press, 1988), p. 21, book II, 1261a, 18–19.
71. Ibid., p. 23, 1262a, 13–14.
72. Ibid., p. 170, book VII, 1330a, 3–6.
73. Ibid., p. 97, book IV, 1295b, 25.
74. Ibid., p. 185, book VIII, 1337a, 21–31. Whereas in *The Republic* Plato abolished the household, in *The Laws* he retains it, though with considerable modifications. Domestic worship was to be restricted, and communal eating was to be introduced not only for men and boys but also for women and girls. Little time, except at night, was to be spent as a family. Newman comments that in *The Laws* the household 'would escape abolition only to be condemned to a somewhat shadowy existence'; W. A. Newman, *The Politics of Aristotle*, vol. 1 (Oxford: Oxford University Press, 1887), p.180.

As a qualifier to these opinions, we must always bear in mind that Aristotle's concept of the polis was based on major exclusions, principally of women and slaves. Citizenship, both for him and Plato, was a highly selective category. None the less, his remarks continue to have considerable resonance for our world, and his proposals, which stop well short of abolishing the household or private property, still have a startlingly radical ring to them. What, we might like to ask, could be the modern equivalent of the *syssitia*, the public meal-tables, and what could families share between them?

One obvious answer is cars. All over the developed world, systems of car-sharing are beginning to proliferate. Instead of incessantly increasing the volume of private traffic on roads, and consequently the number of roads and the general level of pollution, a small minority of families are choosing to plan and ration their use of cars. Instead of owning one or more cars per family, cars are held jointly by car-sharing associations, and then rented out to members of the association as needs arise. Obviously, those who live in isolated places or who need cars as part of their daily work, such as general practitioners visiting the sick in their homes, have little choice but to have a car, or some sort of motor vehicle, of their own. But the number of unnecessary car journeys made by single people in single cars must rank as one of the most absurd features of modernity. In Italy it has been calculated that 80 per cent of cars are used for not more than one hour a day, and carry an average of 1.2 persons. Car sharing, by contrast, is spreading slowly, with some 100,000 people in Europe practising it, mainly in Germany, Switzerland, Austria, Holland and the Scandanavian countries.[75]

The discussion of cars raises the question of public transport and public services in general, to which I shall return in my last chapter. Here instead, still on the theme of sharing, I would like to say something about parks and gardens. The creation of public parks, and their maintenance, is one of the endeavours with which rapid urbanisation has the most difficulty. So great is the drive towards the private and the enclosed that countries in the South of the world have enormous problems in creating green spaces in growing cities. As for cities in developed countries, they sometimes lose the spaces they have. The 'rape of Rome' in the 1950s, when whole areas of green space disappeared into the projects of building speculators, some of them financed by the Vatican, is only one example among many on a global scale.[76] Yet parks are one of the most important expressions of a modern civic community, spaces

75. For further details, www.carsharing.org.
76. A. Cederna, *Mirabilia Urbis* (Turin: Einaudi, 1965).

which families and individuals can share, acknowledging one another. The Victorians, in their systematic creation of urban parks in nineteenth-century Britain, seem to have grasped this as a central element of the relationship between the internal and the external.[77]

Sharing everything

Sometimes too much sharing can take place. In 1968 the family came under radical attack. In that year and those that followed, the question at stake for a minority of youth in the developed countries was not the 'variable rhythm' of family life, but the family itself. In 1971, the members of Kommune 2 in Berlin referred to the middle-class family home as nothing more than an 'air-raid shelter'.[78] In 1970 David Cooper published a famous book whose purpose was enshrined in its title – *The Death of the Family*.[79] In Italy in 1974, Luciana Castellina wrote of 'the exasperated dichotomy between collectivity and family, the latter being conceived of as a lair, a refuge, a system of fortresses where solidarity with one's relatives is the other face of a brutal egoism towards the outside world'.[80]

The freeing of the individual from the values and taboos of such families became one of the movement's most seductive leitmotifs: freedom to move out of the family home, sexual freedom, freedom to use drugs, freedom to wear what you wanted, or not to wear anything at all. The struggle was on to free the individual not only from the family *without* (families as units of social organisation and as powerful metaphors for the rest of society), but also the family *within* (the subconscious imbibing of parental behaviour and values). Few revolutionary movements had ever set themselves such a gargantuan task.[81]

77. H. Conway, *People's Parks: the Design and Development of Victorian Parks in Britain* (Cambridge: Cambridge University Press, 1991). More recently there have been concerted and successful campaigns to develop nature gardens and wild-life havens of many kinds in northern European and American cities. The real problem, though, remains that of maintenance.
78. Kommune 2, *Versuch der Revolutionierung des bürgerlichen Individuums* (Cologne: Kiepenheuer & Witsch, 1971), p. 7.
79. D. Cooper, *The Death of the Family* (New York: Random House, 1970). In Italy alone it sold 60,000 copies during the early 1970s, and in Germany 40,000 copies were printed in six editions between 1972 and 1978.
80. L. Castellina, 'La vertenza famiglia', in *Famiglia e società capitalistica* (Rome: il manifesto, 1974), p. 26.
81. It was not the only political movement of the twentieth century to do so. For the Bolshevik experience, see the balanced introduction by Elisabeth Waters, 'The Bolsheviks and the family', *Contemporary European History*, 4, 3 (1995): pp. 275–92.

Individuals were to find their liberty in the commune. In their very sensitive study of British communes, published in 1976, Philip Abrams and Andrew McCulloch made a list of the ground rules of the 'ideal' commune: all property and money were to be pooled, monogamous relationships were to be discouraged, children would be regarded as the children of the group as a whole, decision-making would be achieved through universal participation and assent. They hastened to add: 'Needless to say, we know of no such communes. On the other hand, all the communes we know may usefully be seen as seeking to approximate to such a condition.'[82]

Little systematic research has so far been done on the fate of these extraordinary experiments in sharing everything and sometimes everybody. In some major cities like Berlin, where large rented apartments were relatively easily available, and where networks of communes were established, the experience was a long-lasting one. This was also the case for many rural communes, especially in the United States. But the majority of the communes in all countries collapsed very quickly. In the autumn of 1970, one British commune described itself in the following optimistic way: 'Our nucleus is now seven or eight adults and three or four kids, our ages between two and forty [. . .] Life is pretty good here and we've hardly begun [. . .] The adults share chores without sex distinction and all pay the weekly sum, finding cash however they can.' Just one year later the collective project had collapsed and the commune had vanished.[83] This was a pattern that repeated itself with dispiriting regularity in all the countries where the ideas of '68 had some influence.

Both external and internal factors contributed to this general failure. At an external level, local government, hardly surprisingly, was very rarely to come to the aid of these radical experiments; the survival for more than thirty years of the 'alternative' quarter of Christiania in Copenhagen, first founded in 1971, is probably the exception which proves the rule.[84] All too often, so-called 'repressive tolerance' soon gave way to real repression, as squatters' and other communes were forcibly broken up. Crack-downs on drug-taking, as well as on illegal occupation of property, were the most common reasons for police intervention.

However, it was the *internal* level of failure that was the more significant. Communes tended, often only after a short period of time, to collapse from

---

82. P. Abrams and A. McCulloch, *Communes, Sociology and Society* (Cambridge: Cambridge University Press, 1976), pp. 38–9.

83. Ibid., pp. 128ff.

84. M. Edwards, *Christiania* (Hamburg: Rowohlt, 1980).

within. One obvious and crucial element here was the degree of individual liberty and choice which communes, in contrast to families, afforded their members. The fact that communes were not families meant that individuals could share and then quarrel, come and then go, very much as they pleased. It was precisely their uncoercive nature that rendered them fragile and transient.

There were also more profound and complicated reasons for failure. Commune members attempted to take a quantum leap into new styles of collective living; yet they brought with them emotional codes and previous socialisation which could embrace only with enormous difficulty the new mores which they themselves often most ardently professed. One recurring example was that of the tension generated by different definitions of love.

On the one hand, there was the communal ideal of shared love, which often ran in tandem with sexual freedom; members of the commune were to share everything, including their beds. On the other hand, romantic love, closely linked to the couple, lived on determinedly. Time and again, communes collapsed as a result of the tension between the two.[85] To make matters more complicated, those who felt possessive and jealous, or appalled at the prospect of sharing or losing their partners, could not give free vent to such emotions, for the latter were regarded, sometimes even by themselves, as illegitimate.

Nor did the communes, by and large, make much progress with regard to new and more liberated roles for women and children. Women more than once found themselves the prey of groups of male predators, who weakly hid their intentions behind the ideology of collective love. Women also often discovered that despite collective rotas they finished up with most of the housework, cooking and childcare. Sometimes they became mothers to all members of the commune, both adults and children. As for children, they certainly enjoyed less suffocating relationships with their own parents, and collective care in some communes was taken very seriously. But often they ran wild and risked making profound attachments to adults who then suddenly disappeared. The transience and instability of the communes did not play in their favour.

On the horns of these dilemmas, and against the brittle surfaces of seemingly inviting critiques like that of David Cooper, very many communes fractured into their individual parts after a shorter or longer period of time. Men, and above all women, reasserted their freedom to choose and their desire for a privatised intimacy. The 'Igloos' of '68 had tried to gather into themselves all of what they considered best in society, and then to make the internal space

---

85. N. Daum, *Des révolutionnaires dans un village parisien* (Paris: Londreys, 1988), p. 126.

they had created totally transparent. As often happens, this was heroic and foolhardy at one and the same time.

Conclusion: families and civil society

In conclusion, I want to leave, if a little reluctantly, the magical and impossible world of the communes of 1968 (and of my youth) to return to the central problem in everyday politics which has been at the centre of this chapter – that of the 'connectedness' of families. Throughout the chapter I have made constant reference to a world external to the intimate and domestic social sphere, but intentionally without ever specifying its contours. I now want to trace a first few distinctions, before discussing civil society and the local state in detail in chapters 4 and 5.

It is obviously of crucial importance not only to inquire into the connectedness of families, but also to ask: connected *to what*? It is one thing to be a member of an Elvis Presley fan club and another to be a member of an anti-mafia association. Without in the least wishing to cast aspersions on the memory of Elvis, it must be obvious that it is the second category of associations, those concerned with civic engagement, that are the focus of my attention here. Robert Putnam has suggested a first, valuable distinction between groups that are *bridging* (or inclusive), and those that are *bonding* (or exclusive). As examples of the first, he cites civil rights movements or youth service groups; of the second, ethnic fraternal organisations or church-based reading groups. The first tend to foster broader identities and reciprocities, the second to bolster specific interests or passions.[86]

Of course, these are not watertight categories. As Putnam himself writes, they are 'more or less' dimensions which help us to differentiate between types of association or social capital. But for the sort of everyday politics under discussion here, it is bridging groups that are the crucial ones. Families that have a predisposition to openness rather than closedness, that manifest empathy towards other families and concern for the great and pressing problems of the contemporary world, need bridging groups urgently if they are not to be rapidly overcome by a sense of their own isolation and the futility of their own good intentions.

A second, important distinction is between bridging groups and neigh-

---

86. Putnam, *Bowling Alone*, pp. 21f. He attributes the invention of these labels to R. Gittell and A. Vidal, *Community Organisation: Building Social Capital as a Development Strategy* (Thousand Oaks, Calif.: Sage, 1998), p. 8.

bourhoods. Pierre Mayol, one of Michel de Certeau's close collaborators, offers us in volume 2 of *The Practice of Everyday Life* a charming celebration of neighbourhood, and in particular of that part of Lyons in which he grew up and to which he returned as a social scientist. For Mayol, the tension between the two terms inside and outside gradually disappears in the neighbourhood, because the one becomes the continuation of the other, with the result that 'the neighbourhood can be called an outgrowth of the abode [. . .] the sum of all trajectories inaugurated from the dwelling place'. Neighbourhood becomes, evocatively, 'the arousal of the sense of smell under the trees in the park, memories of itineraries buried since childhood, joyous, serene or bitter reflections on one's own destiny'.[87]

However, neighbourhood is not enough, nor are there enough neighbourhoods. The sorts of intense, clustered social networks which mark traditional urban quarters, with their strong residential continuities from one generation to another, are certainly precious elements of human contact and reciprocity. In the early 1950s, in the working-class quarter of Bethnal Green, East London, when Michael Young and Peter Willmott asked 'Mrs Landon' to keep a diary of all the people she said 'hallo' to in the street during the course of a week, they found that she greeted no fewer than sixty-three persons, of whom thirty-eight were relatives of at least one other person out of the sixty-three.[88] But sociality of this sort is not at all the same thing as civic engagement, though it may be the terrain from which it grows.

Furthermore, the sort of vital neighbourhood which Mayol evokes is by now a rare species in urban life. Modernity offers us instead the spectacle of walled-off villas with guard dogs and garden gnomes in 'residential' areas, high-rise blocks in working-class peripheries, shanty towns for the millions of recent arrivals in the great metropolises of the South. Its architectural structures have not offered, at least so far, many indications of how inside and outside might reduce the barriers between them and exercise a beneficial influence on one another.

If a first question (connected to *what?*) prefigures the discussion of civil society, a second (*who* makes the connections?) leads back to the themes (individual choice and autonomy) of the previous chapter. In very many

87. M. de Certeau, L. Giard and P. Mayol, *The Practice of Everyday Life*, vol. 2: *Living and Cooking* (Minneapolis: University of Minnesota Press, 1998), pp. 11–13; originally *L'Invention du quotidien*, vol. 2: *Habiter, cuisiner* (Paris: Gallimard, 1994).
88. Young and Willmott, *Family and Kinship in East London*, p. 107.

societies, even in the twentieth century, civic engagement has been an exclusively male affair. When the fishermen in Anita Desai's *The Village by the Sea* travel to Bombay to protest against a proposed fertiliser factory which would pollute their sea and kill their catch, they are bewildered to find women organising a protest march against high prices in the heart of the city: 'Hari and the other Alibagh villagers stood open-mouthed in amazement: they had not brought along a single woman with them, had not thought it necessary, had been sure that they, the menfolk, could manage it all on their own and the women would only be a nuisance.'[89]

Such taken-for-granted gender discrimination is now contested nearly everywhere, though it is far from dead. Women may *formally* be entirely free to join the associations of civil society, but that does not mean that they always can. The structuring of everyday life militates strongly against them doing so, even if they are flanked by sympathetic and loving men. Women have to juggle on a daily basis with too many parts of their own and others lives. The possibilities they have of leaving the house, of being citizens, are thus *informally* constrained.

However, the question of 'who connects?' is not just a gendered one. Families, except in quite specific circumstances, are unlikely to take part *en bloc* in civil society. In Italy in January 2004, when Berlusconi's education minister, Letizia Moratti, moved to penalise public schooling in favour of private education, literally tens of thousands of families took to the streets with their children. The government then denounced political parties and trade unions for making ideological use of minors and threatened to introduce legislation preventing them from doing so. But it is rare to find entire families mobilising in this way, and not by chance was the issue that of schooling.[90]

Civic engagement is much more a question of *individual* choice and participation. It may be that families will delegate (usually by default) one of their members to represent them; more often an individual will choose autonomously to get involved, and then bring back his, or perhaps her, experiences into the heart of a family. Often this is a generational matter. Young people have the most energy and curiosity and are constantly *out* of the home, but they are also those most concerned with themselves, most attracted by the hedonistic aspects of modern consumerism. Often it is the members of a particular generation in history who become most civically engaged, as if a historical conjucture had stamped its mark on them. Putnam found what he

---

89. Desai, *The Village by the Sea*, p. 76.
90. See *Corriere della Sera*, 3 Feb. 2004.

called 'a long civic generation' in the United Sates, born between 1910 and 1940, a broad group substantially more involved in community affairs than those younger than they were.[91] Henri Mendras refers in France to an 'innovatory nucleus' at the heart of the French middle classes, now middle-aged but unrepentant about its involvement in the events of May 1968, still deeply committed to voluntary associations and civil rights.[92] I wonder if the moment has come again when history will suddenly stamp its mark on a generation, and whether it will be possible for this to happen without some preceding catastrophe on a global scale.

I began this chapter with Mill and I would like to end it with Hegel. In all of political theory, there are no pages more densely relevant to the themes that I have tried to discuss in this chapter than the paragraphs dedicated by Hegel in his *Elements of the Philosophy of Right* to the passage from family to civil society. These paragraphs do not make for easy reading, but are worth the struggle.[93]

In them, Hegel examines the moment of what he calls 'dissolution' (*Auflösung*) of the family into civil society. It is a discussion which is as extraordinary as it is neglected in current debates on civil society. He suggests that this moment of dissolution is characterised by three different processes. One is the passage from the family of origin to that of procreation, that is the moment when children leave the family home to begin families of their own. A second is the entry of adult males into modern civil society as independent individuals, each one in competition with another. The last is the dialectical passage wherein the family is the first moment of ethical life, but civil society is its negation.

It would be strange indeed if we were to accept the normative evaluations inherent in Hegel's version of what is happening when family and civil society meet. Neither his version of gender relations – 'woman has her substantial vocation [*Bestimmung*] in the family, and her ethical disposition consists in this [family] *piety*'[94] – nor his famous definition of civil society as that which 'affords a spectacle of extravagance and misery as well as of the physical and ethical corruption common to both'[95] – are ones that are likely to gain wide

91. Putnam, *Bowling Alone*, p. 254.
92. H. Mendras, *La Seconde Révolution française (1965–84)* (Paris: Gallimard, 1988), p. 55.
93. G. W. F. Hegel, *Elements of the Philosophy of Right*, ed. A. W. Wood (Cambridge: Cambridge University Press, 1991), paragraphs 177–88.
94. Hegel, *Elements of the Philosophy of Right*, §166.
95. Ibid., §185.

acceptance today. But what makes Hegel unique is his methodological invitation to concentrate on family–civil society relations, the intensity of his gaze, though it is confined to just a few pages, and his isolation of the moment when family and civil society *touch* each other and come into contact. A modern version of this relationship is at the heart of everyday politics. In it, families would not be isolated in their own consumer dreams and practices, but would be connected, either by women or by men, or by both, to a civil society which, though far from perfect, would be anything but the negation of families' ethical life.

4   The Possibilities of Civil Society

It's 9.30 p.m. on a spring evening in 2003. The meeting was supposed to have started at 9.00, but meetings in Italy (and I imagine in many other parts of the world) never start on time. People are milling around and happily chatting away. I suspect that this is what everyone likes doing *best*, and that the formal meeting that follows is regarded deep down – though no one would ever admit it – as an unfortunate but necessary appendage. The meeting place is a deconsecrated church in the Oltrarno, that part of central Florence which lies on the other side of the river from Piazza della Signoria. The church is a gloomy place, more than a little squalid, with fading frescoes and hard, plastic chairs; but it is also one of the few places available for reunions on this side of the Arno, and it can hold up to 120 people. It's also free. The occasion is an assembly, one of four in different parts of the Oltrarno, to discuss how the neighbourhood can be improved, and what specific requests can be made to the city council. It forms part of a campaign to which the organisers – the local section of the Left Democrats and three neighbourhood committees – have given the grandiose title of the Estates General of Oltrarno. You can say many rude things about the Florentines, and other Italians often do, but you could never accuse them of lacking a sense of history.

I'm not involved in the organisation, but two of my close friends, Fiammetta and Paola, are. One is a psychologist, the other a university teacher. Their faces are tired this evening, but they are both at the entrance giving people forms to fill in so that they can be contacted again, and asking them if they would like to be part of the various commissions – traffic, culture, daily life – which will formulate in detail the requests to go to the city Council. The Oltrarno is one of the few areas of Florence where a traditional sense of neighbourhood, in Pierre Mayol's terms, remains strong. It's a socially mixed quarter, and always has been, with artisans and shopkeepers, students and professional people. Since the early nineteenth century it has also been a favourite part of Florence for foreign residents. But it is full of the problems typical of very many inner-city centres in southern Europe: non-stop traffic in the road outside the ex-church, tiny pavements and no cycle paths, almost no green spaces, air you could cut with a knife, an ageing population who no longer feel safe, and drug dealers in the main square, that of Santo Spirito.

The meeting eventually starts. There are about sixty people present – not a lot – but they form a reasonable cross-section of the population of the quarter. There are working-class women in floral dresses who tell long stories of burglaries and immigrants. There are some of the shopkeepers who boarded up their shops during the European Social Forum the year before because they were convinced that marauding hordes of anti-globalisation protesters were about to pillage everything. The shopkeepers want a Florence of 'real Florentines'. Together with the hotel and restaurant owners and the tour operators they constitute a formidable conservative social and economic bloc in the city; but at least they've come. There's also a venerable old member of the Florentine anti-Fascist Resistance of 1943–44 who talks of the need for civic responsibility, and a young extreme left militant who denounces the whole thing as a waste of time. She has an I-know-the-truth look about her, always a dangerous sign. The majority of the participants are women, middle-aged and middle class, a fact which should not be interpreted in any simply reductive way.

During the course of the meeting there's a good deal of rhetoric and some laughter. At one point a heavily built café owner comes over to whisper something in my ear. He leans his weight against me and puts his arm round my shoulder. I fear my plastic chair is going to give way. It's the sort of physical contact between males that makes Englishmen go rigid and Swedes faint. The meeting has, if we adopt the distinctions mentioned at the end of the last chapter, more of a 'bridging' than a 'bonding' quality about it, being more exploratory than deliberative, more an occasion to listen than to take decisions. The organisers do a good job of not letting anyone speak for too long, but are powerless in the face of the constant hum of conversation at the far end of the church, near the door. The microphone works badly. All in all, it's a typical meeting of Italian civil society – nothing spectacular, requiring much patience, managing to get people together to try and make things better. At the end, lots of people sign up for the commissions.[1] I walk home gone midnight, passing on

1. The commissions made a list of 13 requests to go to the city Council. These were amended and approved by a final assembly of the whole quarter, and then voted on by more than 700 people. The centre-left city government gave the requests a warm verbal

the way a plaque in memory of the poet Elizabeth Barrett Browning, on which are inscribed the first lines of one of her most famous poems:[2]

> I heard last night a little child go singing
> 'Neath Casa Guidi windows by the church,
> *O bella libertà, O bella!* . . .

I wonder what she would have made of the meeting.

An experience of this sort is probably what awaits individuals, all over the world, if they feel the need to be part of civil society, and if they have any time and energy left for it at the end of the day. By and large, people are attracted to modern civil society in order to affirm their individuality. They do not want to be part of a regimented army, as the political militant very often was in the twentieth century. As Marco Revelli has justly written, the modern figures active in civil society 'have neither a flag nor a uniform'. They are not soldiers but civilians.[3]

In many parts of the world – Burma, China, Uzbekistan and so on – it is not possible to be a civilian of this sort. Even among the democracies there exist very great divergences in the quality and strength of associationism, of whatever sort. The 1999 European Values Survey listed the percentages of people in different European countries who declared that they belonged to at least one association. There was a marked difference between east and west. Only in one country, Sweden, did more than half of those interviewed reply that they were members of at least one association (53.4 per cent). The equivalent figure for the United Kingdom was 41.8 per cent and for Italy 24.3 per cent. In eastern Europe the overall average was much lower (18.3 per cent), with 30.8 per cent for the Czech Republic, but just 9.6 per cent for Romania and 4.6 per cent for the Russian Federation.[4] However, these were clubs of all types, from

---

welcome, but then did little in practice, and above all took no steps to encourage a repetition of this experiment in participation from below. In the spring of 2004 there was a first meeting to discuss a possible 'neighbourhood laboratory', but since then nothing.

2. E. Barrett Browning, *Casa Guidi Windows: A Poem* (London: Chapman & Hall, 1851); she lived in the Oltrarno with her husband Robert from 1847 until her death in 1861.

3. M. Revelli, *Oltre il Novecento* (Turin: Einaudi, 2001), p. 284.

4. G. Badescu et al., 'Civil society development and democratic values in Romania and Moldova', available on www.policy.hu/badescu/articolEEPS.doc. Details of membership and volunteering in 'civil society' groups (community action, Third World/

sporting associations to train spotters to watchdog groups against media monopolies. I believe that civil society cannot be regarded as equivalent to associationism of every sort, because then it would lose all specificity; but this is a highly contested terrain, and as in the previous two chapters on individualism and on families, it is time to draw some lines and make some distinctions.

Key words

In the last fifteen years, few terms have been the subject of such intense debate on an international level as 'civil society'. Its history in political theory is a long and fascinating one,[5] but most modern definitions have recourse to two different explanatory areas in order to define it – the spatial and the normative. Although these are distinct one from the other, it is clear that what sort of space civil society occupies (its topography), and the nature and quality of what goes on in that space (its activity) are intimately related.

One widespread usage places the emphasis on 'civil society' as a very broad area of social activity, covering all those associations, institutions and relations that do not belong primarily to the private sphere, the economy or the state. Churches, political parties, associations and interest groups of all kinds fill this vast intermediate area. Civil society in this sense is close to what is usually signified by the English word 'society'. Precisely because it covers so large and amorphous an area, this civil society does not have a precise normative content, though the very choice of defining it in such a wide spatial way is itself a normative one, full of consequences and implications.

With relation to the sort of everyday politics for which I am arguing here, this first attempt at demarcation has to be reinforced by a second one, more attentive to boundaries and content. Contemporary civil society certainly is an

human rights, environment and peace) are to be found in H. Anheier and S. Stares, 'Introducing the Global Civil Society Index', in M. Glasius, M. Kaldor and H. Anheier (eds), *Global Civil Society 2002* (Oxford: Oxford University Press, 2002), p. 245, table 1.1, and p. 363, record 28. Here comparative figures (not only for Europe) are available for membership and volunteering in such groups, but not the comparative total weight of associationism in each country. In the year 2000, Sweden and Holland were the countries with the highest percentage of citizens involved in 'civil society' groups.

5. For the dichotomies of the past, unparalleled in its elegance and clarity is Norberto Bobbio's entry 'Società civile' in N. Bobbio, N. Matteucci and G. F. Pasquino (eds), *Dizionario politico* (Turin: UTET, 1983), pp. 1084–90. See also his 'Sulla nozione di società civile', *De Homine*, no. 24 (1968): 280–97.

intermediate area of associationism distinct from the private sphere, the economy and the state, but it is not only that.[6] It is also an area of social interaction that harbours specific ambitions within the general condition of modern democracy: to foster the diffusion of power rather than its concentration, to use peaceful rather than violent means, to work for gender equality and social equity, to build horizontal solidarities rather than vertical loyalties, to encourage tolerance and inclusion, to stimulate debate and autonomy of judgement rather than conformity and obedience. It aims, in other words, to make the society of modern democracies more civil, though the precise contours of that civility will change and develop from generation to generation, as they did in the past.[7]

Civil society, then, is a place for individuals to protest and organise against arbitrariness and arrogance, to improve the quality of the local environment (in its widest sense), and to link up their own existence with the lives of others far away. It is a learning ground, necessarily plural and tolerant, with a strong transformative dynamic. People do not generally stay in civil society all their lives – it eats up too much time for that. They tend to come and go, but if their experience goes well it is a sort of civic education. It can influence the deeper culture of their families, become part of their daily language, lead them to watch television less often and in a different way (no mean feat). It leaves memories as well as skills that may be reactivated at other moments in what is usually the long course of a single individual's life.

This usage of civil society is thus necessarily more narrow than the first, because not all associations share the aims listed above, but what it loses in breadth it gains in a sense of purpose.

On a larger scale, Mary Kaldor and her colleagues at the London School of Economics have analysed in detail and promoted a nascent global civil society which operates beyond the confines of national societies, polities and economies. This is the world of international non-governmental organisations (NGOs), of powerful transnational bodies like Amnesty International

6. John Keane, in a recurring image, refers to 'citizens living within the nooks and crannies of civil society'; Keane, *Civil Society: Old Images, New Visions* (Cambridge: Polity, 1998), p. 88; Michael Walzer writes of the need for them to be members of 'a smaller, more accessible, less demanding, less dangerous place than the modern state'; Walzer (ed.), *Towards a Global Civil Society* (Providence, R.I.: Berghahn, 1995), p. 1. An important recent contribution is that of Jürgen Kocka, 'Civil society from a historical perspective', *European Review*, 12, 1 (2004): 65–79.

7. See the interesting collection of essays edited by N. Bermeo and P. Nord (eds), *Civil Society before Democracy: Lessons from Nineteenth-Century Europe* (Lanham, Md.: Rowan & Littlefield, 2000).

and Greenpeace, meetings such as the World Social Forums, and of concerted pressure on recalcitrant corporations and governments, democratic or not, to change their ways. Though global civil society, too, is a nebulous project of difficult definition and of more than one internal contradiction, there is important common ground. It lies principally in the desire to strengthen self-determination in both the South and the North of the world, and to contest fiercely the disempowerment and social injustice brought about by unbridled global capitalism.[8]

At first sight, such large-scale battles seem far distant from a mundane little meeting in a deconsecrated church somewhere in the centre of Italy. Yet nothing is more fascinating, difficult and rewarding than the individuation of themes, campaigns and everyday actions which link the micro-politics of such meetings to the macro-politics of world power.

It would be possible, though not permissible in this context, to continue to discuss the nature of civil society at considerable length. Let me just say a few words about businesses. Many present-day debates about the nature of civil society concentrate on the question of what it does and does not include. Should, or can, businesses be part of civil society? If one chooses a very broad and inclusive definition of civil society, including market relations (and this was the primary sense that both Hegel and Marx gave to the term) then the question is a redundant one: firms are automatically part of civil society. But the more precise and normative the definition is, the more complicated life becomes. Firms obviously *can*, and sometimes, though all too rarely, *do* play great and virtuous roles in improving both local and international conditions. Bill Gates's intervention in the African fight against AIDS is only the most clamorous and recent example of a very long history of business philanthropy. Much better, as Will Hutton and others have consistently argued, to foster corporate social responsibility than simply to denounce piously the free-riding transnational corporations of the 1980s and 1990s.[9] At a local level, an enlightened and determined president of a Chamber of Commerce can do a

8. H. Anheier, M. Glasius and M. Kaldor, 'Introducing global civil society', in Anheier, Glasius and Kaldor, *Global Civil Society 2001*, pp. 3–22.
9. See, for example, W. Hutton, 'Capitalism must put its house in order', *The Observer*, 24 Nov. 2002: 'Over the past five years there has been a remarkable growth in leading companies making some attempt to account for their social, environmental and wider economic policies.' And also J. Porritt at the Johannesburg Earth Summit in 2002: 'I would argue that some multinationals have genuinely become "a force for good". By contrast, others are up to their illegitimate stock options in wrong-doing, asset-stripping and short-term profiteering'; 'Sustainable vision', *Guardian Weekly*, 29 Aug.–4 Sept. 2002.

great deal to shift a conservative business culture. But corporate social responsibility is not the same thing as civil society, and cannot be seen as a substitute for it. The two differ in many ways, perhaps above all in terms of primary dynamics and organisational criteria. The primary dynamic of firms, even socially responsible ones, is the making of profits, and their primary organisational mode is that of hierarchy and command. Neither of these sits at all easily with the nature of modern democratic civil society, based on horizontal solidarities rather than vertical loyalties, on aspirations to a socially equitable distribution of economic resources, on non-conformity as much as obedience. This does not mean to imply that the two cannot work together. On the contrary. In that arduous traversing of the sheer face of modern capitalism to which I made reference in chapter 1, the more they try to work together, roped up as it were, the more hope there is for everybody. There are few allies more precious for civil society than far-sighted businesspeople.[10]

I would like to deal briefly with some other key words which are often used in close relationship to civil society, and which are the source of much confusion for nearly everyone except the aficionados of these matters, and sometimes for them as well. One is *public sphere*. In intellectual terms Jürgen Habermas can be said almost to exercise a copyright on this term, because it is above all his work that has led to very wide discussion of it. The public sphere, put briefly and in his own words, signifies 'first of all a realm of our social life in which something approaching public opinion can be formed [. . .] A portion of the public sphere comes into being in every conversation in which private individuals assemble to form a public body.'[11] The public sphere, in other words, is a place (real or virtual) of discussion among citizens, in which

10. For a detailed and illuminating discussion of these relationships at a global level see M. B. Oliviera and A. Simmons, 'Who's minding the store? Global civil society and corporate social responsibility', in Glasius, Kaldor and Anheier, *Global Civil Society 2002*, pp. 77–107. It is perhaps also worth recounting, though this is only a personal impression at a local level, that an increasing number of people who are dependent workers (usually white-collar) in large-scale firms are becoming active in civil society. As they tell it, theirs is a dual identity: one based on work, with its strong ideology and exorbitant time requests; the other on a certain resistance and doubting of this all-embracing and all-pervasive enterprise culture, and an attempt to use residual time for some sort of activity in civil society. It is not easy to establish an equilibrium between these two identities, and it is often the civil society one which first flickers and then goes out.

11. J. Habermas, 'The public sphere: an encyclopaedia article' (1964), *New German Critique*, no. 3 (1974): 49. See also his first and fundamental work on this theme, *The Structural Transformation of the Public Sphere* (1962; Cambridge: Polity, 1989).

opinions are formed and problems clarified. It is not to be confused with the public institutions of the state, though its name seems to imply a close affinity. On the contrary, one of its key modern functions is to put pressure on the representative institutions of democracy, to elaborate and highlight issues in an influential and convincing way.[12]

The public sphere bears a close relationship to civil society, but is not identical to it. The distinction between the two, put very simply, is between an area or sphere for debate which primarily aspires to the discursive formation of public opinion; and one primarily for more structured association, linked closely to organisation and activity. The Florentine meeting I described above could be said to have taken place in the public sphere, but to have been organised and carried forward by civil society associations.[13] However, it must be obvious to all that the two terms are close to each other and overlap.

Social capital is another term frequently used in this field. For Robert Putnam, who has done more to popularise it than any other scholar, social capital 'refers to social networks, forms of reciprocity, mutual assistance and trustworthiness'.[14] Social capital is to be distinguished from physical capital (factories, machinery and so on), financial capital (monetary assets) and human capital (the skills and education of individuals). It is rather the networks of relations between individuals on a micro, or everyday level. The social capital of the inhabitants of London's Bethnal Green in the 1950s (p. 125 above) was constituted by their close-knit relations of kinship and neighbour- hood, and by the frequency with which they greeted each other in the street and visited each other's homes. As with the public sphere, so social capital, too, overlaps with civil society without being identical to it. Social capital, it could be said, constitutes the preliminary resources on which civil society can be, but may not necessarily be constructed.

12. Habermas, *Between Facts and Norms*, p. 359.
13. I shall return to the question of the relationship between political parties and civil society in chapter 5, but it seems to me that a local section of a party which takes an initiative like that of the Estates General of the Oltrarno in Florence belongs clearly to civil society. It is perhaps also worth noting that the term 'public sphere' has sometimes been preferred to that of civil society because it is less value-laden. This seems to me to be a misconception. It is not any old conversation that takes place in a public sphere, but ones that have a specific flavour, even if not a specific orientation. The point has been engagingly made by John Keane. The contemporary public sphere, he writes, is 'the vital medium of naming the unnameable, pointing at frauds, taking sides, starting arguments, inducing *diffidenza* [Umberto Eco], shaking the world, stopping it from falling asleep'; Keane, *Civil Society*, p. 170.
14. R. D. Putnam and L. M. Feldstein, *Better Together: Restoring the American Community* (New York: Simon & Schuster, 2003), p. 2.

Once again, as with civil society and the public sphere, the spiky question of normative values comes rapidly to the fore. Putnam is careful to specify that the basic elements comprising social capital – networking, reciprocity, etc. – can also be applied to groups which would not normally meet with citizens' approval, such as the Ku Klux Klan or the Mafia. Yet there is an element of artificiality in this distinction, because practically all the studies which use social capital as a conceptual tool emphasise its positive effects for society as a whole. Indeed, Putnam's definition of the term includes 'trustworthiness', which is not a quality immediately associated with the Mafia, although it forms part of its own self-presentation.[15] What can be said with a certain confidence is not that social capital is a value-free term, but that it corresponds to a large number of relations and networks in society that most of us would find acceptable. As I wrote at the end of the last chapter, sociality of this sort is not at all the same thing as civil society, though it is often the terrain from which the latter grows.

Modern civil society and *social movements* are closely linked, from both a normative and a temporal point of view. If the most widely accepted definition of social movements focuses on the challenges they offer to the accepted power relationships in a society,[16] it is also true that their dynamic has its point of origin in grass-roots civil society associations, which then expand rapidly and become some sort of forest fire sweeping through society as a whole. As Doug McAdam has written, 'It is there in the existing associational groups or networks of the aggrieved community that the first groping steps are taken towards collective action.'[17] Thus while social capital *precedes* the formation of civil society associations, social movements *succeed* them, in the sense of spreading outwards with great speed from an initial base.

A last term, probably the most popular of all in everyday language, is *community*. How often have we heard appeals, from all parts of the political spectrum, in all parts of the world, for the need to create, or even more often,

---

15. The traditional codes of the Mafia have always emphasised very strongly its trust-worthiness, but the actual history of the organisation is of uneasy coalitions of 'families', shifting and competitive with one another, all too ready to resort to killing and betrayal in their fight for supremacy.

16. C. Tilly, 'Social movements as historically specific clusters of political performances', *Berkeley Journal of Sociology*, 38 (1994): 1–30. See also the 'Introduction' by Mario Diani to M. Diani and D. McAdam (eds), *Social Movements and Networks* (Oxford: Oxford University Press, 2003).

17. D. McAdam, 'Beyond structural analysis: towards a more dynamic understanding of social movements', in Diani and McAdam, *Social Movements and Networks*, p. 284.

re-create community! It is certainly a widely abused term, too often charged with ruralist rhetoric. Its attraction is certainly great, for the word powerfully evokes images of living together, of day-to-day solidarities, of a strong sense of attachment to a place and way of life. Community is what we all want to belong to, but only occasionally do.

However, in historical terms, community has always had too much of a patriarchal, restrictive, conformist and exclusive air about it to be used with any equanimity alongside, or even instead of, civil society. It brings to my mind the peasants' communes of rural Russia before the revolution, with decisions being taken by the assembly of male heads of family and elected village elders, 'a rigid system of authority and command wherein individual activities were tightly controlled for the common good'.[18] Community is what certain shopkeepers at the Florentine meeting wanted to preserve, a neighbourhood of 'real Florentines', whoever they might be. In modern European politics it has been the Haiders and the Bossis, the leaders of extreme neo-localist parties, who have talked incessantly of community as a geographical location to protect – or even invent, as in the case of the northern Italian fiction of 'Padania' – and as a base for exclusion and racism. In modern India, it has been the Hindu revivalist movement that has unleashed what Achin Vanaik has called 'the furies of Indian communalism'.[19] Community and civil society do not go easily together.

I was once travelling on an overcrowded Italian train in the Veneto one Sunday in the mid-1980s. I was alone with my two small children and we were sitting on our luggage in the corridor. The journey was long and the children were exhausted. Inside the compartment facing us were the members of a parish outing, mainly middle-aged women accompanying their parish priest. At a certain point he went off to the dining car to have his dinner. I asked if I could sit down on the vacant seat with my little daughter on my knees until the priest came back. I was met with a wall of silence; they could not say no but they wanted to. The seat 'belonged' to their priest. I sat down all the same and stayed there some fifty minutes until he returned. At that point one of the women hissed at me: 'Vattene! ' (Get out!) I have taken her 'Vattene!' with me across the years. She belonged to a Christian community – probably a strong one – but it had nothing to do with civil society as I understand it.

18. Christine D. Worobec, *Peasant Russia: Family and Community in the Post-Emancipation Period* (Princeton, N.J.: Princeton University Press, 1991) p. 7.

19. A.Vanaik, *The Furies of Indian Communalism: Religion, Modernity and Secularisation* (London: Verso, 1997).

Texture and daily practice

> Mephistopheles: My dear friend, all theory is dull and grey,
> And the golden tree of life is green.[20]

I have not gone over wholesale to the side of the devil, though it is difficult not to agree with his messenger, at least in part. Defining can become an obsession, and we can argue endlessly about conceptual terms without reaching any agreement; such indeed is the sport of a certain academia. But what is important is how concepts inform our actions. In the case in question, if civil society is simply an agglomerate of associations of every sort, an all-embracing term to describe an intermediate space, then it does not add up to anything very much for everyday politics. But if it harbours certain broad ambitions, and has a fairly clear sense of where it wants to go, then it can act as a first magnet of attraction, as well as a sort of education, for an increasing number of individuals.

At the end of her famous book *No Logo*, Naomi Klein wrote that for her the task is to 'build a resistance – both high-tech and grassroots, both focused and fragmented – that is as global, and as capable of coordinated action, as the multinational corporations it seeks to subvert'.[21] I would go along with that, but the aims of everyday politics are both more modest and at the same time more ambitious. At stake is not just a question of resistance (de Certeau uses the same word), sacrosanct though that is, but one of molecular trans-formation. When the lives of individuals and families begin to change on a daily basis, when they begin to look at the choices in front of them in a different way, when they hold back from following the insistent proposals of an invasive material culture, then a transformative dynamic gathers force. This too is subversive, though not in a clamorous way.

Civil society has a crucial role to play in this process. It is not just a social sphere where people's own interests are furthered and guaranteed, but a place where self-interest and the interests of others can combine. It aims to give some collective form to an individual's sense of indignation or anger, or simple desire to do something now. It can respond to requests for information with sober and up-to-date material, offer a wide choice of associations, each with its own distinctiveness, and show that people from different backgrounds can meet, discuss and combine. Civil society, to be successful, needs to be a

---

20. J. W. Goethe, *Faust*, pt 1, ll. 2038–9: 'Grau, teurer Freund, ist alle Theorie,/und grün des Lebens goldner Baum' (trans. Giles MacDonogh).
21. Klein, *No Logo*, pp. 496–7.

place where individuals feel welcome and able to express their opinions freely. It also needs to be an irreverent place, which takes nothing for granted, which is sceptical of all hierarchies, including those in its own midst.

That is what civil society *should* be like, but its actual texture is quite another matter. The truth is that civil society is quite often a mess. That is precisely because of its nature as an area of free association, often without established rules of conduct and procedure, where people may come and go, and where everyone brings their own habits and ways of being from society at large, as well as from their home life. It is no easy task to absorb and amalgamate all this, to find an acceptable collective and democratic form for it, and still move forwards. There are a number of key areas, little discussed, where civil society may stand or fall. They can be called the micro-elements of its daily practice.

The first of these concerns the nature of dialogue. Albert Hirschman, always sharp-eyed, once wrote:

Many cultures – including most Latin American ones I know – place considerable value on having strong opinions on virtually everything from the outset, and on winning an argument rather than on listening and finding that something can occasionally be learnt from others.[22]

Diego Gambetta, taking his cue from Hirschman, has dubbed this general attitude the culture of 'Claro!': 'es claro', 'it's obvious', 'I knew it all along!', 'nothing *you* say surprises me.'[23] He rightly associates such an attitude with a certain form of masculinity, strutting and self-assertive, but it is also linked to long-standing patron–client relations, with powerful men accustomed to passive and respectful audiences. I shall return to patrons below.

The problems of dialogue in civil society do not stop here. Often the attitudes described by Hirschman are accompanied by a strong rhetorical tradition. A speech is a speech, even if it is delivered to a small group of people in a deconsecrated church. In order for its rhetorical form to be properly developed, it needs time, a lot of time, and others are expected to sit patiently through it. Sometimes one rhetorical tradition overlays another, with devastating effects. In southern Europe, the legacy of Communist rhetoric, in which the correct form was always to start from an analysis of the world

22. A. Hirschman, 'On democracy in Latin America', *New York Review of Books*, 10 Apr. 1986, quoted in D. Gambetta, '"Claro!": an essay on discursive Machismo', in J. Elster (ed.), *Deliberative Democracy* (Cambridge: Cambridge University Press, 1998), p. 20.
23. Ibid., pp. 20–1.

situation in general historical outline and then to proceed gradually towards the local or the specific, often combines with a more profound rhetorical tradition, in which discourse is more allusive than explicit and one adjective or verb is never as good as three. The overall result is often lethal in terms of holding and keeping people's attention.

For civil society to achieve a vaguely acceptable texture of dialogue (and without that what sort of civil society is it?), it has to be highly sensitive to the question of time. The preconditions for dialogue can only be assured if there is an agreement on how long each person can speak. Five minutes per person as a rough rule-of-thumb seems an adequate time to many northern European civil society associations. To some in southern Europe it seems like the equivalent of having your tongue cut out.

Nor do our problems stop here. In order to make sure that time limits are adhered to, a coordinator for a meeting has to be agreed on. A coordinator's tasks are not identical to those of the chairperson of a committee in a firm or institution. Not only does the coordinator have to stop the windbags in their tracks, summarise effectively what has been going on, and steer the meeting towards taking some decisions. She or he has also to encourage individuals who have not spoken to come forward, and limit the number of times a single individual can speak.[24] Very often these are gender matters. Many women come to meetings but are too shy to intervene, and confide what they want to say only to a smaller group of friends once the meeting has come to a close. Persuading individuals to speak, giving them self-confidence in the public sphere, is one of the crucial gifts that an effective civil society can confer on a population. Self-control is another.

These considerations may seem to some readers to be entirely obvious and to others overly prescriptive. In reality they are the minimum micro-structural requisites for decent public dialogue. Without them, a meeting of 'civil society', in whatever culture, only reproduces the hierarchies of gender, speech and power of daily life. It also runs the risk of what any seasoned veteran of civil society, like an ancient mariner, can smell in the air: the imminence of the hullabaloo. Everyone speaks at once, the waves of sound mount by the minute, possession of the microphone becomes all-important, and the ship of civil society sinks like a stone.

Time limits, coordination, lack of rhetoric, and the encouragement of the shy are thus essential for the dialogues of civil society. Even so, they may not

24. For other important points of coordination, see Susan George's 'seven commandments' in her *Another World is Possible If . . .* (London: Verso, 2004), pp. 164–6.

be enough. Dialogue also depends on the capacity to listen.[25] How many conversations are in fact nothing of the sort, but only the half-listening of one person waiting for the other to finish, and the half-listening of the other waiting for the first to do the same! Little in the cultural practices of modernity fosters the critical constitutive elements of conversation – those pauses, questions to the other, and general attentiveness which encourage dialogue's vitality rather than its reduction to monologue. Television prefers soundbites to reasoned discussion, confrontations to informed debate. Mobile phones often breed the malpractice of not speaking to the person in front of you, but to someone else whom you regard at that moment to be more important. It is a humiliating business, frequently practised as a demonstration of power.[26]

The conditions for proper collective conversations cannot, then, be taken for granted and have carefully to be created, nurtured and monitored. Often in civil society nothing of the sort happens. Furthermore, dialogue is just one area where the micro-culture of civil society needs to be delineated clearly; another, of considerable difficulty, is that of leadership. In firms, institutions and political parties, leadership is celebrated and sought after almost un-qualifiedly. In the media the personalisation of power and the manufacturing of individual charisma are defining elements of television politics. But in civil society the question is much more complex. If modern civil society harbours certain specific ambitions – to foster the diffusion of power rather than its concentration, to encourage gender equality, to build horizontal solidarities rather than vertical loyalties – then charismatic leadership lies uneasily in its midst. It is obvious to all that certain individuals have more ability and expertise in certain fields than others. Utopian refusal to acknowledge this fact simply leads to paralysis. But the crucial question is: into what sort of cultural and organisational constructs are such capacities to be placed? The Social Forums in Europe and elsewhere have done their best to downplay leadership and limit its duration in time: each spokesperson takes responsibility for representing the movement for only a few months at a time. Inexorably, the media try to make them into 'personalities'.

25. See Marionella Sclavi, *Arte di ascoltare e mondi possibili* (Milan: Le Vespe, 2000), esp. p. 69.
26. I was once invited by a senior Italian politician to lunch. At table, he spent the first fifteen minutes glued to his mobile phone, while I watched him. I then 'phoned my wife and said to her in a loud enough voice for him to hear: 'I have been invited to lunch by X but I cannot understand why. He seems to prefer talking to someone else, and I much prefer talking to you.' He turned off his 'phone for the rest of the lunch, but it was a bit late for my taste.

However, it is all too easy to blame the media. The question is a more individual one, and at its heart lie two profound characteristics of human behaviour: narcissism and adulation. Capable, sympathetic and expert individuals, especially if they are able orators, all too easily come to bask in a leadership role and lose sight of an original modesty. Civil society can quickly breed charismatic leaders, but they are not good for it, and nor is the adulation that is often accorded them. Such mechanisms cannot be eliminated in any easy way, for they have profound roots in the whole history of social relations. Civil society would be foolish to declare their 'abolition'; that would be the sort of gargantuan task that the communes of 1968 set themselves and failed to achieve, unsurprisingly. Instead, we can note their presence, gauge their likely consequences, and try and invent means to contain them. The rotation of offices and responsibilities is certainly one, but a central quandary remains. Civil society has great need of qualified and able individuals, but at the same time it needs them not to be leaders in the sense conferred on that term by the rest of society.

If dialogue and leadership are two questions that press civil society for an adequate response, time is a third. As we have seen, time control is crucial for dialogue; it is also so for participation. Meetings are extremely off-putting if they start late, are poorly coordinated, drag on for an inordinate length of time, and risk ending in uproar. People have better ways of spending their time, or at least more enjoyable ones. This is also a gender question. Women with major responsibilities in the home and to kinship networks have more difficulty than men in getting to meetings, and more difficulty in staying for more than a couple of hours. What happens when is therefore of great significance. If decisions are taken only at the end of an assembly or reunion, and if that end occurs in the small hours of the night, then fewer people will decide, and those will often be of only one gender. The timing of decision-making is of great importance, as is the adherence, as far as possible, to pre-established agendas. Here is a rare recorded testimony to these problems, taken from Portugal in 1975, at a 'popular democracy' meeting in the village of Palmera:

A woman went to the front of the meeting and said she had something to say. She was handed the microphone and said: 'I would like to make an observation. People have been called here to discuss many problems. I came with maximum interest to follow a certain agenda [. . .] there are things which must be dealt with objectively and calmly. In a small village like ours we must not get excited.'

To the Chairman she said: 'We were told that the meeting should finish at midnight and it is now 11 p.m., but we are still on the first part of the agenda. We have problems of heat, flies, etc. There are some points which are more important than ours and we have been hearing about them, but these other problems are also important to us. I apologise but I must insist. I think you have gone on too long, and this leads to confusion. I am sorry. I apologise, but it is my duty to say this.'

The Chairman then replied: 'I must criticise myself. The lady is quite right. I made a mistake. We will go on to the second point of the agenda.'

The second item concerned representation on the committee. The chairman said: 'We have no women. We must have some women. Many of the things we are talking about are of great importance to women and they should be there.'[27]

As a partial and modern answer to problems of this sort, a great deal has been made of the role that information technology in general, and the World Wide Web and e-mailing in particular, can play in establishing contacts between people and accelerating decision-making processes. The advantages are clear for all to see: information is widely and swiftly available for distribution where previously it was restricted to limited groups. During the week of mobilisation in Seattle against the World Trade Organization, the Independent Media Centre registered a million and a half hits, even more than the CNN.[28] The organisation of meetings and campaigns is also greatly facilitated, both at a local and wider level, as the international peace marches of 2003 demonstrated; and collective decisions can take place via e-mail, with all those who have a computer taking part. 'Blogs' (on-line diaries and commentary) have attracted an unexpected number of readers, and within 5–10 years www access will probably be offered as an integral part of the services piped into, and out of, domestic TV sets. All this clearly offers new opportunities for linking households and civil society activities.[29]

But information technology has its dark side. Discussions by e-mail can

27. Quoted in Peter Robinson, 'Workers' Councils in Portugal, 1974–75', M. Phil. diss., Open University, 1989, pp. 246–7.

28. The testimony is that of John Sellers, one of the leading organisers of the demonstrations at Seattle: 'Raising a ruckus', New Left Review, N.S., no. 10 (July–Aug. 2001), p. 83.

29. See the thorough discussion in A. C. Freschi, La società dei saperi. Reti virtuali e partecipazione sociale (Rome: Carocci, 2002); and P. Ferdinand (ed.), The Internet, Democracy and Democratisation (London: Frank Cass, 2000).

become interminable, with those who have the most time and are the most long-winded writing the most. E-mail discussions also have a brittleness about them which face-to-face meetings do not. It only needs one 'flamer', as they are called in e-mail jargon, one person out to provoke and contest, for a 'virtual' discussion to go downhill. Introducing a wide-ranging account of recent American associationism, Robert Putnam and Lewis Feldstein note that the internet and the web 'play a surprisingly small role in most of our stories'.[30] For them, local face-to-face contact, time-consuming though it is, is irreplaceable.

These are only some, perhaps the most significant, of the contested areas in the micro-structuring and daily practice of civil society. At its best, modern civil society is charged with a creative tension which offers the possibility of doing things in a different way, of posing a transformative agenda which is also self-reflexive, capable of changing the ways in which people see themselves and then relate to each other. It is the diametrical opposite of Hegel's 'spectacle of extravagance and misery'. The capacity to listen, the necessity for self-discipline, the respect for time, the art of dialogue, the wariness of charismatic leadership, the encouragement of others in developing their human capacities, not just developing your own – these are all the promissory notes of civil society. All too often they remain only that. Other more prosaic logics and emotions – mirroring the hierarchies and attitudes to be found at work and often at home – gain the upper hand. With the difference that the associations of civil society, by their very nature, have no rigid structures or time-honoured codes, and are therefore particularly vulnerable to dissolution.

Civil society, dictatorship and democracy in the global South

I have spoken of modern civil society as if it were a whole, which of course it is not, and I have concentrated on southern and northern Europe because those are the regions of which I have some knowledge and experience. However, different global regions and different national cultures will produce different histories of modern democratic civil society associationism. I can only allude to these here. In many parts of the South neither economic nor political conditions encourage the prospects for civil society.[31] Arbitrary and

30. Putnam and Feldstein, *Better Together*, p. 9.
31. See the sobering reflections of G. Hawthorn, 'The promise of "civil society" in the South', in S. Kaviraj and S. Khilnani (eds), *Civil Society: History and Possibilities* (Cambridge: Cambridge University Press, 2001), pp. 269–86.

repressive regimes, mass poverty, and the absence of even the most elementary cultural bases all militate heavily against the prospects of informed self-organisation. Viewed from many parts of the world, civil society still appears as a northern luxury, not a global necessity.

None the less, the conditions for its extension have changed significantly for the better in the last thirty years. The availability of information is one valuable index of this change. In developing countries the circulation of daily newspapers grew from 29 per 1,000 people in 1970 to 60 in 1996; radios per 1,000 people similarly increased from 90 in 1970 to 245 in 1997; and televisions, unsurprisingly, enjoyed the most dynamic expansion of all, from 10 per 1,000 people in 1970 to 157 in 1997.[32] Of course, the modern media are what they are, both in terms of control and quality, but it is undeniable that very many people in the world have access to more sources of information – both in terms of quantity and diversity – than they did just a few years ago.[33]

If we probe beneath the surface of standard accounts of countries in the global South, we soon discover that the history of recent civil society campaigns is often a rich one, nowhere more so than in the South's greatest and most numerous democracy, India. The 1980s in India witnessed the growth of new social movements, each of which grew out of specific networks of local associationism. In particular, the Indian women's movement took on a number of novel forms and directions. On the one hand, it pressed the Indian state to improve women's economic and political standing in the wake of the Women's Decade of 1975–85. On the other, radical groups of socialist feminists and eco-feminists had a more explicitly anti-patriarchal and anti-capitalist orientation. Whereas socialist groups concentrated upon fighting women's oppression under semi-feudal relations of production, the eco-feminists sought to protect women from the adverse effects of global projects for technology and consumption.[34]

In India the battles over the destiny of natural resources and who has the right to use them have been fierce. By 1985, only about 10 per cent of India's land was still forest. Who was to be responsible for the forests that remained –

32. UNESCO figures of 1999, cited in UNDP, *Human Development Report, no. 13,* (Oxford: Oxford University Press, 2002), p. 77, Figure 3.3.
33. Ibid., p. 76.
34. On the latter, see in particular V. Shiva, *Staying Alive: Women, Ecology and Development* (London: Zed, 1988). On the Indian movements in general, P. Parajuli, 'Power and knowledge in development discourse: new social movements and the state in India' (1991), in N. Gopal Jayal (ed.), *Democracy in India* (Oxford and New Delhi: Oxford University Press, 2001), pp. 258–88.

the people who were directly dependent on them, or the state which turned a blind eye to deforestation? Women and men in many rural areas as well as indigenous peoples argued strongly for conservation in the name of the *aranyi sanskriti*, the forest culture, in which trees are not viewed as a resource in terms of being a quantifiable commodity, but as the source of light and air, food and water, fertility and sustenance.

The battle over the use of water has also been a bitter and extraordinary one. It is worth quoting at length from an interview with Chittaroopa Palit, one of the leading activists in the Narmada Valley resistance of the 1990s, because it gives us a sharp picture of both who she is and the nature of that movement:

I was born in 1964, to a middle-class Bengali family. My father was an engineer in the Indian Railways and my mother was a college lecturer. My father's work took us all over India, so I learnt early on about the country's extraordinary geographical variety, and how different communities, tribals and poor farmers, lived and worked [. . .] Love of literature – prose and poetry – opened my mind and made me something of a romantic; a streak that eventually pushed me towards work in the villages. But at Delhi University I read economics [. . .]

The Narmada Valley Development is one of the largest projects of all, involving two multipurpose mega-dams – Sardar Sarovar, in Gujarat, and the Narmada Sagar, in Madhya Pradesh – that combine irrigation, power and flood-control functions [. . .] The four state governments involved have seen the Narmada's waters simply as loot, to be divided among themselves. There was no question of discussing the matter with the communities that had lived along the river for centuries, let alone respecting their riparian rights [. . .] We found [instead] that there were perfectly viable, decentralised methods of water-harvesting that could be used in the area. Tarun Bharat Sangh and Rajendra Singh of Rajasthan were able to revive long dried-up rivers in almost desert-like conditions by mobilising local villagers' collective efforts to build tanks on a large scale. In Gujarat, remarkable pioneering work [. . .] has recharged thousands of wells and small water-harvesting structures using low-cost techniques [. . .]

The rhythm of activism is also dictated by the pattern of the seasons. Every monsoon, as the people of the Valley face the rising waters, we hold a mass meeting. People from the various villages affected will come together for a whole day, sometimes two, to discuss the situation [. . .] Most of the time, we are fighting with our backs against the wall and we often have only a certain number of options to choose from – state officials to confront, buildings to occupy, sympathetic supporters to call on, and so forth. So the range of disagreement is limited and, in practice, there is a great deal of consensus about these decisions [. . .] Of course, we defend our right to call for international solidarity; but we also believe that it is possible for the resources of Indian civil society to sustain popular struggles – and that to do so builds and affirms support for the movement.[35]

After campaigns involving tens of thousands of people, brutal police repression and an independent review deeply critical of the project, the World Bank withdrew its support in 1993. It had previously made a $450 million loan for the Sardar Sarovar dam. However, seven years later a ruling of the Indian Supreme Court went the other way, in favour of the project. It was a terrible blow to the movement after fifteen years of struggle.

In the campaigns about water, forests and land, Indian civil society has had recourse to that moral vocabulary which, in historical terms, has nearly always been adopted by communities threatened by external modernisation. It has appealed to concepts of *dharma* (righteousness) and *nyaya* (justice). It has also done so by reviving the great tradition of non-violent direct action, and of that which Ghandi termed 'Satyagraha', which he defined as the vindication of truth not by the infliction of suffering on an opponent but on one's self. Even though the movement appeals to time-honoured practices and rights, it has been far from merely backward-looking, because it has constantly tried to redefine the terms of debate within the modern Indian polity, raising fundamental questions about nature and human beings, development and survival, autonomy and identity, women and men.[36] Time and again, the democratic Indian state has responded with beatings and arrests, as well as the third-degree torture to which Palit and her colleagues were at one point subjected. Theirs is an epic and tragic story, seemingly far removed from the quiet of civil society in the North, but actually connected in very many ways: in its self-organisation from below, in the will to contest decisions taken over the heads of people, in the need for one part of the world to support another.[37]

35. C. Palit, 'Monsoon risings: mega-dam resistance in the Narmada Valley', *New Left Review*, NS, no. 21 (May–June 2003): 81–100.
36. Parajuli, 'Power and knowledge', p. 273.
37. During the struggle against another dam project in the Narmada valley, the Maheshwar dam, the German NGO Urgewald, led by Heffa Schücking, succeeded in convincing the German government to refuse an export guarantee for Siemens, which

Many of the expressions of civil society aspirations and organisation in the South have come in the last years of authoritarian regimes, prior to their fall and the establishment of democracy. The South African township-based civic organisations, or 'civics', based on resistance to apartheid and non-violent direct action, were one of the most extraordinary of these. The 'civics' movement not only fought the regime but also tried to lay the basis for popular, democratic control at a local level. In townships like Alexandra, just north of Johannesburg, with a population of around 350,000 living in an area of less than two square miles, in the 1980s and early 1990s the movement built up its own dense network of street-based democracy. It had its own idea of community-controlled development projects, and struggled to establish equity along class, gender and generational lines. It mobilised those who had had no experience of politics – the unemployed, individual men and women sharing rooms in hostels, entire families of very poor people. South Africa's 'civics', as one of its leaders, Mzwanele Mayekiso, has written, took 'the idea of independent civil society a long way, possibly as far any social movement in the world'.[38] It did so while continuing to ask uncomfortable questions about the texture of that movement and its strategy: 'Can township civics represent poor and working people and the small but important black middle class at the same time? Can we represent people with homes as well as the homeless? Can we confront the diverse issues that divide people and that cross-cut our various identites? [. . .] Can we overcome leadership styles that are sometimes not as conducive to democratic practice as we might want, and as our movement requires?'[39]

There are other examples of great vitality and courage in the organisation of civil society groups in the face of dictatorial regimes. Subject to constant harassment and repression, civil society had no way of working in openly democratic ways, but could at least in its day-to-day activity express different values to those of the regime, and thus a covert aspiration to democracy. In Chile, after Pinochet's triumph, popular economic organisations – soup kitchens, artisan workshops, shopping cooperatives and communal planting groups – sprang up as a means for ensuring survival and comradeship when all formal politics had ceased to exist. In the 1980s, as elsewhere in Latin

was preparing to ship millions of dollars' worth of electro-mechanical equipment out to India. See also Arundhati: Roy, *The Algebra of Infinite Justice* (London: Flamingo, 2002), pp. 129–63.

38. M. Mayekiso, *Township Politics: Civic Struggles for a New South Africa* (New York: Monthly Review Press, 1996), p. 12.

39. Ibid., p. 13.

America, Chilean women's groups allied with unions, human rights organisations, neighbourhood associations and many other groups to push for an end to the authoritarian regime.[40] The most famous example of civil society mobilisation against a hated regime was, of course, that of eastern Europe. It was indeed the success of that experience and its simultaneous theorising by figures such as Václav Havel and Adam Michnik that provided the impetus for the widespread theoretical discussion of civil society from 1989 until the present day.[41]

It is crucial to recognise that once democracy was established, all these experiences – South African, Chilean, east European – faltered very gravely. It is one of the great ironies of modern politics that such impressive civil society movements, pressing hard for the re-establishment of democracy, should in the end be rendered innocuous not by their authoritarian opponents (though these exacted a high enough price in terms of repression and bloodshed), but by democracy itself. Many are the elements that contributed to this debacle:[42] the difficulty of finding an institutional role for these movements within representative democracy and the politicians' refusal to invent one for them; the cooptation of leadership into political parties and the consequent pursuit of individual careers, often leading to self-enrichment; and the re-assertion of time-honoured political practices such as patronage and corruption. All these contributed to a widespread feeling of disillusion and demobilisation. I shall return to many of these phenomena below.

Civil society, then, has no guarantee of health in the conditions of modern democracy. None the less, I would suggest three general reflections to support the idea of its being a permanent feature of the modern world. The first is that even if civic associationism is transient – intense but passing – it is a difficult plant to kill, and often re-emerges at a later date in another form. Often, too, there are kinship and generational connections behind its survival, with involvement sometimes skipping a generation to pass directly from grand-parents to grandchildren. Secondly, in spite of the great variety of civil-society groupings, they have a basic common ground which I have tried to delineate,

40. T. Fitzsimmons, *Beyond the Barricades: Women, Civil Society and Participation after Democratisation in Latin America* (New York: Garland, 2000), pp. 139ff.
41. A. Michnik, *La Deuxième Révolution* (Paris: La Découverte, 1990); see also V. Havel et al., *The Power of the Powerless*, ed. John Keane (Armonk, N.Y.: M. E. Sharpe, 1985).
42. For South Africa, the group of essays collected in G. Adler and J. Steinberg (eds), *From Comrades to Citizens: The South African Civics Movement and the Transition to Democracy* (London: Macmillan, 2000).

and which is not just relative to one part of the world, but potentially universal in character. And third, civil society is at its most effective when it is consciously formed of alliances, between classes, genders and generations.

Nowhere in the world has there been more need of the ambitions of modern democratic civil society – to foster the diffusion of power rather than its concentration, to encourage gender equality and social equity, to build horizontal solidarities rather than vertical loyalties, to use peaceful rather than violent means, to encourage debate and autonomy of judgement – than in most of the Middle East and of North Africa. There the possibilities of civil society are crushed between an extremely strong and suspicious state on the one hand, and an overpowerful kin and clan system on the other. The two are intimately linked by networks of patronage and advantage. Such networks have their points of departure in kinship solidarities as well as tribal and local loyalties, and their point of arrival in government bureaucracies, state agencies and other favour-dispensing organisations.[43]

Where intermediate zones do exist, they are the terrain of often bitter conflict between religious and political discourses. In the last twenty-five years, ever since the Iranian revolution of 1979, there has been a very determined attempt in many Arab countries – Algeria, Lebanon, Egypt and so on – to reactivate the *umma* (the community of believers) as the focus of all public space and discourse. The traditional and the modern have combined to produce new elaborations of 'Islamic economies', the 'Islamisation of knowledge', and the policies of the 'Islamic state'.[44] Various contemporary Islamic currents compete for hegemony on this terrain. The dominant one is the Salafi orientation, conservative and fundamentalist, with its insistence on a literal reading of Shari'a law and its consequent emphasis on authoritarian and patriarchal structures, on allegiance and obedience. Most Arab states have seen this fundamentalist challenge as a mortal threat, and have reacted accordingly. As Sami Zubaida has written: 'Arbitrary and oppressive

43. S. Zubaida, *Islam, the People and the State* (London: I. B. Tauris, 1993). See also R. A. Norton (ed.), *Civil Society in the Middle East*, 2 vols (Leiden: E. J. Brill, 1995 and 1996). For a radically alternative view, stressing traditional tribal practices as the basis of a civil society defined generically as promoting 'cooperation and trust for the purpose of accomplishing social goals', see R. T. Antoun, 'Civil society, tribal process and change in Jordan: an anthropological view', *Journal of Middle Eastern Studies*, 32 (2000): 441–63.

44. V. Nasr, 'Lessons from the Muslim world', *Daedalus*, (summer 2003): 67–72; see also D. F. Eickelman and J. Pescatori, *Muslim Politics* (Princeton: Princeton University Press, 1996), pp. 46–79.

government on the one hand, and a civil society increasingly controlled by Islamists with tenuous claims to pluralist democracy on the other, do not appear hopeful for a civil society based on civility and tolerance.'[45]

The case of Egypt is instructive. Mustafa Khamil al-Sayyid has offered a recent, detailed account of the arbitrary powers of the Egyptian state, its control over associational life, its dominance of the media, and its brutal repression of dissent and dissenters, above all those who support Islamic fundamentalism.[46] From the moment in 1981 that Husny Mubarak took over as president after the assassination of Anwar al-Sadat, he reconfirmed the restrictive Law 32 of 1964 on citizens' societies and Law 40 of 1977 on political parties. The Ministry for Social Affairs has denied registration to certain associations, most notably the Arab Organisation for Human Rights and its Egyptian chapter. Egypt has quite a rich associational life and some tradition of judicial autonomy, but the space for constructing civil society, or even a public sphere, is thus perforce limited. This does not imply a necessary lack of community. Diane Singerman's study of the *sha' bi* (popular) quarters in central Cairo in the early 1990s reveals the degree of everyday connectedness of families to informal and formal networks, as well as the degree of negotiation and bargaining characteristic of these quarters.[47] It also shows how oversimplified the usual characterisations of the Egyptian family as patriarchal and authoritarian may be, and how much contestation takes place between genders and generations within households. But all this, even if it is 'participative' as Singerman rightly claims, remains at a community level, far distant from the 'civics' of the South African townships. The historical terrain seems to be completely different, and the resulting political quandary is a terrible one. A tiny, educated minority carries forward the fight for civil rights in Egypt and elsewhere in the Arab world, but any advance on this front is most likely to benefit those fundamentalists who have no sympathy with civil liberties of any sort.

45. S. Zubaida, 'Civil society, community, and democracy in the Middle East', in Kaviraj and Khilnani, *Civil Society*, p. 242.
46. M. K. al-Sayyid, 'A civil society in Egypt?', in Norton, *Civil Society in the Middle East*, vol. 1, pp. 269–94.
47. D. Singerman, *Avenues of Participation: Family, Politics, and Networks in Urban Quarters of Cairo* (Princeton: Princeton University Press, 1995). She notes that the adjective *sha' bi* 'demarcates a wide range of indigenous practices, tastes, and patterns of behavior in everyday life' (p. 11).

The enemies of civil society

The example of Egypt has already delineated in summary form some of the most potent obstacles to any project for civil society in the modern world. I would now like to analyse these in a more general and systematic fashion. In doing so I would like to stress that there is no linear pattern to history which sees civil society starting from Northern homelands, and steadily triumphing in the rest of the world. It is enough to reflect for a moment on what happened to the civil society of Weimar Germany in the 1930s to realise how vulnerable the North is, let alone the South.

Patron–client relations

In chapter 1, I mentioned the ubiquity of unequal dyadic relationships between patron and client, with one person dependent on, or beholden to another. These relationships take many and complex forms but are of predominant importance in the Middle East and the Mediterranean countries, in Latin America and South-East Asia, in Japan and India, in eastern Europe and in some parts of sub-Saharan Africa. They are far from absent, if not so prominent, in the English-speaking and other European democracies.

In a seminal article of 1972 on political change in South-East Asia, James C. Scott offered a model of these relations which has stood the test of time. The patron–client relationship, he wrote,

> may be defined as a special case of dyadic (two-person) ties involving a largely instrumental friendship in which an individual of higher socio-economic status (patron) uses his own influence and resources to provide protection or benefits, or both, for a person of lower status (client) who, for his part, reciprocates by offering general support and assistance, including personal services, to the patron.[48]

Scott added three further distinguishing features to this definition of patron–client links: their basis in inequality, their face-to-face character, and their diffuse flexibility. The first two are self-explanatory, while the third merits a word or two of further explanation. Scott had in mind, as he explained, the multiple layers and variability over time of a patron–client relationship. A

---

48. J. C. Scott, 'Patron–client politics and political change in Southeast Asia', *American Political Science Review*, 66, 1 (1972): 93.

landlord might – the example is his – have a client who was connected to him by tenancy, friendship, past exchange of services, the past tie of the client's father to his father, and ritual god parenthood. Over time, a patron and a client might ask different favours of each other: the patron in preparing a wedding, winning an election campaign, or finding out what his local rivals are up to; the client in need of help in paying his son's tuition, filling out government forms, or getting food and medicine when he falls on hard times.[49]

On the basis of his fieldwork, Scott was convinced that the 'active clientele' of a single patron was unlikely to exceed one hundred persons. Many Mediterranian politicians, both past and present, might want to adjust this figure upwards. Certainly, the wider the social situation under consideration, the more complex the pyramids of loyalty and dependency become. Patrons make alliances with each other, the periphery builds its contacts with the centre, and elaborate hierarchical systems are established.[50]

Complex and diffuse patron–client relations have a pressing relevance for modern everyday politics, and for the possibilities of civil society in particular. They are not a phenomenon that belongs to a fast disappearing rural or 'undeveloped' past, but rather one which is constantly reinventing itself and finding new forms under modernity. Olivier Roy, with reference to the two very different cases of Algeria and Tadjikistan, has written of the disappearance of traditional societies and the 'retraditionalisation' of political relations.[51] The reinvention of patron–client relations finds a highly favourable environment in a global neoliberal economic context, where the emphasis is placed on informal and flexible relations rather than on contract, and on privatisation rather than public control. All this weighs heavily against a political project which has as one of its essential points of departure horizontal solidarities and the creation of citizenship, rather than vertical loyalties and the creation of clientelistic dependencies.

Naturally, it is important not be too manichean about this contrast. All social relations have a necessarily informal side to them, and the wheels of bureaucracy and government are always oiled by personal contacts and friendship. Crucial, though, is the sense of limit, the legal context and the

49. Ibid., p. 95.
50. A classic analysis of a clientelistic system of this sort is P. Allum, *Politics and Society in Post-war Naples* (Cambridge: Cambridge University Press, 1973).
51. O. Roy, 'Patronage and solidarity groups: survival or reformation?', in G. Salamé (ed.), *Democracy without Democrats: The Renewal of Politics in the Muslim World* (London: I. B. Tauris, 1994), pp. 270–81.

strength of public ethics in which these informal contacts take place.[52] Let us return for a moment to the case of Egypt, and to the popular quarters of central Cairo in the 1990s. A young woman tries to get the necessary papers to register as a temporary employee at a daycare centre. She goes a number of times to the civil registry which is housed in the police station, but makes no progress. The clerk treats her badly, and she is unable to find out exactly what she needs or how long it will take:

> So I asked my friend Huda if her father (who was also the father of my brother's fiancée) knew anyone at the police station. She said he did, a police officer named Ustaaz Mu'hammad [. . .] he [Huda's father] went with me to the office and introduced me to his friend who told me to get another copy of my birth certificate [. . .] When I came back he said that only one stamp was missing. I asked if I could take care of it now, he said no, but that I should take the papers home (so they would not get lost or misplaced) and return with them in the morning. At 8.00 a.m. I returned and he stamped the paper to send it to the Ministry of Health for approval. Then he said I should come back in twenty-five days. Nearly a month! [. . .] He said, 'It's not in my hands, what do you want me to do?' I had made all that effort, all those visits, and tired myself out [this occurred during the terrible July heat] and all of this was because he wanted money out of me. The paperwork could have taken an hour to finish but they want your money.[53]

Singerman comments that the girl had had few expectations of government efficiency or due process, and blamed herself for not mastering the art of 'informal politics'. The story is enlightening on a number of levels. It reveals, first of all, something which Scott's examples do not – the highly gendered nature of patron–client relations. The young woman is clearly at a disadvantage because of her sex (although she confides in Singerman that her older sister is much better at 'dealing with bureaucrats and merchants'). After

52. In a recent article on the question of civil society and patronage, Luis Roniger first states, rightly, that 'at the level of principles, the logic of civil society and democracy runs counter to the logic of patronage and clientelism'. Later in the same article, though, he appears to backtrack on this fundamental point, asserting instead that 'sometimes patronage can be seen to reconcile public and private authority and formal and informal rules of the game'; L. Roniger, 'Civil society, patronage and democracy', in Alexander, *Real Civil Societies*, pp. 72 and 75.
53. Singerman, *Avenues of Participation*, pp. 140–1.

initial failure, she appeals to men for help – Huda's father and his policeman friend. They do help, but not enough. It is also a story of absence rather than presence – that of the missing (male) patron who would have resolved the question swiftly on her behalf. She is not on any rung of a patron–client ladder, and in the end will either have to wait or pay money – even to the policeman 'friend'. In a system where informal networks dominate, corruption is always round the corner. The girl is alone in another sense as well: there is no civic network to take up her case, no movement for reform from below, only an 'informal politics' of clientelistic connections; or, as in this case, failed connections.

Overpowerful families

The story from Cairo is also illuminating because of the passing mention of kinship networks – Huda's father being the father of the girl's brother's fiancée. Here, too, the story is a negative one – the linkage is too weak and the girl's own family is obviously unable to help. But side by side with powerless families of this sort, there are many overpowerful ones, especially in societies like those of the Middle East, where, as we have seen, kinship and clan relations have led traditionally to a familist relationship between families, civil society and the state. The syndrome here is not the one analysed at the beginning of chapter 3, of the enclosedness of many modern families in democratic societies, separated off by a consumption cocoon and by time constraints from the wider world and its concerns. It is rather of families which relate outwards but in a heavily instrumental way, so that the general interest is subordinate to that of an extended family group or clan. In a society dominated by these primary relations, it is difficult for a civil society to grow, because there is little or no autonomous intermediate space in which individuals can express themselves. Individuals remain first and foremost family members, parts of an overall family strategy. In recent times that strategy may be less patriarchal and more debated than in the past, but it still remains the essential point of reference.

In historical terms, it is worth comparing for a moment Palestinian and Israeli societies in the era of the British Protectorate, because it is possible to discern how elements in both obstructed the creation of a modern civil society. In the Palestinian case, the overriding power of extended families and clans (*hamulas*), and their constantly feuding character, meant that it was difficult to find an accord among themselves, let alone with respect to the outside world. In the Israeli case, the power of the family was much more strictly limited, with the kibbutzim movement strongly stressing the need to contain and transform the traditional Jewish family of the Diaspora. The settlers were thus much more active than the Palestinians in the creation of associations, health services, etc., and much aided by financial support from abroad. But the sort of society they created, given the basic tenets of Zionism, was very much a 'bonding' rather than a 'bridging' one, exclusive and not inclusive, with dire consequences for all.[54]

The overweening presence of families and clans in any given society is heavy with consequences for its public institutions. Nepotism becomes an accepted practice. When this is linked, as it most often is, both with patron and client relations and with widespread corruption, then the state assumes a highly negative aspect. Once again it is worth stressing that such conditions are not simply the residues of 'underdevelopment', but involve modern and dynamic elaborations of traditional power relations. They find their most extreme, but far from uncommon form in personal, family-dominated dictatorships, in which wide-ranging powers are conferred on close kin. Saddam Hussein's regime in Iraq was one such. These patrimonial or neopatrimonial regimes, as they are often called, are characterised by a concentration of power and wealth in a single male figure, surrounded by his cronies and relatives. It is he who supervises the appropriation of public resources for private ends, and distributes them according to personal whim and favour. Associations and societies are permitted to exist only if their loyalty is unquestioning, and their autonomy severely limited.[55]

54. M. Simoni, 'La costruzione di due nazioni. Famiglia e società civile in Palestina (1900–1948)', *Passato e Presente*, no. 57 (2002): 125–46. See also M. Muslih, 'Palestinian civil society', in A. R. Norton (ed.), *Civil Society in the Middle East*, vol. 1 (Leiden: Brill, 1995), pp. 243–68.

55. In Max Weber's original use of the term, patrimonialism referred in ancient societies to the system in which personal, traditional authority gradually became more extended spatially and dependent on different forms of interpersonal relationships. The children and slaves of the household were settled on the land, each with their own holdings, cattle and responsibilities, and the patrimonial leader gradually formed his own administration, 'a staff of slaves, *coloni*, or conscripted subjects', as well as 'mercenary bodyguards and armies'. In the economic field, patrimonialism leant itself to a wide variety of different possibilities, but 'the important openings for profit are in the hands of the chief and the members of his administrative staff [. . .] There is a wide scope for actual arbitrariness and the expression of purely personal whims on [their] part'; M. Weber, *The Theory of Social and Economic Organization*, ed. Talcott Parsons (New York: Oxford University Press, 1947), p. 347. For neopatrimonialism in the global South, see Theobald, *Corruption, Development and Underdevelopment*, p. 64, and R. Theobald, 'Conclusions: prospects for reform in a globalised economy' in A. Doig and R. Theobald (eds), *Corruption and Democratisation* (London: Frank Cass, 2000), pp. 153–4.

Suharto's regime in Indonesia, which lasted for thirty years from 1968 to 1998, is a pertinent example of such tendencies. Ruling over a nation of some 200 million people, the largest Muslim country and the fourth most populous nation in the world, Suharto accumulated a personal fortune variously valued as between 9 and 20 billion dollars. His wealth was deposited in Swiss bank acounts but also in 'charitable foundations' known as *yayasans*. These are essentially slush funds into which money can be paid without being audited or attracting taxation. They are a unique way of accumulating riches while disguising or 'atoning for' the fact by undertaking charitable works. Suharto's regime is especially relevant here for the part played by family members and the wealth accumulated by them, which is said to have equalled that of its central patriarchal figure. Suharto's six children, including the infamous Hutomo Mandala Putra, better known as 'Tommy', had dominant interests in hundreds of companies. In 1987 one of Suharto's sons received the first commercial television licence in the country, in 1990 his foster brother received the second, and in the same year Suharto's daughter Hardyanti received the third. His son 'Tommy' responded to a court case against him by having the judge murdered. The fall of the regime finally opened up possibilities for a different sort of history, in which other dynamics became possible, though certainly not predominant.[56]

Corporations and media empires

At first glance, transnational corporations seem a very long way from regimes like that of President Suharto. They are ultramodern, most of them have their territorial headquarters in the US, and they wish to be considered on a global scale as forces working for the good of humanity. Yet they can hardly be considered natural friends of civil society, global or local, and much of their ethos and modes of practice has more to do with power- and resource-hungry dictators than they would care to admit.

As I mentioned at the beginning of this chapter, neither the primary dynamic of firms, even socially responsible ones, nor their primary organisational mode sits at all easily with the nature of modern civil society. This is even more true when we are dealing with transnational corporations, which are tied to an iron logic of achieving global supremacy in their specific sectors and subjected to ceaseless, unsparing and often short-term judgements on their overall economic performance. To this latter, in the last analysis, all else

56. D. Kingsbury, *The Politics of Indonesia* (London: Oxford University Press, 1998), esp., ch. 10, 'Corruption and the first family', pp. 198–218.

is sacrificed: job security for their workforces, environmental conditions, and even sometimes, as in the case of Enron, any semblance of legality. In the Indian case of dam construction cited above, the corporations were all on the side of the authorities because the appropriating of rivers and natural resources from those who lived on and by them was the necessary precursor to the corporations' own large-scale trade in water and energy markets.

However, the question is one not just of economic interest, but also of knowledge. The corporations are greedy for control of knowledge and circumspect about the conditions for its diffusion, even when matters of life and death are at stake. Their performance over cheap drugs for AIDS victims in Africa was revelatory in this respect. Corporations need to dictate their own terms, to enjoy not just high global profits but high global profiles. As a result, their names are everywhere, the result of billions of dollars spent on publicity, and on communicating a certain sort of very partial knowledge to mass audiences all over the world.

Indeed, it is in the media that the processes of concentration of power and knowledge are at their most menacing. Rupert Murdoch's empire now extends to millions of viewers on five continents. His is not a regime which depends on repression, tear-gas, threats of electrocution, police beatings or any of the other habitual modes of authoritarian regimes (and even, as we have seen, some democratic ones). There is no compulsion, other than habit and convenience, to watch his channels, no obstacle to changing programme or switching off the television. At the end of the day, as Murdoch is fond of repeating, it is the consumer who decides. But the argument is a disingenuous one, to say the least. Murdoch is as power-hungry in his own field as Suharto was in his, and infinitely more significant on a world scale. The politics and programming of his world empire do not, obviously, present a single, monolithic viewpoint but a carefully attuned pluralism within a single, quite rigid frame of values and priorities.[57] The ubiquity of his channels on a global scale and their underlying priorities make him a formidable enemy of any civil society dedicated to the freedom of information.

57. Shawcross, *Murdoch*, p. 424: 'Murdoch believes that the Americanising of the world is not only profitable for his business, but a great good in itself. But even he asked, in an interview for this book, "Are we going to homogenize the whole world with satellite and cable, with no room for local culture? I think there is a danger".'

Conclusion: civil society and the state

We seem to have come very far from the little deconsecrated church in Florence where nothing much happened on a spring evening in 2003. Yet there is more than one connection between that seemingly insignificant event and Rupert Murdoch's massive media empire. One link, obvious enough, is that if fewer people habitually watched television of an evening, participation in meetings might be higher (though much, I would argue, also depends on the quality and texture of those meetings). Another, perhaps less obvious, is that the fates of both the little meeting and the great empire depend, in the last analysis, on the political action of states, whether at local, national, or supranational level. The Estates General of the Oltrarno in Florence could only have survived and flourished as an experiment in participatory democracy if local government had welcomed it as such and tried to encourage similar experiences elsewhere in the city. It did not. Rupert Murdoch has come as far as he has because of the absolute unwillingness and incapacity of national and supranational institutions to confront seriously global oligarchical control in the media. What states do, or choose not to do, in other words, is of crucial significance for the destiny of civil society, at both a local and a global level.

There exists a broad spectrum of possible attitudes on the part of states towards the sort of modern civil society I have been trying to analyse and describe in this chapter. One is outright hostility. This is the attitude of authoritarian and dictatorial regimes all over the world, and the many pages of Amnesty International's reports are full of the way in which regimes continue to imprison, maim and kill those who dissent, or who dare to meet and organise.

A second possible reaction, less draconian than the first, is that of suspicion. Civil society is permitted but controlled. Meetings are infiltrated, and participants always have the sensation that their conversations in the public sphere are being in some way noted and recorded.

Suspicion, though on a very different level, is also the attitude of many democratic politicians who regard civil society as a disturbance which it would be better to do without. Real politics, for a considerable part of the political class in the democratic world, is solely that which takes place inside representative institutions. Politicians are elected for a term of office, they must be free to get on with the job, and they will be judged by the electorate at the end of their term. This attitude, still very prevalent, can be likened to the instruction to be found at the front of public buses all over the world: 'Please do not disturb the driver.' It is in the corridors of houses of parliament, in committees and conclaves, that politics takes place, not in everyday life. Politicians should be left in peace to get on with the job.

A third attitude could be named the Machiavellian ploy. The representatives of the state astutely profess sympathy and understanding for the aspirations of civil society, but in reality do very little about it. This is a strategy that aims at exhaustion by rhetoric; all the right noises are made for a considerable period of time, at endless conferences and debates, but nothing happens or changes. Civil society retires exhausted. Or else its leaders are coopted into political parties, and steadily become more distanced from their origins, which they come to regard as exhilarating but juvenile.

The last, appearing on the far horizon like a life-boat, is appreciation. State institutions and personnel, unlike the Indian Supreme Court in 1990, make it clear how valuable civil society is for the well-being and robustness of democracy. Civil society is encouraged rather than left to languish, and its members are considered as valuable citizens rather than mere trouble-makers. Public spaces for meetings, functioning microphones, and the availability of public transport in the evenings become priorities for local government, not afterthoughts. At a national level, public service broadcasting – broadly based, free of advertising, autonomous and informative – is considered a political imperative, not a commercial choice. In the work–life balance, so crucial to the potential of civil society, legislation might be enacted to allow more time for people to be citizens; such was the intention, at least in part, of the legislation for a 35-hour working week in France.

Civil society cannot substitute for the state nor take the place of more formal political organisation. Neither can it survive or prosper without the help of state institutions at all levels. On the other hand, democracy itself is a poor cow without the vitality and criticism of those associations which lie between the private sphere and the state, and which harbour ambitions for democracy's enrichment. It is to the democratic state, as well as to the state of democracy, that the last chapter of this book is dedicated.

5 Making Democracy Work

Some problems in modern democracy

It is possible to say many things in favour of democracy in its present form, but one is not that it has an everyday quality. Indeed, it does not even have a weekly, monthly or annual character. The first great movement of the industrial working class in the contemporary world, the British Chartists, demanded in their petition of 1838, signed by 1,200,000 people, that annual parliaments be instituted as a means of ensuring a greater interplay between electors and elected. They were refused. For most of those who have the privilege of living in democratic political systems, active politics on an individual level is reduced to a question of minutes, not days. If we are fortunate to live long lives, we will perhaps vote (an activity of some three minutes) twelve times at a national level, and the same number at a local one – some seventy-two minutes in all, perhaps one-third of the television viewing that we do *daily*. Depending on where we live, there may also be national referenda and, exceptionally, elections to a supranational body like the European parliament. I say 'we', but it is an improper use of the pronoun. The 'we' of modern democracies is an ever more uncertain collective entity, as increasing numbers of people do not bother to go to the polls at all. Disaffection is widespread.

John Dunn has rightly warned us not to expect too much of democracy. It is, as he writes, a state form – nothing less and nothing more. As such its reputation does not rest on its 'prowess at mass spiritual edification or the transformation of souls'.[1] He continues: 'In the modern democratic republic, it is the citizens who must change themselves. They cannot hope for their state

1. J. Dunn, *The Cunning of Unreason: Making Sense of Politics* (London: HarperCollins, 2000), p. 255.

to do this for them. If the purposes which govern state power within these polities are to become wiser, less myopic or more austere, it is we who must change, not the states to which we belong'.[2] At the end of his *Elements of the Philosophy of Right*, Hegel introduces the state in all its magnificence, entrusted with the task of reconciling the particular with the universal, and of giving expression to the highest level of ethical life. But such a grandiose view of state power, democratic or otherwise, is both illusory and dangerous.

On the other hand, we should not consider democracy a political form that has been fixed once and for all. If it were, it would not belong to human history. Nor is it without potential with regard to the pressing problems that have accompanied us throughout this book. In this last chapter I wish to argue in favour of a number of linked propositions, which can be presented on an ascending scale of complexity.

The first and simplest is that modern democracy, now as in the past, is capable of significant improvement, and that it can be made to work in a much better and fuller way than it does at the moment. If it is left as it is, neither bolstered nor reformed, it is highly vulnerable to all manner of predators.

The second is that the history of democracy has been marked by a constant tension between two different forms – the representative and the participative (or direct) – whose relationship needs serious theoretical reconsideration. If direct democracy was the basis of the Athenian model, with male citizens deciding the fate of the *polis* directly in assembly, representative democracy was (and is) government *on behalf of* rather than *by* citizens, with decision-making entrusted to representatives elected to parliaments. The first, to use the famous distinction drawn by Benjamin Constant in 1819, was the liberty of the ancients, the second that of the moderns; the first, in his words, ensured the 'sharing of social power' through constant participation, but the second guaranteed individual liberties and allowed men 'the enjoyment of security in private pleasures'. This latter was for Constant the form both most feasible and most desirable in modern and complex societies.[3]

For most of the nineteenth and twentieth centuries, these two views of the proper workings of democracy – direct and representative – were considered antithetical. Indeed, from the Marxist point of view, counterposed as it was to that of liberals such as Constant, direct democracy was to replace the representative form in the passage from capitalism to socialism. The young Marx

2. Ibid.
3. B. Constant, 'The liberty of the ancients compared with that of the moderns' (1819), in Constant, *Political Writings*, ed. B. Fontana (Cambridge: Cambridge University Press, 1988), p. 317.

wrote that representative democracy was nothing more than 'the sophistry' of the bourgeois state,[4] and the young Gramsci, following on Lenin's heels, established an uncompromising binary opposition between 'representative democracy (which is bourgeois) and direct democracy, which is proletarian'.[5] In their vision, democracy had to escape the narrow confines of politics to inhabit the economic sphere as well. However, all over the world, this promise of proletarian democracy was never fulfilled. Indeed, long before the fall of the Berlin Wall it was clear that Communist societies had no internal democratic dynamic whatsoever.[6]

In 1989 representative democracy triumphed, to some definitively, but at the very moment of its global victory, as we shall see below, its fragility and inadequacy became more apparent. Representative democracy, rather than being perfectly attuned to the modern age, revealed an urgent need of its elder sister.[7] In the 1990s democracy's two modes, far from being mutually exclusive, began to be seen as potentially of mutual benefit, the one conducive rather than detrimental to the other. The experience of the participatory budget at Porto Alegre, Brazil, which I shall recount in detail at the end of this chapter, is only the best-known example of a vital experiment with a *combined* form of modern democracy.

The third and last proposition bears the stamp of de Tocqueville. In part 2 of *Democracy in America* he wrote:

4. K. Marx, 'On the Jewish question', in Marx, *Early Political Writings*, ed. Joseph O'Malley (Cambridge: Cambridge University Press, 1994), p. 36.
5. A. Gramsci, 'Menscevismo e libertà' [unsigned], *l'Unità*, 31 July 1925, quoted in M. Salvadori. *Gramsci e il problema storico della democrazia* (Turin: Einaudi, 1970), p. 7.
6. In contemporary European history there have been some *glimpses* of what an alternative, more direct and popularly based democracy might look like. One such was the Paris Commune of 1871, another the first months of Soviet democracy after the Russian Revolution, another the period of popular rule in Barcelona between 1936 and 1937. These experiments never lasted and most often ended in brutal repression, and not just by right-wing forces.
7. This had also, a little strangely, been the conclusion of Constant way back in 1819. Having argued fiercely in favour of separating ancient and modern concepts of freedom on a number of grounds, including that of modern man's lack of time for, and limited influence on the political process, he none the less concluded his address to the Athénée Royale by exhorting male citizens to 'an active and constant surveillance over their representatives': 'The danger of modern liberty is that, absorbed in the enjoyment of our private independence, and in the pursuit of our particular interests, we should surrender our right to share in political power too easily'; Constant, *Political Writings*, p. 326.

If men living in democratic countries had no right and no inclination to associate for political purposes, their independence would be in great jeopardy, but they might long preserve their wealth and their cultivation: whereas if they never acquired the habit of forming associations in ordinary life, civilisation itself would be endangered.[8]

Democracy cannot hope to survive and flourish, and with it humanity as a whole, without considering, far more seriously than has been done previously, the necessary relationship between democracy as a political system, and civil society as a network of everyday associations, intimately connected to that system. It would be simply foolish to ignore this relationship, or pretend that civil society and democratic politics are in some sense pitted against each other. There may indeed be tensions between the two, but they are of the creative sort, and democracy has everything to gain from them. If the 'habit of forming associations in ordinary life' is not encouraged, and there is a great deal, as we have seen, in modernity that does not encourage it, then democracy is unlikely to survive. Democratic politicians all over the world seem to lack any sense of Tocquevillian urgency in this regard.

However, my third proposition does not just consider the relationship between the democratic state and civil society. It extends to embrace the relationship between democracy and the everyday activities of families. If families are not to remain profoundly unaware of the terms in which they are in the world, and if they are not to follow the merely private 'work and spend' itineraries that are so strongly suggested to them every day, then they need the support and encouragement of democratic states. The forms of this encouragement have not been the subject of much enquiry.

On this important theoretical point neither Constant nor de Tocqueville, nor many others, have had much to say. For Constant family relations were simply to be enjoyed, far from the intruding eye of the ancients' omnipresent state. For de Tocqueville, the question was more complicated. Under the conditions of democracy in America, according to him, family relations became more relaxed, the powers of the father figure diminished, and kin were drawn more closely and more informally together. But there was a negative side to all this. 'Democracy', de Tocqueville wrote, 'loosens social ties, but tightens natural ones; it brings kindred more closely together, while it throws citizens more apart.'[9] How this gap between strong kin groups and distant citizens is to be bridged has remained

8. De Tocqueville, *Democracy in America*, vol. 2, p. 107.
9. Ibid., vol. 2, p. 197.

a little-examined rebus of modern politics. De Tocqueville himself felt that the vitality of associationism and political institutions under the general conditions of democracy would constantly remind a citizen, 'and in a thousand ways, that he lives in a society'.[10] History has not proven him right, either for the United States or other 'mature' democracies.

The democratic state, at least in present circumstances, cannot afford to ignore this problem, but must rather invent new ways of intervening. Not, I hasten to add, as 'the redeemer of souls', nor as the 'highest expression of ethical life', nor with the severity of Sparta or Thrace as Constant presented them, but rather as a *facilitator*, an institution that creates the conditions for possible, but in no way obligatory everyday journeys to take place. I shall examine some specific forms of this facilitating process below, but ideally its outcome would be strikingly different from the highly damaging familist relationships between family, civil society and the state which I outlined in chapter 3.

Three propositions, therefore, lie at the basis of this last chapter: that democracy can be greatly improved; that it must now seek to combine both representative and participatory forms; and that the democratic state has a crucial facilitating role to play in linking an active civil society with family life. I wish to illustrate all three themes with particular regard to local conditions, where democracy should theoretically be most soundly based, but where it is so often found lacking. Before proceeding, though, I must add a number of caveats and clarifications.

In the final pages of the novel suitably entitled *Democracy*, written by the historian and novelist, Henry Adams, and published in New York in 1880, his heroine, Madeleine Lee, has had enough: '"I want to go to Egypt," said Madeleine, still smiling faintly. "Democracy has shaken my nerves to pieces."'[11]

Madeleine Lee had been exhausted by a particular, and not especially attractive form of democracy – that of the shady deals, intrigues and power-broking of Washington DC. It was a type of democracy that Adams both deplored and regarded as inescapable. However, what concerns us here is not Adams's political sensibility, but Madeleine's exhaustion. Democracy can indeed be a very nerve-wracking and tiring business, and in a certain sense the more democratic it becomes the more it exhausts its participants. How much easier it would be to delegate all to others! Or, even more simply, to entrust our fate to one of those populist figures who increasingly infest modern

---

10. Ibid., vol. 2, p. 105.
11. H. Adams, *Democracy: an American Novel* (London: Meridian, 1994), p. 189. Adams was both the grandson and great-grandson of Presidents of the USA.

democracies, and who promise startling resolutions to our problems in return for the adulation of their person. There is a constant danger of losing the democratic challenge by asking of people more than they can possible hope to deliver. Certain of the meetings in Lisbon that marked Portugal's tormented transition to democracy in the mid-1970s, and which I mentioned before, ended at four in the morning, and workers had to begin the morning shift at six. There was obviously no future for participation of that sort.[12]

This same problem can also be examined from an objective rather than a subjective angle. If we wish to combine representative and participative democracy (and for the latter to be not merely consultative) then there can be no doubt that decision-making processes will be lengthened as a result. Democracy in a deliberative form is a long-winded affair. As such, it runs considerable risks: not this time of the exhaustion of individuals but of the paralysis of institutions.

A third and connected danger lies in creating an ethos of obligatory participation. Jacobin 'democracy', that of year II of the French Revolution, took from Rousseau the idea that people could, in certain circumstances, be forced to be free. The theme of forcing people to do what they do not want to do, in the name of a greater good, has a long and very undistinguished history. If democracy is to be radically improved, it will certainly not be by exhuming ideas of 'false consciousness', or by exerting peer pressure on families. A democratic state has a very delicate role to play in this regard. It can make suggestions, create possibilities and forums, encourage discussion and suggest alternatives, but it must, in order to merit the epithet 'democratic', leave it at that. Individuals and families must be free to make their own choices, properly informed. If they choose not to be part of civil society, not to take part in the organs of participative democracy, even not to vote, so be it.

What sort of democracy are we talking about? There are probably more definitions of democracy than there are democratic states. My working definition is adapted from that of the Swedish sociologist Göran Therborn. It denotes a form of state which (1) has a representative government elected by (2) an electorate consisting of the entire adult population, whose votes (3) are cast by secret ballot at regular intervals and carry equal weight, and who (4) are allowed to vote for any opinion without intimidation either by the state itself or by organised elements of society.[13]

12. Robinson, 'Workers' councils in Portugal', p. 248.
13. G. Therborn, 'The rule of capital and the rise of democracy', *New Left Review*, First Series, no. 103 (May–June 1977), p. 4. My adaptation includes the addition of 'or by organised elements of society', with March 1933 in Germany very much in mind.

This is a definition which concentrates above all on the minimum requisites of the electoral process of representative democracy. It should be regarded as a starting point for modern democracy, not as encapsulating its essence once and for all. Even so, as Therborn shows, democratic states have had great difficulty in meeting these conditions, and if they have done so it has been much later in their history than is commonly assumed. The United States, for instance, which in certain aspects got off to a flying start, could be identified as democratic under these criteria only around 1970. It was then, bowing to the pressure of civil rights movements in the south and ghetto rebellions in the north, that the federal government began to enforce the Fifteenth Amendment (of 1870) for the whole of the country.[14] Similarly Switzerland, which had boasted one of the most advanced of European constitutions in the mid-nineteenth century, only managed to grant the suffrage to women in 1971.

Historically, the principal categories of exclusion from democracy have been those based on class – more or less crudely defined by property, income, occupation or literacy; on sex, with great discrepancies (New Zealand enfranchised women as long ago as 1893); on ethnicity, where the racist exclusion of poor and degraded minorities has been generally and vigorously applied; and on political opinion, widely employed during the course of the twentieth century.[15] Indeed, one of the most delicate and difficult questions lies in the area of opinion. Should those whose declared aim is to destroy democracy, such as neo-Nazi and racist groups, be allowed to organise none the less and present candidates in representative elections? Under the terms of this definition the answer is unequivocally 'yes'. While it is difficult not to feel sympathy for those who after the Second World War demanded the permanent banning of any neo-Fascist or neo-Nazi groupings, an essential test of modern democracy lies in its ability to defeat its opponents without succumbing to their methods.

A last question regards the universality of democracy. More than once democracy has been denounced as a hegemonic tool for the richest nations of the world, a political system which has been exported, or even imposed, on the wings of economic and cultural imperialism. The rhetoric of democracy, so the argument continues, masks the real relations of power at a global level and the relative impotence of the South of the world compared to the North. In addition, it runs roughshod over other political traditions, often more deeply embedded in the culture of certain regions of the world. At the present time,

14. Article 1 of the Fifteenth Amendment reads: 'The right [. . .] to vote shall not be denied or abridged [. . .] on account of race, colour, or previous servitude'.
15. Ibid., pp. 36ff.

it is not difficult to understand the popularity of such a viewpoint, especially in the light of President Bush's wish to export democracy by invasion and the force of arms.

Yet it would be a grave error to fall back on a comfortable relativism at this point, with anti-Americanism being the pretext for justifying the existence of any sort of indigenous arbitrary power. There are at least two good reasons for insisting on the potential universality of democracy. The first is that, as both Marcel Detienne and Amartya Sen have pointed out recently,[16] in the pre-history of democracy it is possible to find many instances from all over the world of groups and peoples coming together to deliberate and decide. Such political behaviour was not just the prerogative of Athens, important and sophisticated as that early example was. In the society of the Ochollo in southern Ethiopia, as described by the anthropologist Marc Abélès, men and boys over the age of puberty deliberate over their communal affairs in plenary sessions.[17] Meetings take place inside a circle of raised stones, hollowed out in the form of seats. The person whose turn it is to speak comes forward so that he is facing the assembly. As Detienne comments, 'Up to now, there is no reason to believe that the Ochollo took their inspiration from the agora of Ithaca and its high stone seats.'[18]

Similarly, Sen points out that the ancient Greek example probably had more points of contact with the Egyptians, the Iranians and the Indians, than with the Goths, the Visigoths or the many other peoples of an imagined 'Europe'. A series of Buddhist 'councils' in India, the largest of which took place at Pataliputra (today's Patna) in the third century before Christ under the aegis of the Emperor Ashoka, insisted on public discussion without violence or animosity, and with respect for the opinions of different sects. Many centuries before the 'civic republicanism' of the Italian city-republics, there were numerous instances of popular assemblies and elected councils in the villages and cities of the ancient kingdom of Bactria, covering much of today's Pakistan and Iran, and in the Maurya empire in India.[19] Of course, these examples are not the same thing as modern representative democracy, but they go to show how the preconditions of democracy – open debate and

16. M. Detienne, *Comparer l'incomparable* (Paris: Seuil, 2000), ch. 5, 'Des pratiques d'assemblée aux formes du politique. Approche comparative', pp. 105–27; A. Sen, *La democrazia degli altri. Perché la libertà non è un'invenzione dell'Occidente* (Milan: Mondadori, 2004), pp. 3–40.
17. M. Abélès, *Le Lieu du politique* (Paris: Société d'ethnologie, 1983).
18. Detienne, *Comparer l'incomparable*, p. 114.
19. Sen, *La democrazia degli altri*, pp. 16–18 and 24–5.

tolerance of different points of view – were far from solely present in a certain Mediterranean and then western European world.

The second reason for insisting on the potential universality of democracy is the modern mirror of the first. All over the world in the twentieth century and at the beginning of the twenty-first, individuals and groups, some extremely courageous, have fought for the cause of democracy. For the most part, they have done so not because it forms part of the ideology of American imperialism, but because they consider it to be the fairest political system yet invented, even if it is far from perfect. Often they have been minorities in their own countries, sometimes, as in China, very small minorities, but that does not mean that we should ignore their efforts. Nor should we ever let the arbitrary concentration of power be justified in the name of a dubious cultural relativism.

Expansion, crisis and disaffection

In the global expansion of democracy historians have usually distinguished a number of successive phases.[20] The first 'long' wave of democratisation covers the period from the first decades of the nineteenth century to 1926. By that time there were just twenty-nine democracies in the whole world – though the figure would be much smaller if the definition I have just outlined above was rigidly applied. Mussolini's assumption of dictatorial power in Italy then began a 'reverse wave', which saw the number of democracies shrink to twelve by 1942. This was democracy's darkest hour. After the Second World War, as was only to be expected, there was a return to expansion, which reached its peak in 1962 with thirty-six countries enjoying democratic government of one sort or another. In the 1970s and 1980s there was a further expansion, primarily in Catholic countries, beginning in Portugal and Spain and then sweeping rather uncertainly through south and central America. However, the really dramatic breakthrough took place in the twelve years after the fall of the Berlin wall. In 1988 only 66 states out of the then total of 167 in the United Nations claimed democratic credentials. By the year 2000 120 out of the 192 member countries in the United Nations, or 62.5 per cent did so. For the first time democracy had acquired majority status on a world scale.[21]

This enormously significant fact, one of the few in this book to constitute a

20. My obligatory point of reference is S. P. Huntington, *The Third Wave: Democratization in the Late Twentieth Century* (Oklahoma: University of Oklahoma Press, 1991).

21. L. Diamond and M. F. Plattner, 'Introduction', in Diamond and Plattner, *The Global Divergence of Democracies* (Baltimore: Johns Hopkins University Press, 2001), p. x, table 1.

firm basis for optimism,[22] has to be inspected carefully. Larry Diamond and Marc Plattner have made a first broad division of the 120 democratic countries of the United Nations, separating them into 'electoral' and 'liberal' democracies. To belong to the first category, it is sufficient to satisfy a single criterion: that of holding 'regular, free and fair' elections among competing parties. The second and more demanding category, that of 'liberal' democracy, requires a further five criteria. The first concerns civil liberties. A democracy can only be considered liberal if freedom of belief, expression, organisation, protest and assembly is properly safeguarded. Secondly, under the rule of law all citizens must be treated equally and due process be secure. Thirdly, the judiciary must be independent and neutral, not subordinate to the executive or any political faction; at the same time, institutions of 'horizontal accountability', such as the central bank or the 'watchdog' for the media, have to be autonomous and endowed with effective powers. Fourthly, in a liberal democracy there must be clear evidence of the existence of an open and pluralist civil society; an essential part of it consists in free mass media. Lastly, the armed forces must be clearly under the control of the democratically elected government.[23]

Applying these criteria to the 120 democracies of the United Nations, Diamond and Plattner concluded that only 75 out of 120 qualified as liberal.[24] There would be much to discuss here. What, for instance are 'free mass media' in an economic structure of media markets which perforce lead to narrow oligopolies, and where public television is under ever greater threat? What are to be considered the 'effective' powers of 'watchdogs'? How draconian with regard to civil rights do anti-terrorist laws have to be before old-established democracies can no longer be considered liberal? And so on.

However, I want to draw attention to another aspect, which has to do with the propositions with which I began this chapter, and with the central argument of the whole book. None of these democracies, except in the most perfunctory of ways, combines participatory and representative systems. In all of them politics is an excessively *separate* sphere. As such there is no sense or

22. A. Sen, 'Democracy as a universal value', *Journal of Democracy*, 10, 3 (1999): 'among the great variety of developments that have occurred in the twentieth century, I [do] not, ultimately, have any difficulty in choosing one as the preeminent development of the period: the rise of democracy'.
23. Diamond and Plattner, *The Global Divergence*, pp. x–xi. For further elaboration, see L. Diamond, *Developing Democracy: Toward Consolidation* (Baltimore: Johns Hopkins University Press, 1999), pp. 11–12.
24. Diamond and Plattner, *The Global Divergence*, p. xii, table 2.

culture of everyday politics, no mechanisms by which ordinary lives are connected to extraordinary problems. The structures and practices of democratic politics, as they exist now, are old and worn, often isolated in antiquated and protracted rituals, always a long way away from the electors. However much democracy's expansion is to be celebrated, it has no inevitable dynamic of forward march, nor inbuilt quality control. These two aspects – expansion and quality – are closely linked, for if the quality of present-day democracy is not radically improved, its continued existence will be in jeopardy.

I wish to conduct a brief exercise of quality control in a number of key areas of modern democracy; they concern the role of the media, the nature of political parties, and electoral expenditure. There could be many others as well, but the economy of this book imposes a certain selection.

Media and the politics of the person

At two previous stages in this book I have touched upon the question of the media – first in relation to families and then to civil society.[25] As far as the political sphere is concerned, modern communication processes, and television above all, offer enormous potential for the democratic process. People are connected as never before, global events reach their homes on a daily basis, and their opportunities to be properly and well informed have greatly increased. The reality of modern communication is something quite different. The iron cage of commercial interest, in which programmes are bound tightly to audiences, publicity and markets, has come to determine the destiny of democratic politics with regard to much of the media. This cage functions in a number of different ways. The first has to do with ownership. A modern oligarchy of transnational corporations or single individuals and their families have come to control a great part of the world's media. In the United States six companies alone exercise an inordinate influence. In the United Kingdom four groups own 85 per cent of the daily press. Mexico's Televisa and Brazil's Globo, two of the world's greatest media monopolies, are controlled by individuals and their families, and encompass all aspects of production and distribution of television, radio, film, video and much of the advertising industry.[26]

If we concentrate only on television, we can see just how far a restricted modern oligarchy heavily influences the possibilities of the medium, as well as

---

25. See above pp. 107–11 and 159.
26. UNDP, *Human Development Report, no. 13 (2002)*, p. 78 and fig. 3.4. See also Ginsborg, *Silvio Berlusconi*, pp. 104ff.

the potential of politics. By and large, those who own and control modern television are not interested in making available to the general public a constant flow of documentaries, well-balanced and educative news programmes, and reports from the South of the world. Quite the opposite. Such programmes have low audience ratings, and as a result no great allure for advertisers. Athough they would greatly profit viewers in terms of general political culture, they are economically unprofitable for media magnates.

Furthermore, those who control modern media have their own political agendas, which have little to do with liberal democracy, let alone democracy which combines participation and representation. Their political influence may be direct, as in the case of Berlusconi, or indirect, as with Murdoch and Roberto Marinho, owner of the powerful TV Globo network in Brazil.[27] If they are not directly in the political arena, then media corporations, newspaper barons or media magnates will most often back those politicians who promise to hinder their expansionary activities least, and to keep the public 'watchdogs' without bark or bite.[28] If sometimes they have been philanthropists, they have never shown the least interest in civil society, nor in the diffusion of power rather than its concentration.

Democratic politics is also heavily conditioned by commercial television in another way. Programming all over the world is characterised by short timespans, frequent interruptions, archetypical narratives, dramas and minidramas, and is oriented to the creation of charismatic figures, who may be show presenters, religious figures (such as Padre Pio), sportsmen or women, or the commercial channel's owner himself. Television producers and programmers theorise this television texture in terms of the short attention spans

27. Marinho's young and almost unknown candidate for the presidential elections in Brazil in 1989, Fernando Collor de Mello, successfully won the presidency only to squander power in record time. For an interesting comparison, see E. Canaglia, *Berlusconi, Perot e Collor come political outsider* (Soveria Mannelli: Rubbettino, 2000). An interesting intermediate case is that of Thaksin Shinawatra, who was the proprietor of a significant telecommunications empire in Thailand but was not a television magnate, and who became the country's prime minister in January 2001, just two months before Berlusconi triumphed in Italy. For his victory, see 'Tycoon or Thai con?', *The Economist*, 11 Jan. 2001.

28. After Rupert Murdoch threw the weight of his newspapers (*The Sun* and the *News of the World*) behind Mrs Thatcher in the 1979 British elections, she wrote to thank *The Sun*'s editor Larry Lamb, and in 1980 knighted him for his 'services to journalism'. When Murdoch took over *The Times* and the *Sunday Times* in 1981, his bid was not referred to the Monopolies Commission. The pledges he gave on editorial independence were soon to be flouted, but no action was taken against him.

of the general public and their need for escapist entertainment. Theirs is a self-fulfilling prophecy. The more this diet is served up, the more people become accustomed and even dependent on it, like junk food. The possibilities of television thus become self-limiting.

Democratic politics fits very poorly into these kinds of logic.[29] It has a logic of its own, sceptical of overly charismatic figures, needy of reasonable amounts of time to explain difficult problems and different points of view, and dependent on accurate information and proper investigative journalism. Its narratives are often undramatic, but necessary to the process of forming civic consciousness.

With the counterposition of these two logics – of commercial television and democratic politics – it is quite shocking to see how democratic politicians of all persuasions are acquiescent in the first and unmindful of the second. Their attitudes towards the fate of public television, to which I shall return below, are highly ambiguous. However, it is not just public broadcasting that is at stake, crucial though that is, but the very constitution of the modern political persona. We return here to the question of narcissism, which I raised with respect to civil society. Politicians celebrate their television personalities, practise their sound bites, and accept television's time constraints without criticism. Image is all-important. Berlusconi's facelift and hair implant are only the most explicit manifestation of an absolute concentration on self and self-image:

> Mais moi, Narcisse aimé, je ne suis curieux
> Que de ma seule essence;
> Tout autre n'a pour moi qu'un coeur mystérieux
> Tout autre n'est qu'absence.
> O mon bien souverain, cher corps, je n'ai que toi![30]

The Narcissus of antiquity and modern democratic politicians have their differences. He was certainly more beautiful than they are, and also much stiller. Today's politicians are never still; they are always running – or rather being ferried in their official cars – from one studio, committee meeting or public occasion to another. Such a frenetic pace prevents them, for the most part, from elaborating anything but short-term aims, closely linked to themselves and their own careers. The media urge them along this path, and

29. T. Meyer with L. Hinchman, *Media Democracy: How the Media Colonise Politics* (Cambridge: Polity, 2002).
30. P. Valéry, 'Fragment du Narcisse', in *Oeuvres*, vol. 1 (Paris: Pléiade, 1962), p. 128.

they acquiesce, but all this takes them a long way away from de Tocqueville's version of democratic personal relations: 'In democracies no great benefits are conferred, but good offices are constantly rendered; a man seldom displays self-devotion, but all men are ready to be of service one to another.'[31]

Political parties

In many ways political parties have served democracy well. Especially in the era of mass parties (in Europe roughly between 1860 and 1960), they channelled the voices and needs of many parts of the population, including those who had never previously taken part in politics, into a national arena. They also served as educators and as centres of sociality and social solidarity.[32] We must be careful, though. Mass parties are now looked back to with nostalgia and with more than a little idealisation, rather like the working-class communities which many of them linked to politics for the first time. In reality, in all their manifestations – religious, right-wing and left-wing – they managed to organise only a minority of the population, were often undemocratic in their internal practices, and showed a clear tendency towards oligarchy. But when all is said and done, they performed valuable roles for representative, and even participatory, democracy.

Time has moved on, and with it party systems. Peter Mair has suggested a valuable way of looking at these transformations, in relation not just to civil society but also to the state.[33] Put briefly, his thesis is that whereas once mass parties were, and in some parts of the world still are, linked organically to society, agents bearing societal interests into the state arena, more recently these links have loosened, and those with the state have increased. Parties have transformed themselves into 'semi-state agencies':

> The state, which is invaded by the parties and the rules of which are determined by the parties, becomes a fount of resources through which these parties not only help to ensure their own survival, but through which they can also enhance their capacity to resist challenges from newly mobilised alternatives.[34]

31. De Tocqueville, *Democracy in America*, vol. 2, p. 176.
32. Some fine architectural monuments remain as testimonies to these functions, such as the art nouveau Maison du Peuple di Bruxelles (Victor Horta, 1899), with its enormous and splendid assembly hall.
33. P. Mair, *Party System Change: Approaches and Interpretations* (Oxford: Clarendon Press, 1997), esp. pp. 93–119.
34. Ibid., p. 106.

Such a state of affairs will be familiar to Italians, accustomed as they are to the practices of a long-standing '*partitocrazia*'.

At the same time a number of other changes take place. According to Mair, where parties' principal goals were once social reform, or at least amelioration, now they are politics as a profession. Where once there was mobilisation, now there is containment; where once they boasted of representative capacity, now they insist on managerial skills and efficiency. Parties converge where once they diverged.[35] At the same time mass membership has declined radically. If in the 1960s in European democracies some 15 per cent of the electorate were members of parties, by the end of the 1980s that proportion had shrunk to 10.5 per cent, to decline still further to 5 per cent by the end of the century. The percentages were particularly low in the newly democratised eastern European countries and in the larger states like Germany and Britain.[36] In the United States, too, party membership has declined. If the number of voters contacted by parties has increased, as a result of more resources and wider possibilities of communication, the number of those working for parties at election times has radically decreased.[37] Inside parties, of both the left and right, the power of leaders has increased exponentially. There were always local and regional barons within parties, with their own followers and power bases, but at least in mass social-democratic parties significant political debate did at one time take place. Nowadays loyalty to leaders, with an eye to career advancement, is probably the strongest driving force.

All these factors do not make modern political parties natural allies for civil society, or for participatory politics. The autonomous manifestations of civil society are viewed with suspicion, as disturbances for the professional politics that takes place in parliament. As I mentioned at the end of the last chapter, parties often react by coopting individual leaders of civil society, offering them status and financial rewards of which impoverished civil society associations can only dream. By and large, parties, when they are not overtly hostile, take an *instrumental* attitude to civil society. By doing so, they increase the gap between the two.

35. Perhaps it is above all this last point which leads Mair to write about the emergence of the 'cartel party', in which all parties become part of a cartel, creating a restricted system and enjoying the patronage and spoils of the state. This is certainly true, but divergences can remain strong, as we see in the BPL–Congress contest in India, the Casa delle Libertà–Ulivo clash in Italy, and other such cases.
36. P. Mair and I. van Biezen, 'Party membership in twenty European democracies, 1980–2000', *Party Politics*, 7, 1 (2001): 5–21. The Italian percentage (for 1988) was 4.05, the highest of the major democracies.
37. Putnam, *Bowling Alone*, pp. 39–40.

Yet this need not be so. Mair is right when he notes that the era of party-based democracies is not necessarily on the wane, and that each change in the party system produces, in time, a further elaboration of party forms. The time is nigh for such a process to begin again. It is difficult to sketch its contents in detail, but it is possible to make some suggestions, both theoretical and practical.

At a theoretical level, modern democracies with active civil societies may be said to function along two different axes. The first and dominant one is that which connects political parties to representative democracy. The greater part of the energy and intelligence of parties is absorbed in the traditional practices of representative democracy: contesting elections, representing established interests, organising within institutions such as parliaments and distributing jobs. There is little time left for anything else. But another, albeit weaker axis – that which connects civil society to participatory democracy – calls increasingly for attention. Citizens in democracies all over the world, as we shall see at the end of this chapter, are demanding to participate in new ways in the democratic decision-making process. Political parties ignore these requests at their own peril. If they do not find ways of interacting with them, of linking the two axes, then their reputation will suffer a further decline and the separation of politics from society can only increase.[38]

A reorientation of political parties in this direction is no easy task. In the 1970s and 1980s the German Greens were the party that experimented most with alternative party forms and practices. They insisted at first on rotating leaders in office, on gender equality, on the 'imperative mandate', which was supposed to bind parliamentarians to party resolutions, and on openness to non-members. Their aim was to link leaders to the grass-roots of the party, and both to the social movements of German society. However, most of these measures were abandoned once the party began to undertake the business of government at both local and national level. The 'movement-party' became a 'party-party' as the need for professionalism and continuity in office became paramount.[39]

---

38. An informed and cautiously optimistic commentator like Paul Webb concludes at the end of a detailed survey that 'the area in which party performance seems most obviously flawed is the fostering of political participation'; P. Webb, 'Political parties and democratic control in advanced industrial societies', in Webb, D. M. Farrell and I. Holliday, (eds), *Political Parties in Advanced Industrial Democracies* (Oxford: Oxford University Press, 2002) p. 449.
39. See A. Demirović, 'Grass roots democracy: contradictions and implications', and C. Offe, 'From youth to maturity: the challenge of party politics' in M. Meyer and J. Ely (eds), *The German Greens: Paradox between Movement and Party* (Philadelphia: Temple University Press, 1998), pp. 141–64 and 165–79.

None the less, the experience of the German Greens cannot be said to have closed the debate. On the contrary; the question of internal democracy, or the lack of it, remains one crucial difference between parties. So, too, does Max Weber's famous distinction between living 'for' politics and living 'from' politics. Those who feed constantly at the 'state trough', as Weber called it, are clearly to be distinguished from those who bring a sense of probity and vigour into modern politics.[40]

Further down the scale, renewal is likely to be founded on an open and frank alliance between civil society groups and the rank-and-file members of parties. When the local section of the Left Democrats invented the Estates-General of the Oltrarno in Florence it was moving exactly in this direction. Leaderships must be cajoled into recognising that they cannot do without active, critical memberships, that citizens active in civil society are precious animals, that adulation and spin doctors are no substitute for serious debate, and that financial capital is no substitute for social capital.

Electoral spending

For the moment the trend is very much in the opposite direction. The mention of financial capital brings us to one of the weakest points of modern democracy, and one in the most urgent need of reform. Electoral spending in nearly all democracies has spiralled completely out of control. The attitude of the public institutions of the United States regarding this question has been disastrous. In 1974, in the wake of the Watergate scandal, marked by President Richard Nixon's illegal use of hidden slush funds, moves were taken to reform the system; the Federal Election Commission was established as the watchdog of campaign fund-raising. However, the reforms were challenged on the grounds that government has no right to establish how much a citizen can spend to make his or her voice heard. In 1976 the Supreme Court, in the case of *Buckley v. Valeo*, found in favour of the objections. Any limits on electoral spending, according to the Court, represented 'substantial [. . .] restraints on the quantity and diversity of political speech [because] every means of communicating ideas in today's mass society requires the expenditure of money'.[41] No clearer constitutional invitation exists for economically

40. M. Weber, 'The profession and vocation of politics', in Weber, *Political Writings* (Cambridge: Cambridge University Press, 1993), pp. 318 and 321.
41. J. H. Birnbaum, *The Money Men: the Real Story of Political Power in America* (New York: Times Books, 1996), p. 34.

dominant interests to buy up media space in order to determine the outcome of elections.

Although limits remain in the American case, they are easily circumvented. Let us take the example of the election of Michael Bloomberg as mayor of New York. He has a large publishing business based in the city, 8,000 employees, a radio station and a very influential cable television company specialising in financial information for banks and stock market operators. He spent an estimated $60 million on his election campaign, a sum which broke all previous records for New York elections. After he had won, the *New Yorker* commented: 'the contest proved that in politics, as in so many other realms of modern life, money trumps all'.[42] Bloomberg is not alone. There is a growing list of American billionaire politicians – Ross Perot, Steve Forbes and Jon Corzine are among them – who have spent their way to electoral victories by buying unprecedented amounts of television advertising. Spending on presidential nominations and election campaigns has increased in the United States from $35 million in 1964 to over $700 million in 1996, fivefold even in constant dollar terms.[43]

In other countries, too, the influence of 'big money' makes itself felt. In Brazil in 1989 Collor de Mello gathered in an estimated $120 million during his successful presidential campaign. Reform followed, but in 1994 Fernando Cardoso received an official $32.3 million in private donations and 54.3 per cent of the vote, against Lula da Silva's $4 million and just 27 per cent of the vote.[44] Of course, money does not determine everything – eight years later Lula won – and there have been examples, especially in the United States, of huge expenditure accompanying eventual failure. But in these money stories there are three cardinal lessons for democracy, all of which are quietly hidden away by most democratic politicians. The first is that the lack of radical limitations on electoral expenditure ensures that the gross economic disparities in society are automatically transferred into the democratic sphere.

42. E. Kolbert, 'His Honor', *New Yorker*, 19 Nov. 2001.
43. S. J. Wayne, *The Road to the White House, 1996: The Politics of Presidential Elections* (New York: St. Martin's Press, 1996), pp. 30 and 46, quoted in Putnam, *Bowling Alone*, p. 39 n22. See also W. Hutton, *The World We're In* (London: Little, Brown, 2002), who comments: 'Without reform of campaign finance, the US might as well concede that its democracy is a hollow shell in which public conversation and public discourse are auctioned to the rich' (p. 370).
44. M. D'Alva Gil Kinzo, 'Funding parties and elections in Brazil', in P. Burnell and A. Ware (eds), *Funding Democratisation* (Manchester: Manchester University Press, 1998), pp. 116–36, esp. p. 130, table 6.2.

Together with disparities of knowledge – major political parties have foundations, think tanks and policy institutes at their disposal – and disparities of media time, they go a long way to delegitimising totally the democratic system.[45]

Second, electoral spending raises an ethical question of more than marginal importance. In the face of the dramatic needs of a significant part of the world's population, it is difficult indeed to justify such enormous and continually spiralling electoral costs. The money, to put it simply, could be better spent – in increasing for instance the percentage of national GNP dedicated to development funds, a point I tried to make right at the beginning of this book. And third, with such enormous private funding, it is difficult for politicians to maintain even a vestige of impartiality. Democracy and cronydom come to intertwine, and the slippery slope to corruption beckons to all.[46]

In all the three areas, then, in the media, in party politics, and in electoral spending, there are considerable grounds for disquiet, and a need for fundamental reform. Other areas in the practice of democratic states – gender bias, bureaucratic procedures, parliamentary institutions, the treatment of minorities, failings in judicial autonomy – could come under similar scrutiny. Levels of belief in democracy *per se* remain strong among the populations of most democratic states, but the same cannot be said for more specific attitudes towards politicians, parties and institutions.[47] Let me take just the example of Sweden, generally considered one of the most stable, successful and welfare-based of all democracies. In 1968, 60 per cent of the respondents to the Swedish Election Study said that they did not agree with the statement that 'parties are only interested in people's votes not in their opinions'. By 1994 that percentage had declined dramatically to 25 per cent. A similar decline was to be found with regard to the activities of the Riksdag, the Swedish parliament.[48] The difficulties of the Swedish economy in the 1990s may well be part of the explanation, but there are less contingent and more specifically political causes at work.

45. See T. H. Dye, *Top Down Policymaking* (New York: Chatham House, 2001).
46. For some useful case studies, see R. Williams (ed.), *Party Finance and Political Corruption* (London: Macmillan, 2000).
47. R. D. Putnam, S. J. Pharr and R. J. Dalton, 'Introduction: What's troubling the trilateral democracies?', in Putnam and Pharr (eds), *Disaffected Democracies* (Princeton: Princeton University Press, 2000), pp. 3–27.
48. S. Holmberg, 'Down and down we go: political trust in Sweden', in P. Norris (ed.), *Critical Citizens: Global Support for Democratic Government* (Oxford: Oxford University Press, 1999), p. 107, fig. 5.1.

The statistics from Sweden and from many other countries would be less troubling if anti-democratic forces were not gathering in strength. We can discern two kinds of experimentation with alternatives to democracy, for the time being obliged to abide more or less by the rules of electoral, if not liberal, democracy. One of these is a media-based populism which finds expression in a series of more or less charismatic figures – Menem in Argentina, Berlusconi in Italy, Shinawatra in Thailand. Another is an exclusive form of communalism – sometimes localistic, sometimes religious, always intolerant. As Achin Vanaik and Praful Bidwai write of the Indian case: 'It is only Hindu communalism that can transform altogether the character of the Indian state and society, pushing it towards viciously authoritarian forms.'[49]

The expansion of democracy is one of the key dynamics of political modernity, but it is not the only one. There are others, for the moment minoritarian, but flexing their muscles and ready to challenge if democracy falters. This makes it all the more urgent to render our democracies more robust and convincing at an everyday level.

The facilitating mechanisms of a democractic state

It is one of the bizarre aspects of political labelling that neoliberalism has come to be associated so strongly, all over the world, with a series of positions that much of nineteenth-century liberalism itself did not hold. The destruction of public services and public space, the precariousness of work, the absolute sway of market values over all other considerations – these would have horrified not only John Stuart Mill and William Gladstone, but many others besides. The liberal Joseph Chamberlain, who dedicated much of his early political career to municipal reform in the gaunt industrial conditions of nineteenth-century Birmingham, wrote: 'Private charity is powerless, religious organisations can do nothing, to remedy the evils which are so deep-seated in our system [. . .] I venture to say that it is only the community acting as a whole that can possibly deal with evils so deep-seated.'[50] And his fellow reformer, the pastor Robert William Dale, described the atmosphere in the Birmingham ward meetings in the late 1860s. Speaker after speaker insisted

49. A. Vanaik and P. Bidwai, 'Communalism and the democratic process in India', in J. Hippler (ed.), *The Democratisation of Disempowerment* (London: Pluto, 1995), p. 132. For a broader reflection, especially on the difficulties of transitional periods, A. Przeworski, *Sustainable Democracy* (Cambridge: Cambridge University Press, 1995).
50. E. P. Hennock, *Fit and Proper Persons* (London: Edward Arnold, 1973), p. 174.

that great monopolies like the gas and water supply should be in the hands of the corporation; that good water should be supplied without stint at the lowest possible prices; that the profits of the gas supply should relieve the pressure of the rates. Sometimes an adventurous orator would excite his audience by dwelling on the glories of Florence, and of other cities of Italy in the Middle Ages, and suggest that Birmingham too might become the home of a noble literature and art.[51]

Naturally, their view of the local democratic state and its functions bore the imprint of the age in which they were active, and of the social-imperial ambitions of the Victorian era. But there is nothing to stop us from trying to invent an early twenty-first-century version of what local democracy *might* look like, worthy of the tasks that a global age imposes on it.

The local state and civil society

Claus Offe, in an interesting essay of 1997, dedicated to what he calls the 'micro-aspects of democratic theory', has written of the need to create 'supportive institutional background conditions' which provide the context in which citizens reach decisions and take actions in the course of everyday life. For Offe, the nature and viability of these conditions are 'an open question of democratic theory, as well as [. . .] its most important one'.[52] In this delicate area, the democratic state is poised between the devil and the deep blue sea. On the one hand, too vigorous an interventionism smacks of an invasion of privacy and an excess of pedagogy. On the other, too little signifies abject surrender in the face of all those fiercely present factors – of which markets and the media take pride of place – which do condition choice in modern life to a great degree.

Once, in isolated rural worlds like that which surrounded the city of Florence in the 1930s, a limited number of elements framed the lives of peasant families – the sermons of the parish priest on a Sunday, the cycle of the seasons, the gossip and secrets of everyday life in large kinship groups and small communities. Only echoes reached them of the great city or the authoritarian regime.[53] Today, in most of the North of the world and much of

51. Quoted in D. Marquand, *Decline of the Public* (Cambridge: Polity, 2004), p. 53.
52. C. Offe, 'Micro-aspects of democratic theory: what makes for the deliberative competence of citizens?', in A. Hadenius (ed.), *Democracy's Victory and Crisis* (Cambridge: Cambridge University Press, 1997), p. 103.
53. G. Contini, *Aristocrazia contadina. Sulla complessità della società mezzadrile. Fattoria, famiglie, individui* (Siena: Protagon, 2004), esp. ch. 1, 'Il mondo di un bambino contadino alla fine degli anni '30: Natalino Carrai'.

the South, individuals are by contrast distant from nature but subject to a veritable bombardment of information; much of it, as we have seen, to do with their everyday consumption. Many of them also find their time heavily constrained. In these conditions, the local democratic state cannot simply turn a blind eye. It has responsibilities, fundamentally of a facilitating nature.

The first of these is spatial in quality, relating to the deliberative activities of its citizenry. As a preliminary measure the local state can guarantee the conditions in which such deliberation takes place: halls or meeting rooms can be clean and painted, equipped with a microphone that works, heated in winter. Such places must be distributed throughout the city and made available free of charge. There is nothing more dispiriting than sitting on the narrow school benches in one's children's school, trying to reach decisions while the caretaker (justly from his point of view) is waiting to lock up and go home. It is unlikely that citizens will acquire 'the habit of forming associations in ordinary life', to take up de Tocqueville's phrase again, or participate in Habermas's 'communicative democracy' if they are not provided with vaguely decent conditions in which to do so. There are, after all, many attractive alternatives.

If a first responsibility is spatial, a second is informational. It is not the job of the local state to distribute a great deal of propaganda in order to justify the line of action of its local ruling party (or parties). Incumbent on it, rather, is the provision of information of a detailed and reasonably impartial character which can serve as the basis for choices to be made. If citizens are to be asked to participate in democracy (and if they do not, it will be a very unbuttressed sort of democracy), then they have the right to be decently informed. This function is never adequately fulfilled by the creation of one or two websites: these have their uses, but can in no way substitute for more traditional channels of communication, like the posting of letters into individual homes. Merz's question 'Do we revolve around houses or do houses revolve around us?' comes back to tease us. The local democratic state has to reach homes, not in order to create armies of faithful clients, but to create the conditions for debate and informed pluralism.

A third responsibility is administrative. If civil society associations or meetings in the public sphere make demands on local government, timescales have to be established both for replies and for eventual action. Local administrators and politicians cannot spend all day meeting one street committee after another; they have many other things to do. On the other hand, they cannot promise action in a vague and conciliatory way – the most common of attitudes – and then do nothing at all, or at most a little something in the months prior to their standing for re-election. There have to be clear guidelines about how long citizens can expect to have to wait, and what can be done when. Ingenious solutions to these fundamental questions have been proposed in Porto Alegre, as we shall see in a moment.

The last responsibility is the most demanding and long-term of all – that of creating a different cultural climate in which politics takes place. If politics can come to be viewed, at least in part, not as the distant actions of the ambitious and unscrupulous, nor as the clinging on to clientelistic ladders, but as part of the texture of everyday life, then it is conceivable that quite new dynamics and perspectives would open up for democracy as a whole.

States and families

In its theorising of the relationship between states and families, neoliberalism has always had very clear ideas.[54] Democratic states were not to 'nanny' their citizens, to provide a wide panoply of public institutions and welfare measures to help families. Too much provision of this sort would only breed dependence on the state, and deprive families and individuals of a necessary sense of enterprise and self-sufficiency. In any case, according to the neoliberals, the state had no right to interfere, except minimally, in the private domain of families. And even if it wanted to, so they concluded, it could not, because the rising costs of welfare provision made public intervention ever more problematic.

The net result of these political attitudes has been that all over the democratic world, even where neoliberalism has not triumphed in formal political terms, there has been a major shift towards states *delegating* to families rather than *providing* for them. Families have been thrown ever more on themselves. In this way familist tendencies, that is the assertion of the primacy of family interests to the detriment of others, have been much reinforced, but consciously from the top downwards. The neoliberal state, in the highly sensitive area of relations between families, civil society and the state, basically invites families to sink or swim by themselves. In so doing it aspires to a double political result. It encourages families to think, more or less exclusively, in private terms (private health care, private schools, private parks, private beaches, and so on); and it negates the essence of modern civil society, in the sense of it being formed by 'bridging' groups dedicated to horizontal solidarities, social equity and the diffusion of power. Not that

54. P. Abbott and C. Wallace, *The Family and the New Right* (London: Pluto, 1992).

associationism, under this model, ceases to exist, but it assumes an over-whelmingly 'bonding' aspect, of groups serving particular interests, made up of like-minded persons who may or may not be committed to charitable actions. The transformative potential of civil society thus diminishes or disappears. Families are definitively separated from any such dynamics, and firmly anchored instead to conventional 'work and spend' itineraries.

Naturally, different democracies lend themselves more or less easily to such a political perspective, for each has a different and deep-rooted societal paradigm. The United States has been a prime candidate for neoliberal discourse, given the country's historic accentuation of private enterprise and responsibility, and the consequent residual nature of its public welfare provision. Paradoxically, Catholic countries, too, are well suited to such discourse. Spain and Italy, for instance, though they indulge in a high degree of rhetoric in the public sphere about the importance of families, actually make very modest provisions for them. They have 'familist' welfare regimes that assign a maximum of welfare obligations to the household.[55] Behind such choices lingers the long-standing conviction that women are better off at home than at work, caring for households and relatives. The cumulative effect is once again to devolve constant and heavy responsibility on the central female figure in the household, and to limit accordingly her range of everyday possibilities. Any affirmative tension towards gender equality, one of the central principles of a flourishing civil society, disappears by sleight of hand.[56]

What sort of policies, then, could the democratic state adopt in order to promote different sorts of dynamics between itself, civil society and families? The Scandinavian experience offers some clues. Since 1976, Finland has granted parents of children under the age of four the right to shorten their working day by two hours, and Sweden has done the same for parents of children under the age of ten.[57] Time is of the essence, for it is only with reasonable work rhythms and reasonable provision for childcare that parents can hope to achieve a satisfactory time balance: between work, family time, individual time, and some space to participate in public sphere discussions.

55. See G. Esping-Andersen, *Social Foundations of Postindustrial Economies* (Oxford: Oxford University Press, 1999), p. 45. The author prefers the term 'familialistic' to 'familist', perhaps to distinguish his treatment of the subject from previous ones, though this is not made explicit.
56. L. Balbo, 'Le ipotesi, gli interrogativi', in Balbo (ed.), *Vincoli e strategie nella vita quotidiana: una ricerca in Emilia-Romagna* (Milan: Franco Angeli, 1990), p. 10.
57. UNDP, *Human Development Report No. 6* (1998); L. Balbo (ed.), *Time to Care* (Milan: Franco Angeli, 1987), esp. pp. 15–72.

However, the problems are more complex and wide-ranging than merely temporal ones, crucial though these are. If democratic states are really to act as facilitators in this context, then they have to consider and debate in wider theoretical terms.

One critical area is that of informal as opposed to formal democratic practice, day-to-day contact as opposed to municipal or parliamentary procedures and rules. In far too many democracies, families are reduced to regarding the offices of the state, or for that matter of the welfare state (if it exists), as sites for negotiation, the extraction of favours, and discretional privilege based on clientelistic contact. They become wheedlers in the face of the state. This is not just, as we saw in the last chapter, in the case of Egypt (where little enough democracy exists), but also of Mexico and the greater part of India, as well as many states of southern Europe.[58] The rules of democracy are there but not its essence; rather like Paris in 1793–4, when the ultrademocratic Jacobin Constitution was closed reverentially in its casket in the National Assembly, while all around its provisions were being flouted daily. The *rectitude* of the informal practice of democracy could, but rarely does, extend to many spheres. To hospitals, for instance, where consultants all too often sweep through wards followed by junior doctors, with hardly enough time to pause to talk to patients or anguished family members before going off to their lucrative private practices.

Another unusual but critical area is that of the mental care of families. With families thrown more on themselves, and closed in self-referential terms, there is an increasing incidence of their implosion. On news bulletins there are regular reports of 'inexplicable' family crimes, of children killing parents, or men killing their whole families. In this area, the need is very great for a public service which is widely available rather than residual.

Naturally, this is a demand that can be made with some degree of sense only in democracies that have enough public wealth to entertain such possibilities. In many others, as we have seen in chapter 1, even the most basic of health requirements are lacking. However, for all types of democracies, both rich and poor, perhaps the greatest service that the democratic state can perform is to try and increase the social connectedness of families. From an 'internal' point of view, family tensions and poisons can sometimes be lessened if members of the family turn towards the outside and are encouraged to see themselves in a different perspective. And from an 'external' point of view, it is only by

58. M. Ferrera, 'The "southern model" of welfare in social Europe', *Journal of European Social Policy*, 6, 1 (1996): 17–37.

pooling resources and sharing experiences, by setting objectives and struggling together to achieve them, that citizens are made and democracy fortified.

Reinventing the public

A reinvigorated democracy, capable of playing to the full the facilitating role that I have sketched above, stands little chance of making progress unless it has reflected seriously about the role of the public domain in its affairs The public domain can in the first place be described in physical and material terms. It is constituted by the principal services which the democratic state offers to its citizens – educational, welfare, judicial, administrative – as well as the assets which the state owns – land, railways (not everywhere), art treasures, and so on. But the public domain can also be described, as David Marquand has done very recently, in terms of values and ethics, as something much more, and more intangible, than the mere sum of the different parts of the public sector. For him it is 'a dimension of social life [. . .] symbiotically linked to the notion of a public interest', inspired by the values of citizenship, equity and service.[59] Neither personal interest nor market power has a place in this domain, which exists to serve citizens and in turn be protected by them. The public domain, as Marquand writes, 'is both priceless and precarious – a gift of history, which is always at risk'.[60] Ideally, its values extend far beyond the physical confines of the state, to enter into the minds of its citizens and frame their way of conceiving democracy.

This conception of the public domain is potentially of great value for everyday politics, for if treasured and internalised it forms a potent vehicle for reform. It is from the resources of the public domain, both material and cultural, that the local state can hope to live up to its responsibilities in the spatial, informational and administrative spheres, to create the conditions for the deliberative competence of citizens. An effective public ethos of this sort can also meet and check familism head on. Politicians who adopt its framework in their own daily practice, and not just at a general rhetorical level, can no longer ignore the modest civil society meetings of citizens, but would recognise in them the valid, if often exasperating, aspiration to link participative and representative democracy. A different set of priorities emerges at the top of the political agenda, accompanied by a different language: that of self-discipline in the place of self-interest, of modesty in the

---

59. Marquand, *Decline of the Public*, p. 27.
60. Ibid., p. 2.

place of arrogance, of transparency instead of subterfuge, of politics as the need to develop both one's own human capacities and those of others. These are the possible moral and political bases on which connections between the local and the global can be made. Civil society cannot accomplish such a great task by itself.

Sadly, the historical record of the public domain has not lived up to these aspirations. There have been moments in the history of democracies when the public domain has approximated to such an image – in Gladstone's reforming Victorian state, during Roosevelt's New Deal, and in the determined building of a new France by a public-minded technocracy after the Second World War. But over time in most democracies the public domain has not distinguished itself. Far from it: in the 1960s and the 1970s the public *domain* was indistinguishable from the public *sector*, and the latter was characterised chiefly by its economic inefficiency and lackadaisical attitudes.

In analysing this historic failure, it is possible to draw out a number of recurring themes. One is lack of accountability: the professionals who formed the highest echelons of the various parts of the public sector became increasingly answerable only to themselves, or at most to other professionals – almost never to a general public in whose name they operated. Another is overcentralisation. The triumph of centralised planning in the 1940s and 1950s, in the shadow of a seemingly triumphant Soviet model, meant that traditions of local reform and local control were all too easily abandoned. Another still is the constant infiltration of private interests into the public sphere. It was not only in Italy's public administration that functionaries adopted a proprietary attitude to their jobs, which they regarded, usually with reason, as theirs for life. Those who should have known better did not: 'democratic' political parties of all persuasions filled (and still do fill) the public sector with their placemen. Trade unions adopted uniformly corporative attitudes towards public sector workplaces. The interests of their members came first, those of the general public second. Unsurprisingly, widespread corruption was not slow to follow.[61]

Given this catalogue of misdeeds, it is not surprising that public sectors in late twentieth-century democracies were economically inefficient and incapable of dealing with the tasks ascribed to them. Naturally, there were structural reasons for this failure, not only subjective ones. Demographic

61. One exemplary study will have to stand for a bibliography that is tragically all too long: R. Wade, 'The system of administrative and political corruption: canal irrigation in South India', *Journal of Development Studies*, 18, 3 (1982): 287–328.

changes meant that welfare states had to cope with increasing numbers of ageing people, the costs of health care rose, public sector industries could not compete in increasingly global markets, and democratic states entered into fiscal crisis. By the end of the 1970s the public terrain was more than ripe for the neoliberal attack. Sweeping cuts took place (and continue) in public sector services. The whole idea of public ethics was ridiculed. What was needed instead were privatisations and the application of market values to the public sector. Hospitals, schools, universities, and public managers of all sorts were to compete one against the other. Those who won were rewarded with resources, those who did not were left to their own fate. The public sector became the realm of targets and performance indicators, as well as of perpetual monitoring and auditing. Accountability was not to a general public interest, defined and debated locally or nationally; rather it was to special government agencies and to single, atomised families, conceived of purely as 'consumers' of services.[62]

The debate on the effectiveness of this neoliberal onslaught has been long and furious, and I shall not enter into it here. There have been some successes (in terms of lowering the price of services, eliminating parasitical areas and increasing cost efficiency) and many failures (in terms of safety, quality and coverage, as well as the motivation and security of the public sector work-force). What is very clear, though, is that democracies after the neoliberal cure are unhappier, as well as more privatised, places, incapable of offering collective answers to the formidable challenges that face them. The time is long overdue to take up again the historical challenge of the public domain.

In this context a few indicators of a way forward will have to suffice. The first regards human resources. In spite of everything, there remain in public service in democracies all over the world millions of teachers, doctors, social workers, judges, broadcasters, local and national civil servants, and so on, who are both upright and conscientious, and who are in desperate need of a public philosophy and of political signals which would give a wider sense and purpose to their everyday activity. The service ethic can be revived and set to work. It will be all the more effective if it is set in a context of local account-ability and constant interchange between users and providers, between civil society associations and the local state. The goods of the public domain should not be treated as commodities, something the neoliberals have done, but on the other hand jobs in the public sector cannot be treated as sinecures or

62. See A. Gamble and T. Wright, 'Introduction', in Gamble and Wright (eds), *Restating the State?* (Oxford: Blackwell, 2004), pp. 3–4; C. Leys *Market-Driven Politics. Neoliberal Democracy and the Public Interest* (London: Verso, 2001).

personal property, as has often been the case in the past. Public sector trade unions should no longer behave as ostriches, their heads buried in the corporative sand. In what are often very rich societies, the financial resources have to be found to make a viable reality of a new public domain – not a shoddy, lazy, corrupt sort of place, but a beacon for a different sort of relationship between services, ethics and politics. There is no iron law of history that condemns the public domain to the first of these images rather than to the second. It is time to try again.

In all this, there is one public institution that has an absolutely central role to play, and that is the public broadcaster.[63] The role of public broadcasting is diminishing daily, and its increasing subordination to the commercial model is ever more apparent. Discussions of its privatisation are frequent, as are the controls exercised over it by politicians – directly as by Berlusconi in Italy, comprehensively as by Putin in Russia, indirectly as by Blair, whose management of the media (and of the BBC in particular) was condoned by the Hutton report. It is high time that some ground rules were redrawn for this most important of public institutions, as crucial as is an autonomous judiciary to making democracy work. The public broadcaster cannot be expected to function in the same way as private channels, or compete with them for audience levels. It has a different function, fundamentally that of information, documentaries, and attention to local realities. It too is potentially a facilitator, but it must be left alone by the politicians to evolve its own ethos of public service, investigation and responsibility.[64] John Lloyd of the *Financial Times* has written recently of the need for a media journalism which defies its own instincts, which acts as an adjunct to activity and reflection, and 'which presents to its audience first drafts of history which are absorbing and subtle, strong on narrative but attentive to the complexity and context of every story'.[65] To attain these goals journalists themselves have to question the routines and practices which present television modes impose upon them.

A reformed public service may not at first attract enormous audiences, but if it is part of a general rethinking and if reforming politicians do not lose their

63. For the case of the United States, see D. Barsamian, *The Decline and Fall of Public Broadcasting* (Cambridge, Mass.: South End Press, 2002).

64. In many democracies, public television channels are simply part of the spoils of holding political office. In Italy in the 1970s the first channel of the RAI 'belonged' to the Christian Democrats, the second to the Socialists, the third to the Communists. This is a pernicious model, still a long way from being eradicated in Italian and other cultures.

65. J. Lloyd, *What the Media are Doing to our Politics* (London: Constable, 2004), p. 203.

nerve, then the constancy of its presence and the quality of its alternative will gradually win the day, or at least part of the day, in the homes of people all over the world.

Deliberative democracy and Porto Alegre

Deliberative democracy derives its name from the dual meaning in English of 'deliberation' – both to discuss and to decide. The notion has at its core the idea of making policy by involving all those who will be affected by a decision, or their representatives.[66] The method employed is debate in a structured and collaborative context, founded on adequate information and a plurality of opinions, with clear time limits for reaching decisions. Deliberative democracy, at its best, is not an open-ended talking shop; it is rather a honed instrument for bringing a large number of people into the most important activity of democratic politics, that of making informed and wise decisions in reasonable amounts of time.

Deliberative democracy has a number of significant advantages. Luigi Bobbio has outlined three of the most important.[67] In the first place, it produces better decisions, because in the course of discussion problems come to be redefined and new mediations and solutions proposed. Second, deliberation enhances the legitimacy of decisions, because they are the fruit not of a single decision-maker but of a plurality of persons, some of whom may not agree with the final decision but all of whom recognise the legitimacy of the procedure that has taken place. Third, deliberation strengthens civic virtues, because it teaches people to listen, to be more tolerant, and to build trust among themselves.

It is crucial for our purposes to distinguish between consultation and deliberation. The former is what many present-day democratic politicians have in mind when they talk of citizens' participation. People will be listened to, sometimes patiently, sometimes not, and then politicians will decide. Because the voice of the people, in its raw state, is usually cacophonous and inchoate, it is all too easy for politicians to adopt paternalistic, even dismissive, attitudes towards it. 'Consultation' is very often a political ruse, and should be exposed as such. On the other hand, deliberation implies the active involvement of citizens in a decision-making process. It has to do with learning and with empowerment.

66. J. Elster, 'Introduction', in Elster, *Deliberative Democracy*, p. 8.
67. L. Bobbio, ' "Non rifiutarti di scegliere": un'esperienza di democrazia deliberativa', paper presented to the annual meeting of the Società Italiana di Scienza Politica, Siena, 13–15 Sept. 2001, p. 5.

If deliberative democracy works well, it is the crucial mechanism that connects participation to representation. It cannot replace representative democracy, which is the result of a formal voting process with opinions rightly protected by the secrecy of the ballot box. But it can and indeed should flank it, with the liberty of the ancients coming to the aid of that of the moderns. The power and responsibility of representatives are not negated or even diminished. They are, rather, modified, enriched and sometimes constrained by the deliberative activity that is taking place around them.

The exact relationship between participation and representation cannot be fixed once and for all, but is the subject of present-day experimentation. Sometimes the deliberative process is so rich that politicians will regard themselves as bound by its findings. Sometimes, it is less intense and widespread, and the autonomy of representatives must be considered correspondingly greater. In modern European democracies, the case studies are still limited, even non-existent in many regions, and the play between the two forms of democracy has yet to acquire a richness of light and shade. The experiments of citizens' juries, of the German *Plannungszelle*,[68] of Danish empowerment of parents in the primary school system, of British public health panels have all been precious, even if many of them have been much closer to consultation than to deliberation in the sense I have outlined above. Caution, as well as politicians' fear of losing some part of their power and patronage, has tended to prevail.[69]

The practice of deliberative democracy need not be confined only to the political sphere. Democracy at the workplace has a long and contested history, made up of some historic victories (such as workers' representatives sitting on major companies' boards in Germany and Sweden), but also many defeats and disappointments.[70] Employers are naturally very reluctant to share any part of

68. The German 'planning cell' is formed by a group of twenty-five people from across the social spectrum, who work together for a strictly limited time. With the help of two moderators, they learn about an issue delegated to them by a commissioning body, and choose between alternative solutions. Their recommendations are then fed back into the policy process.

69. See U. Khan (ed.), *Participation beyond the Ballot Box* (London: University College London Press, 1999). Khan comments: 'Doubts remain as to whether the desire to involve both users and public will extend as far as a willingness to transfer to the community a significant degree of power over agenda setting, policy appraisal and policy implementation' (p. x).

70. Perhaps the most significant was the failure in Sweden of Rudolf Meidners's 1975 proposal for collective investment funds, which would gradually have given workers a dominant stake in Sweden's major companies: R. Meidner, *Employee Investment Funds: an Approach to Collective Capital Formation* (London: Allen and Unwin, 1978).

their power with their employees, seeing in any such concession the beginning of an insidious process of losing overall control. However, this is a very short-sighted approach. Workers, too, are stakeholders. Neoliberalism would like to keep their rights to a minimum, rendering them both subordinate and 'flexible'. A more collective and socially responsible approach would stress the need for their inclusion and even their deliberative rights. The almost complete absence of any employees' voices in the strategic decision-making process of transnational companies is a striking indictment of modern capitalism.[71]

The most extensive and justly renowned experiment in deliberative democracy comes not from Europe, nor from Japan nor from the United States,[72] but from Brazil. At first sight, the city of Porto Alegre with 28 per cent of its 1.3 million population still living in shanty towns in 1989, with its mass poverty and illiteracy, and its setting in a wider national context of limited traditions of democracy, would seem an unlikely place for a complicated experiment in deliberative democracy. If literacy and a long-term democratic culture were to be considered preconditions for participative democracy, then Porto Alegre would be a non-starter. Instead, local activists, radical Catholic groups and politicians, with the Partido dos Trabalhadores (Workers' Party) playing an important role, have slowly created an impressive tradition of popular deliberation since the end of military rule in 1985. They have done so, not at the margins of the local government system, but at its core, in control over the spending priorities of the city's budget. The process by which these priorities are established and then enacted has come to be known as the Orçamento Participativo, the 'participatory budget'.[73]

The first thing to note about this process is its annual character. Different parts of it take place regularly at different moments in the calendar year. The participatory budget is not an open-ended discussion nor a mere consultation, but a series of decisions made according to a seasonal timetable which is clear

71. Cf. Will Hutton, 'Did I get it wrong?', *Observer*, 9 Jan. 2005, where he writes of he need to incorporate 'values of inclusion, commitment and fairness in the bedrock of capitalism'.

72. For a detailed and fascinating account of some Chicago experiments in this field, see A. Fung, *Empowered Participation: Reinventing Urban Democracy* (Princeton: Princeton University Press, 2004).

73. The literature on the Orçamento Participativo is by now extensive. I have found particularly useful M. Gret and Y. Sintomer, *Porto Alegre. L'espoir d'une autre démocratie* (Paris: La Découverte, 2002); G. Allegretti, *L'insegnamento di Porto Alegre. Auto-progettualità come paradigma urbano* (Florence: Alinea, 2003); H. Wainwright, *Reclaim the State: Experiments in Popular Democracy* (London: Verso, 2003), pp. 42–69.

for all to see. Such a procedure produces a sense of continuity and achievement, with citizens being able to evaluate results at the end of one annual cycle, and before the beginning of the next.

The period between March and June marks the first stage of the process. In March a series of preparatory meetings takes place all over the city, with members of the municipal administration illustrating the previous year's achievements and outlining their plans for the coming year. Then between mid-April and mid-May citizens come together in sixteen territorial assemblies and (since 1994) six thematic ones to vote their list of priorities for the year. The thematic assemblies, dedicated to general problems like health care, provision for young people, etc., usually take place directly in the Municipal Council building, so as to symbolise the opening up of representative institutions to the city as a whole. The whole process is aided and facilitated by twenty coordinators from the city's Coordination Committee for Relations with the Community.

At the end of this first phase a solemn meeting of the Municipal Council takes place, when the priorities voted on by the assemblies are handed over to the local administrators. They, with their technical staff, must now work on the feasibility of the proposals (July–August). Then, from September onwards they are flanked in this activity by the popularly elected Council of the Budget (COP), consisting of forty-eight delegates elected directly from the assemblies. Finally in November and December the budget is approved by the Municipal Council of the city of Porto Alegre.[74]

The decision-making process is a complex one, changing from year to year, and I have given no more than a bald summary of it. A number of points stand out from what is now the fifteen-year history of the Orçamento Participativo. The first is the steadily increasing number of citizens who take part – from just 1,300 in 1989 to 31,300 in 2002. Their social and gender composition is also revealing, with the number of women growing from 46.7 per cent in 1993 to 57.3 per cent in 2000. A clear majority of those taking part are poor people with only primary education, and the same goes for councillors elected to the Council of the Budget. A significant number come from the city's ethnic minorities, who until recently had even been forbidden to shop in the same supermarkets as white citizens.[75]

A second point made by all observers, and by the participants themselves, is that this open method of financial decision-making is the best antidote to a

74. Allegretti, *L'insegnamento di Porto Alegre*, ch. 6, pp. 113–43.
75. S. Baierle, 'The Porto Alegre thermidor? Brazil's "participatory budget" at the crossroads', *Socialist Register* (2003), pp. 306 and 307, table 1.

deep-rooted culture of clientelism, favouritism and corruption. It is very much more difficult for patron–client relations to gain the upper hand in so transparent a participative democracy. It is also the case that a new mode of administrative behaviour is imposed on the local bureaucracy. Technicians are not left to their own deliberations, but forced to come out of their offices and explain in comprehensible language what they consider possible or impossible, and why. This, too, forms part of an invaluable educative process for all concerned.

The material results have been impressive, especially given the lack of economic resources: 9,000 families, who a decade earlier lived in shacks, now have decent homes made of brick; 99 per cent of the city's population have treated water, and the sewerage system covers 86 per cent of the city, compared to 46 per cent in 1989. Over fifty schools have been built, and the number of school students continuing their education at university doubled between 1989 and 1995.

There are, of course, considerable difficulties with the Porto Alegre experience which should on no account be masked. It is difficult to make progress in an isolated way, at a local level, if the general economic conditions of the population as a whole worsen. The relationship between the leadership of the Workers' Party and the autonomy of assemblies and delegates is a delicate one. Above all, there are still relatively few people involved – 30,000 is a small number compared to the overall city population of 1,300,000. The limited numbers of participants forcefully underlines the importance of combining both representative and participative democracy, the one guaranteeing a formal vote to very large numbers of people, the other constant involvement for an as yet smaller number. The crucial point about the relationship between the two – between representative and participatory democracy – is that *the activity of the second guarantees the quality of the first*. If it works well, deliberative democracy guarantees transparency, constantly questions financial choices, builds wider circles of decision-making, and plays a crucial role in the formation of a small but expanding group of experienced, educated and active citizens, who have an ethic of public service in their very bones.

Conclusion

At the end of this long political argument, I want to say a final word about participative reformism. In the social democratic tradition of government, as in the liberal and conservative traditions, reforms have overwhelmingly been a top-down process, a series of measures that descend from the institutional sites of politics towards the population. They are received passively (and sometimes gratefully) by families or individuals, who share the fact that they are beneficiaries, but are in every other respect isolated from one another. Participative reformism, on the other hand, is based on flows in both directions: upwards, as in Porto Alegre, from the population towards institutions, and back down again, once final decisions have been made. Perhaps the traditional image of climbing and descending is the wrong one, and it would be better to talk of a circular movement, involving different staging posts. The important point is that in this conception of reformism, politics is not confined to institutions, but reaches out to involve people in its workings, to give them elements of control over it, to create an ongoing dynamic of civic culture and deliberation. Participative reformism has a different quality from its predecessors, for it has the potential to touch everyday life in many of its most routine and intimate aspects: in shopping, in the finding and making of time, in the texture of conversations that take place around the kitchen table, in the capacity to listen, in its inbuilt request for human modesty and its attention to developing the capacities of others, in the possibility of linking romanticism not just to small screens but to the real problems of an extraordinarily diverse world. The natural starting place for such a politics is the home and then civil society and then the city, but its natural ambit is the world. Under its mantle, in so dark a moment for humanity, we can perhaps find the collective strength to start again.

Rachel Whiteread, *House 1993* (1993)
(courtesy of Rachel Whiteread and the Gagosian Gallery, London;
photograph © Sue Omerod).

Mario Merz, *Igloo: Do we revolve around houses or do houses
revolve around us?* (1985)
(courtesy of the Archivio Merz, Turin; photograph © Tate, London 2005).

Index